Dealing with DNA Evidence: A Legal Guide

Since it entered the criminal legal practice, DNA has become an indispensable weapon in fighting crime. It allows both the unambiguous identification of the criminal from traces of biological material left at the crime scene and the acquittal of innocent suspects.

This book explains in plain English how DNA evidence is obtained, what the various types of DNA test are, the weaknesses of DNA testing, and how DNA evidence can successfully be challenged in court in order to minimise its impact on the case, or even dismiss it completely.

Defence strategies for refuting DNA evidence are presented and discussed, emphasising that DNA evidence should be treated as just another piece of evidence and that, on its own, it is often not enough to convict someone of a particular crime. Written specifically for those studying or practising criminal law, this text gives the reader an in-depth understanding of DNA evidence in criminal practice.

Andrei Semikhodskii is Director of Medical Genomics Ltd.

Dealing with DNA Evidence:
A Legal Guide

Andrei Semikhodskii

Routledge·Cavendish
Taylor & Francis Group
LONDON AND NEW YORK

First published 2007 by Routledge-Cavendish
2 Park Square, Milton Park, Abingdon, Oxon OX14 4RN

Simultaneously published in the USA and Canada
by Routledge-Cavendish
270 Madison Ave, New York, NY 10016

*Routledge-Cavendish is an imprint of the Taylor & Francis Group, an
informa business*

© 2007 Andrei Semikhodskii

Crown copyright material is reproduced with the permission of the
Controller of HMSO and the Queen's Printer for Scotland

Typeset in Times New Roman by
RefineCatch Limited, Bungay, Suffolk
Printed and bound in Great Britain by
MPG Books Ltd, Bodmin, Cornwall

British Library Cataloguing in Publication Data
A catalogue record for this book is available from the British Library

Library of Congress Cataloging in Publication Data
A catalog record for this book has been requested

ISBN13: 978–1–84568–049–7 (hbk)
ISBN10: 1–84568–049–9 (hbk)

To my parents Genrikh Semikhodskii and
Valery Semikhodskaya and my daughter Anastasia

Contents

Preface

At a criminal trial, the task of the defence team is to deal efficiently with any evidence adduced by the prosecution against the accused. When faced with scientific evidence, the lawyer has to understand it and the prosecution scientist who presents it, as well as the scientist who is working for the defence team. At the cross-examination of the prosecution expert, the barrister has to use this knowledge to highlight the drawbacks of the prosecution analysis to the jury and has to be able to question the expert about subtleties of their scientific expertise. This is especially true for DNA evidence as it is one of the most scientifically demanding types of evidence available to the prosecutor.

Forensic DNA analysis and evaluation of DNA evidence is a scientific discipline in its own right, relying on human genetics, molecular biology and statistics. When faced with DNA evidence the defence should include in its team experts in one or several of the above mentioned disciplines. It is not unusual to have several experts representing these various disciplines arguing a case on behalf of the prosecution or the defence in the same courtroom (see, for example of *R v Doheny and Adams* [1997] 1 Cr. App. R. 369). At the same time it falls to the skills of the lawyer to develop a successful strategy for dealing with it. Obviously, a lawyer can hardly be a specialist even in one of the above areas, let alone all of them. However, the aim of this book is to provide the lawyer with an overview of how DNA evidence is obtained, the ways it can be interpreted and its weak points, in order successfully to deal with it in the courtroom.

Approaches to DNA evidence evaluation are similar to those applied to other evidence used for identification purposes, like fingerprint evidence, glass evidence or shoe print evidence. This means that despite the high cogency that gives it the aura of infallibility, DNA evidence should be treated as any other type of evidence and as such it can be successfully challenged in the courtroom. Understanding how DNA evidence is obtained and evaluated allows lawyers to find pitfalls in evidence and in data interpretation, and use their skills in dealing with other identification evidence to highlight them to the jury. Providing lawyers with such information is the main goal of this book.

A match between the defendant and a biological sample recovered from the crime scene does not and should not automatically mean conviction, even if it is a complete match. DNA is a means of identification and, as any other means of identification, it is prone to errors, uncertainties and conflicting interpretations. DNA analysis can be compromised by a large number of factors such as environment, contamination, bad laboratory practice and human error to name just a few. The results obtained are subject to incorrect evaluation due to errors in logical thinking or the use of an inappropriate population database. In many cases even correctly obtained and analysed DNA results are ambiguous and open to several opposing interpretations. Understanding these factors and how they affect the evidence is important for a lawyer in determining how much probative value the DNA evidence adduced by the prosecution has.

In this book I will try to explain how DNA evidence is obtained and interpreted, to highlight the pitfalls of DNA analysis and DNA evidence interpretation, and also, to discuss possible strategies which can be employed when challenging DNA evidence in court. The book is designed to be read by lawyers, barristers and judges, as well as by legal students who wish to know about the use of DNA in the courtroom. On pages 166–172, there is a glossary of terms and acronyms which may not be familiar to the legal readership.

The first chapter gives a general introduction to key concepts of genetics and biology of DNA. It provides the reader with the scientific background necessary for understanding how DNA evidence is obtained. The chapter explains different types of DNA markers which are used for forensic DNA examination, outlines technology of DNA analysis and explains how DNA testing is performed in the laboratory.

The second chapter provides the reader with information about forensic DNA analysis. Various types of samples used for obtaining DNA evidence are discussed in conjunction with relevant legislation. SGM genotyping, forensic Y chromosome and mtDNA testing are explained together with forensic applications of non-human DNA testing and future approaches in forensic DNA analysis. This chapter also explains the principles of parentage testing and kinship determination for forensic purposes.

The third chapter explains how results of DNA testing are converted into DNA evidence. Three major approaches of evidence interpretation, the frequentist, the logical and the full Bayesian, are discussed and advantages and disadvantages of each one are outlined. The concept of random match probability is introduced and the calculation of this parameter is explained. Evaluation of mixtures and non-autosomal DNA evidence is dealt with in the later part of the chapter.

The fourth chapter introduces criminal DNA databases. The role of the UK's national and regional DNA databases in criminal investigation process is explained. The chapter discusses the rules of retention and removal of samples and genetic information from the databases and also covers relevant legislation.

Pitfalls of DNA testing are examined in the fifth chapter. Biological and technical factors affecting the results of DNA analysis are outlined. Various types of human error, including contamination of samples, are discussed. A separate section is devoted to technical problems associated with LCN DNA testing.

The sixth chapter continues to explore errors in DNA analysis. The effect of genotyping and reporting errors on DNA evidence is outlined and the approaches for estimating them are discussed.

The errors of DNA evidence interpretation are reviewed in the seventh chapter. Logical errors like the prosecutor's fallacy and the defendant's fallacy and their effect on the trial are discussed. In addition the chapter examines other types of evidence misinterpretation such as the uniqueness and the false positive fallacies, and other difficulties related to evaluation of DNA evidence. The chapter concludes with a discussion of the reasons for the frequency of evidence interpretation errors.

The eighth chapter deals with DNA evidence during the trial. The chapter discusses matters associated with pre-trial disclosure of DNA evidence against the accused, the guidance for presenting results of DNA analysis in court and the role of the prosecution expert witness during the trial. Whether or not conviction solely on the basis of DNA evidence can be justified is also examined in this chapter.

A number of strategies for challenging DNA evidence are outlined in the ninth chapter. Among others, possible routes of attack include challenges to continuity, hearsay, privilege, technical and laboratory issues and issues of evidence interpretation.

The tenth chapter discusses post-convictional DNA testing and its importance for correcting miscarriages of justice.

The final chapter deals with ethical issues around the use of DNA for criminal investigations. The implications of storing DNA samples from suspects and convicted criminals in a database are highlighted. The chapter concludes by discussing issues related to the use of the stored samples and the information derived from them.

Forensic DNA testing and its application to criminal investigation is a new and rapidly evolving discipline. There are many good books dealing with the way DNA evidence is obtained and analysed. One major disadvantage of these books is that they aim at the forensic audience and even those few which are written for legal practitioners require a solid technical and mathematical background. In addition, most books on DNA evidence describe in detail various technical aspects of DNA analysis but do not deal with legal aspects associated with this type of evidence. In this book I try to present both technical and legal aspects of DNA evidence in a plain and simple way. Because much of the readership will not have a background in sciences or mathematics beyond school, I try to write about complicated scientific and statistical issues in simple terms. Those who have scientific backgrounds in biology or statistics and would like to read about some topics in depth, I would like to direct to the reference section which lists various sources used in writing this book, as well as referring them to the following excellent books dealing with DNA evidence.

Forensic DNA Evidence Interpretation edited by Buckleton, Triggs and Walsh (2005) is without doubts an encyclopaedia of current knowledge of forensic DNA examination. This book, written by world renowned experts in the field, deals in depth with almost every aspect of obtaining DNA evidence and is an excellent introduction to this subject. This is a 'must have' book for anyone who is interested in how DNA evidence is obtained and evaluated.

Technical aspects of DNA testing are covered in depth by John Butler in his book *Forensic DNA Typing* (Butler, 2005) which could be considered as a bible of STR genotyping and forensic DNA analysis. Written for forensic scientists and students, the book does not require prior knowledge of biology as all key scientific concepts are covered in sufficient detail.

Interpretation of forensic evidence has been the subject of a number of books. David Balding's *Weight-of-evidence for Forensic DNA Profiles* (Balding, 2005) introduces the weight-of-evidence approach in dealing with DNA evidence. The book presents this complicated subject in a clear and comprehensive way but requires understanding of basic statistics. Statistical evaluation of evidence is the subject of the book by Aitken and Taroni *Statistics and the Evaluation of Evidence for Forensic Scientists* (Aitken and Taroni, 2004). This book presents basic concepts of statistics and covers various types of scientific evidence, including DNA evidence. It describes approaches that are currently used for scientific evidence evaluation and discusses numerous logical errors in evidence interpretation.

In their classic book *Interpreting Evidence*, Robertson and Vignaux (1995) discuss evidence interpretation in the context of the trial. The book is written in an accessible way with minimum focus on technical details and is aimed at the legal audience.

Legal aspects of DNA testing in the UK and other countries are explored in *Genetic Testing and Criminal Law* (Chalmers, 2005). This book is a good source of current legislation in various jurisdictions with regards to DNA sample collection and the use of DNA results in criminal process but does not deal with how DNA evidence is obtained and evaluated.

The law is stated as at 1 April 2006.

Table of Cases

Table of Statutes and Regulations

Chapter 1

Introduction to criminal DNA analysis

1.1 The DNA revolution in the criminal justice system

Solving a crime is a difficult task. The challenge faced by a criminal investigator, though simple, is not trivial – correctly to identify the perpetrator and bring him/her to justice. This can be achieved in a number of ways, by examining eyewitness accounts and physical evidence recovered from the crime scene. Among the physical evidence, DNA evidence has possibly the highest probative value of all, on a par with fingerprint evidence, in identifying an individual.

According to the Locard exchange principle, one of the most fundamental concepts in forensic science, 'the dust and debris that cover our clothing and bodies are the mute witnesses, sure and faithful, of all our movements and all our encounters' (Locard, 1930). This means that when a person comes into contact with another person or substance, s/he bound to leave physical traces of his/her presence. The Locard principle denotes forensic science as the science of discovering associations between samples found at the crime scene and a reference sample.

The aim of forensic DNA analysis is to identify the source of biological evidence collected at the scene of crime. The seminal discovery in the early 1980s by Professor Sir Alec Jeffreys of a technique which enabled the use of DNA for human identification purposes has revolutionised forensic science. The criminal justice system now relies heavily on DNA-based evidence. All over the world, thousands of people have been convicted of various crimes with the help of DNA evidence, and hundreds of wrongfully convicted people have been exonerated. DNA analysis has become an indispensable police tool, as it allows unambiguous identification of the criminal by traces of biological material left at the crime scene and the acquittal of innocent suspects, based on DNA evidence. The importance of this silent but faithful witness in fighting crime cannot be underestimated.

Before the advent of DNA, biological evidence was analysed by serological methods, which are based on examination of blood groups and various human proteins. DNA testing completely replaced its predecessor within five years of its introduction. Now, DNA analysis is a routine tool of police investigation with police forces worldwide relying heavily on forensic DNA testing. In parallel with developing DNA testing technology, national criminal DNA databases have appeared in various countries. At the moment, UK and most European countries have DNA databases used by law enforcement agencies to combat crime.

There are several reasons which made DNA the method of choice of forensic examination:

- DNA has very high discrimination power. No two people, with the single exception of identical twins, have identical DNA. Current forensic DNA genotyping systems allow achieving discrimination power of one in several billion, ensuring that every DNA profile obtained is virtually unique.
- Individual's DNA profile is constant and does not change with time. Many biometrical parameters used for human identification change during the lifetime of the individual. DNA does not. It is also impossible to replace one individual's DNA with another's.
- Different types of cell have identical DNA complements. DNA obtained from different sources from the same individual will have an identical pattern, regardless of the biological origin. A DNA profile of a seminal stain from one crime scene can be compared to that of a droplet of blood recovered from a different scene and if the semen and blood were deposited by the same individual, identical DNA results will be obtained.
- DNA is stable and reliable data can be produced from very old and decayed biological samples. DNA is more robust than proteins when subjected to harsh environments and is capable of withstanding both natural and man-made environmental injury. The high molecular integrity of DNA allows forensic scientists to analyse long-buried samples as well as samples that have been subjected to high temperatures and chemical treatment. Even when biological material is severely degraded DNA evidence can still be produced using modern forensic approaches.
- DNA is inherited. Family members have similar DNA profiles. Using sophisticated data analysis tools it is possible to identify a culprit with reasonable confidence by analysing DNA of close relatives.
- It is possible to generate millions of exact copies of DNA by specific enzymatic reactions which allow genetic information from exceedingly small amounts of biological material to be obtained. Modern day technology is so advanced that a single hair, skin flake or small droplet of sweat left at the crime scene is often sufficient to obtain a full DNA profile, which can be used to identify the perpetrator.

DNA testing can provide a vast amount of other information besides the conventional DNA profile. It is possible to determine the gender of the donor, his/her ethnic origin, hair, eye and skin colour, predisposition to certain diseases and even biological age. As new technologies develop and understanding about the function of human genes increases, this array will only expand. No other type of evidence is capable of producing so much information about the individual whose biological sample is analysed.

1.2 DNA – function, structure and location

1.2.1 Function and structure of DNA

Deoxyribonucleic Acid (DNA) is a complex biological molecule that encodes the complete genetic information of an organism. Written in our DNA is a record of each person's individuality, a shared history of human evolution, and information that can provide insight into a person's future health. In layman's terms DNA is a software code which encodes all the information necessary for an organism to function, as well as the information required for its development and procreation.

Discovered by the Swiss biochemist Johan Friedrich Miescher in 1869 who called in 'nuclein', it was not until 1953 when James Watson and Francis Crick, working in Cambridge, revealed the structure of DNA and provided a simple model which explained how genetic information is passed from generation to generation. This fundamental discovery of the twentieth century opened a new era in biology and medicine and had an impact on various other fields from computing to forensic science.

According to the Watson and Crick model, one single DNA molecule consists of two intertwined strands making a double helix. Each strand has a polysugar-phosphate backbone from which protrude the nucleotides (bases) – A (adenine), T (thymine), G (guanine) and C (cytosine), the order of which determines the function of the genes. The two strands which form a DNA molecule are called complementary strands. The strands are held together by weak hydrogen bonds between the opposing bases thus forming base pairs (bp). The bonding between the opposing bases observes a strict base-pairing rule – adenine pairs only with thymine (an A–T pair) and cytosine with guanine (a C–G pair). This ensures that once the information on the nucleotide sequence is obtained for one of the strains it is easy to deduce the sequence of nucleotide of the complementary one.

Each human DNA molecule consists of various types of DNA sequences – sequences coding for genes, sequences coding for the elements which regulate the activity of genes, pseudogenes (or 'fossil genes', genes which are not needed any more and are not in use but which could have had some important function in the past) and sequences with no known function. The fraction of the coding DNA in the human genome is very small and constitutes about 1–2 per cent. The rest is thought to have either no function or the function is not yet identified.

The total DNA complement of a cell is called the genome. The size of the genome is usually stated as the total number of base pairs. Genome size is thought to parallel the complexity of an organism – however, this rule does not always hold. The human genome is approximately three and a half billion bp long, which is similar to that of many mammals such as mouse, rat or chimpanzee, while bread wheat has a genome which contains in excess of 15 billion bp. It is estimated that the total number of human genes is in the region of 25,000 to 40,000.

1.2.2 Genomic and mitochondrial DNA

DNA is present in almost every human cell. Within a cell, DNA can be found in two compartments, called organelles, the nucleus and the mitochondria. This compartmentalisation of DNA occurred at the very beginning of life on Earth and is a feature of all animal or plant species. This means that there are two evolutionary distinct types of human DNA – nuclear or genomic DNA, which is located in the nucleus, and mitochondrial DNA (mtDNA), located in mitochondria.

Genomic DNA is what most people think when they read about 'DNA' or 'human DNA'. This type of DNA constitutes more than 99.7 per cent of the total cell DNA contents. Genomic DNA is organised into small structures called chromosomes, which are made of DNA and protein. The chromosomal number of individual cells in humans varies. Somatic cells are diploid, i.e., they have two sets of chromosomes, each given by one parent. All body cells with an exception of gametes (sex cells) are somatic cells. In humans, somatic cells have 23 pairs of chromosomes, making the total human chromosome complement of 46. Sex cells have a haploid (single) set of chromosomes. The sex cells are formed from a particular type of somatic cell by the process of meiosis, a specialised form of reductive cell division. This results in production of sperm cells in men and egg cells in women, both containing 23 chromosomes. When an egg is fertilised by a sperm, haploid genomes of the male and female gametes fuse resulting in a diploid fertilised egg, a zygote, containing 46 chromosomes.

mtDNA is located in mitochondria which are small cellular organelles serving as cell power plants. They produce energy for all cellular biochemical processes including cell division and chromosome replication.

Mitochondria are semi-autonomous self-reproducing organelles and have their distinctive genome. There are somewhere between 200 and 400 mitochondria in most human cells. DNA in a mitochondrion is organised into one small circular chromosome. Because of these unique features, mitochondria are believed to originate as a result of a symbiotic relationship between primitive eukaryotic organisms and an unknown species of aerobic bacteria. Mitochondria have an unusual mode of inheritance – they are passed only via the maternal line and although an individual gets an equal share of chromosomes from each parent, s/he inherits mitochondrial DNA exclusively from the mother.

All 100 trillion cells making up a human body originated from just a single cell – the zygote. Human cells are grouped into 220 different tissue types performing different functions but remarkably each and every one of them, with the important exception of gametes, is identical in terms of their DNA. This means that it will make no difference which cell or tissue type is analysed – blood, saliva, bones or muscle – barring mutations and some genetic abnormalities discussed below, the results of DNA profiling will be identical no matter what cell or tissue type is used for analysis.

Each sperm and egg cell is unique in terms of DNA and should one analyse them individually one would get different results from cell to cell. However, in practice, sperm cells are analysed millions at a time (e.g., from ejaculate or a vaginal swab) and the resulting DNA profile will be identical to that obtained from somatic cells as individual differences between each sperm will balance each other.

DNA in cells remains constant during the human life. The only variation in DNA between the cells is due to mutation. Although mutations are very rare they may affect forensic analysis and complicate interpretation of the results, especially in paternity disputes, kinship determination or identification of missing persons.

1.3 Human chromosomes and mtDNA

1.3.1 Human chromosomes

Humans have 23 pairs of chromosomes, 46 in total – two sets of 22 autosomes (chromosomes not involved in sex determination) and a pair of sex chromosomes (chromosomes which take part in sex determination). Chromosomes are numbered from 1 to 22 with chromosome 1 being the largest and 22 the smallest. The sex chromosomes are named X and Y. The X chromosome is among the largest human chromosomes while the Y chromosome is one of the smallest with only a handful of genes on it. Normal males (males with no chromosomal abnormalities) have one X and one Y chromosome, while normal females have two X chromosomes. The karyotype or chromosomal complement of an individual is indicated by providing the total number of chromosomes and the sex chromosome constitution. Thus, a karyotype of a normal male is indicated as 46, XY and that of a normal female 46, XX.

A matching pair of chromosomes is termed a homologous pair. Homologous chromosomes have the same structure and order of genes and very similar DNA sequence. One chromosome from a homologous pair is inherited from one parent and the other one from the other parent.

In rare cases, some individuals may have chromosomal abnormalities, which fall into two categories – numerical abnormalities, when the total number of chromosomes is different from 46 and structural abnormalities, when the total number of chromosomes may be 46 but one (or more) chromosome has some structural transformation. The most well known examples of numerical chromosomal abnormalities are Down's syndrome, when an individual has three chromosomes 21, the phenomenon called a trisomy, and sex chromosome abnormalities when individuals have karyotypes like 47, XXX, 47, XXY, 47, XYY or 45, X. People with chromosomal abnormalities often have visible physical signs and impaired intelligence and can be easily identified by a medical professional. In some cases, however, depending on the type of abnormality, they may appear both intellectually and physically normal.

When a DNA profile from an individual with numerical chromosomal abnormalities is analysed, an extra DNA component can often be found and at first glance a single profile can be mistaken for a mixed one (DNA profile with more than one contributor). Although an experienced forensic scientist will be able to identify chromosomal abnormality in an individual by analysing his/her reference sample, when crime scene samples are profiled (which are in many cases mixed samples) it can add additional uncertainty, and the knowledge of whether or not a potential contributor has a particular chromosomal abnormality will assist in data interpretation. This is discussed in more detail in Chapter 5.

1.3.2 mtDNA

Mitochondrial DNA is a single circular DNA molecule of about 16,569 bp. An mtDNA molecule contains a coding region, which encodes only 37 genes, and a non-coding region, which is 1,122 bp long and contains elements necessary for gene regulation (Budowle et al, 2003). Usually, a mitochondrion contains 2–10 copies of mtDNA. The average number of mitochondria in somatic cells is about 200–400 but it can be as high as 1,000 while a sperm cell contains just a single mitochondrion.

Most interesting from the forensic point of view is the non-coding area of mtDNA. This region, which encompasses 610 bp, contains two areas which were found to be the most variable between individuals – hyper-variable regions 1 (HV1) and 2 (HV2), nucleotide positions 16,024–16,365 and 73–340 respectively.

mtDNA has increased stability due to the small circular double-stranded structure and extra layers of protective biological membrane, and is present in high numbers in each cell. Because of these features the main application of mtDNA testing is cases when little or no chromosomal DNA can be recovered from a sample (Buckleton et al, 2005c). When old or degraded biological material is analysed mtDNA is often the only source of DNA which can be isolated. mtDNA has been successfully used in analysis of bone tissues which might be several thousand years old. In forensic analysis mtDNA is an indispensable tool for identification of victims of mass disasters such as plane crashes, natural disasters or acts of terrorism or when a distant relative has to be used as reference sample (Buckleton et al, 2005c).

1.3.3 Inheritance of chromosomes and mtDNA

All humans except identical (monozygotic) twins are thought to be genetically different. Because monozygotic twins originate from a single zygote, they are genetically identical. A child gets one set of chromosomes from the father and the other one from the mother. There are two special cases to this rule. Boys inherit a Y chromosome from their fathers and then pass it on only to their male offspring (Figure 1.1). All children inherit mtDNA exclusively from their mothers but only girls then pass it on to all their children (Figure 1.2). These two modes of inheritance are called patrilineal and matrilineal respectively. As for the autosomes, there is 50 per cent chance of a child inheriting one of the parents' two chromosomes. Only sex chromosomes do not strictly obey this rule – girls have a 50 per cent chance of inheriting a specific copy of the mother's X chromosome but 100 per cent chance of inheriting the father's only X chromosome. The same is true for

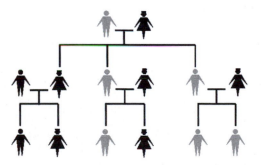

Figure 1.1 Inheritance of Y chromosome (patrilineal inheritance). Tinted figures have Y chromosome.

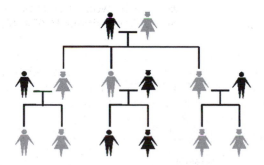

Figure 1.2 Inheritance of mtDNA (matrilineal inheritance). Tinted figures have mtDNA.

boys with the exception that they have a 100 per cent chance of inheriting the father's Y chromosome. These particular features of inheriting sex chromosomes and mtDNA are widely used in forensic DNA testing for human identification as well as in testing for paternity and kinship.

If one were to analyse DNA from members of one family one would find that, depending on how close the relationship is, the individuals will have different proportions of common genetic material (Table 1.1). By studying common DNA markers between two individuals it is possible to infer how closely the individuals are related. This principle underlines the basis of DNA relationship testing.

1.4 Genes, loci and markers

When describing results of DNA testing, scientists often use terms such as genes, loci, markers and alleles. Each of these names denotes a concept that it is necessary to understand in order to be able to interpret DNA evidence correctly.

A gene is a specific sequence of nucleotides encoding the information required for constructing structural proteins and enzymes essential for biochemical reactions. A gene always occupies a specific position on a chromosome, called a locus. The role of genes in the survival of an organism is of paramount importance. Even the smallest of changes in the DNA sequence can cause the complete breakdown of their function directly leading to reduced viability of the individual concerned. Because of this, DNA sequences coding for genes are under extreme selective pressure, which results in very low variability in gene sequences between individuals and even species. Thus the average difference in sequences of homologous genes (genes performing the same function and thought to have descended from a common ancestor

Table 1.1 Proportion of common genetic material between relatives

Degree of relationship		Proportion of common genetic material
	Identical twins	100%
First degree	Parent Child Full siblings / non-identical twins	50%
Second degree	Half siblings Uncle / aunt Nephew / niece Grandparent	25%
Third degree	First cousin Half uncle / aunt Half nephew / niece	12.5%

gene) between human and mouse is about 10 per cent while that between human and chimpanzee is less than 1 per cent.

Nuclear, but not mitochondrial, genes contain intronic and exonic regions. Exons are specific DNA sequences located within a gene, which encode genetic information. Exons are separated by introns, non-coding sequences, which until recently were thought of as superfluous DNA but are now suspected of playing an important part in the regulation of gene activity. One gene can have several exons and introns and span a region of 100,000 nucleotides or more.

If one were to compare exonic sequences of a particular gene between a lawyer from London, an Australian aboriginal and a Zulu shepherd, one would probably not find any differences between them, notwithstanding fundamental differences in physical appearance and ethnic background. However, intronic and other non-coding sequences are under significantly less evolutionary pressure and if one were to compare those areas between the above individuals, big differences could be observed. Forensic DNA testing is concentrated on analysing DNA sequences located in non-coding areas whereas, for medical purposes, information about coding sequences is important.

Genetic variation is analysed by studying DNA markers. A DNA marker is a specific region on a chromosome which is used to assess genetic variation. Here, genetic variation means variation in DNA sequence, which can be either variation in the sequence of the genes or variation in non-coding regions. The terms 'genetic marker' and 'DNA marker' are often used interchangeably. Strictly speaking, 'genetic variation' should be used only to reflect variation between coding sequences while 'DNA variation' can be used to describe either. Following this logic, the term 'genetic marker' should be used only to describe markers which reflect genetic variation while 'DNA marker' can be used to describe any variation within DNA.

A DNA marker occupies a specific location on a chromosome which by analogy with genes is also called a 'locus'. In forensic reports, the terms 'locus' and 'marker' are often used interchangeably. Because individuals with normal karyotype have two copies of each chromosome, there are also two copies of each DNA marker. There is often more than one variant of the same marker present in a population. These are called 'alleles' or 'allelic variants'. Some forensic DNA markers have more than 20 different alleles while, for some other markers, only two or three alleles are known. When an organism has two identical alleles the marker is called homozygous; when the alleles are different, it is termed heterozygous (and the organism is also called homozygous or heterozygous with respect to this marker). The combination of alleles at a given locus is called a 'genotype'. Depending on the combination of alleles, a genotype can be either homozygous or heterozygous.

The actual differences in the DNA sequence between different alleles are called 'genetic polymorphisms' (when talking about differences in gene sequences) or 'DNA polymorphisms' (when talking about differences in any DNA sequence). The term 'polymorphism' can also be used to describe the presence of several alleles of a particular gene or DNA marker in a population. A population is said to be polymorphic with respect to a specific marker when (1) it has at least two alleles present and (2) the common allele is found in less than 95 per cent of the members who constitute the population in question.

In any polymorphic population, alleles at any given locus are present with a specific frequency. The allelic frequency is determined as the proportion of a specific allele at a given locus among all alleles present in the population. Allelic frequencies vary depending on the type of population, race and ethnic background. All calculations or probabilities of a DNA match and other DNA statistics are based on allelic frequencies. This is discussed in more detail in Chapter 3.

1.5 Human genetic variation

Looking at people from various countries and continents it is easy to see how different they are. This is because large amounts of genetic variation exist between human populations. Genetic (and DNA) variation comes from two major sources – chromosome recombination and DNA mutation.

1.5.1 Recombination

Chromosome recombination is 're-shuffling' of genetic material that occurs in the meiosis, the process of formation of sex cells. During the first stage of meiosis maternal and paternal chromosomes, which usually show some genetic differences, pair together, exchange homologous fragments in reciprocal fashion and then separate. The chromosomes thus produced differ from both the maternal and paternal ones. In the second stage chromosomes are independently sorted into gametes with each homologous chromosome having a 50 per cent chance of ending up in a specific cell. This combination of independent assortment and recombination ensures enormous genetic variation between gametes of a single individual. When an egg and a sperm fuse, the resulting zygote will have 50 per cent of maternal and paternal genetic material, however, the DNA sequence of most chromosomes will be different from that of each parent.

One chromosome where recombination is extremely rare is the Y chromosome, as it does not have a pair (in women, who have two X chromosomes, they exchange fragments during meiosis). This ensures that Y chromosome is passed virtually unchanged from father to son. The only significant source of DNA variation in Y chromosome is mutation. At the same time, Y and X chromosomes, although structurally rather different, pair together during the first stage of meiosis and can sometimes exchange regions. In extreme cases this can result in males with the karyotype 46, XX and females with karyotype 46, XY. Non-disjunction (non separation) of paired sex chromosomes often produces numerical chromosomal abnormalities described earlier.

1.5.2 Mutation

Human DNA is not a static entity. It can undergo different types of changes. If such changes happen in gametes, they can be inherited by future generations and become fixed in the population, thus increasing DNA variability. If a change happens in other types of cells it will not be passed on and will disappear when the cell or the organism dies. Any change in a DNA sequence is called a mutation. Mutations which affect sex cells are very important for paternity and relationship testing as they may cause DNA variants in children which are absent in their parents. Mutations in other types of tissue may affect results of DNA profiling causing discrepancies between DNA samples taken from different tissues (e.g., blood at the scene of a crime and a mouth swab of the suspect). We will see how mutations could affect the results of forensic DNA testing in Chapter 5.

There are several types of mutations which cause both structural and sequence differences in DNA. Large-scale mutations cause gain or loss of whole chromosomes or their parts. Smaller scale mutations cause deletions, insertions or inversion of DNA fragments, as well as individual nucleotide substitutions (e.g., A is replaced with G).

Mutations can be either spontaneous or induced. Spontaneous mutations are rare and result from errors in DNA replication. Induced mutations are caused by environmental factors, such as radiation, chemical substances, smoking, etc. The frequency of these mutations depends on the type and duration of the agent (mutagen) and for some it can be very high.

Most mutations are benign for the carrier. If a mutation happens in a non-coding region it will not lead to any changes in gene machinery. A deleterious gene mutation in many cases will be inconsequential to the carrier as it will lead to the death of only the affected cell. Just a very small number of mutations can lead to abnormalities of cell division which can cause cancer.

The frequency of mutations between nuclear and mtDNA is different. The mutation rate in mtDNA is about 20 times that of nuclear DNA. Different genes and DNA markers have different mutation rates. The frequency of mutations in coding DNA is significantly lower than that in non-coding DNA. This is because non-coding DNA is thought to be under less selective pressure and consequently more tolerant of changes than coding regions. The mutation rates of forensically important DNA markers have been estimated and published (Butler, 2005). Theoretically all of the alleles that exist today for a particular DNA marker have resulted from a few original variants through mutations over a very long period of time.

1.6 DNA markers

Forensic DNA testing relies on the process called 'DNA fingerprinting' discovered in 1984 by Professor Sir Alec Jeffreys of Leicester University (Jeffreys et al, 1985). This technique allowed unambiguous identification of an individual by analysing his/her DNA. When properly conducted, DNA-based testing not only provides exclusionary evidence, it can provide positive evidence of a person's identity without bias.

The term 'DNA fingerprinting' was coined to allude to the traditional use of fingerprints as a means of human identification. Although widely accepted at the time, this term is somewhat confusing and the analogy between conventional and DNA fingerprinting is not helpful. Since then 'DNA fingerprinting' has been superseded by the terms 'DNA profiling' and 'DNA typing' in forensic literature and expert witness statements, and I will use 'DNA profiling' throughout.

Two factors affect the accuracy and reliability of results obtained by DNA profiling – the number of DNA markers tested and their discrimination power. The more markers analysed, the more powerful and reliable are the results of DNA analysis. The discrimination power of a DNA marker is a function of the number of allelic variants of this marker that can be found in a particular population as well as the frequencies of these alleles. As a rule, the more alleles for a particular marker are present in the population, the more informative will be the marker.

When analysing DNA for identity testing one is presented with a very simple problem – what are the chances of the same DNA variant being found in the DNA profile of another individual? Assuming the individuals are not related, these chances depend on the frequency of this variant in the population.

More than 97 per cent of DNA is identical between all people and if it were analysed no difference would be found between any two randomly selected individuals. However, there are certain areas of DNA which are unique virtually to each individual and they can be used for studying differences between people. Among these, areas of highly variable DNA called STR (Simple Tandem Repeats) and VNTR (Variable Number Tandem Repeats) are the ones commonly used for forensic DNA testing. Recently, a new type of DNA marker, called SNP (Single Nucleotide Polymorphic DNA), has also been found to be very promising for these purposes.

Various forensic DNA technologies differ in their ability to differentiate between two individuals. Since it was first used there has been a significant evolution in the adoption of a number of DNA testing techniques and marker systems. The rise and fall in popularity of different marker types reflects continuous improvement of technology and of the way genetic variation is assessed. New marker systems supersede old ones in terms of information obtained, reliability of interpretation and cost.

1.6.1 VNTR

VNTR, also called minisatellites, was the first DNA marker system success-fully used for human identification. Discovered by Jeffreys in 1984 (Jeffreys et al, 1985), VNTRs are short identical segments of DNA aligned head to tail in a repeating fashion (Figure 1.3). They are interspersed in the human genome but often clustered near the end of the chromosomes. The usual length of a repeat unit is 6–100 nucleotides; it is repeated up to several hundred times.

The most common method of VNTR analysis uses Restriction Fragment Length Polymorphism (RFLP) to uncover genetic variation. This method of detection is based on a remarkable ability of some enzymes, called restriction enzymes, to recognise and cut a specific DNA sequence. If the DNA flanking a VNTR is cut with a restriction enzyme, the size of the resulting DNA fragment can vary depending on the number of repeat units within the VNTR. The resultant small DNA fragments are then separated on a gel under electric current by the process of DNA electrophoresis. The smaller the restricted fragment (i.e., the smaller the number of repeated nucleotides) the faster it migrates in the gel. After the separation the DNA fragments are transferred onto a nylon membrane and made visible by a radioactively labelled DNA probe which has a homologous sequence to the fragment of interest and under special conditions, recognises and binds to it. This results in a stripey DNA pattern shown in Fig. 1.4. In his original research Alec Jeffreys used a multi-locus probe (Figure 1.4a) which recognised various loci at the same time. The resulting bar code-like pattern was very complex and difficult to interpret. Subsequent modification of the technique led to develop-ment of single loci probes (SLP), probes which recognise only specific loci (Figure 1.4b). These probes produce a two-band pattern, comprised of bands inherited from each parent.

Although VNTR was a very useful DNA marker system it had several disadvantages which limited its application. Radioactively labelled DNA probes are usually used for detecting VNTR, so special premises equipped

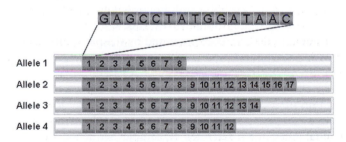

Figure 1.3 The structure of a VNTR locus.

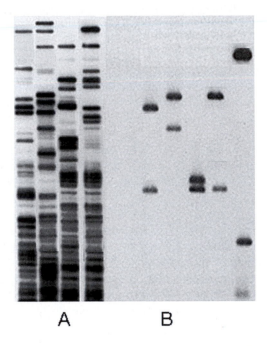

A   B

Figure 1.4 Results of multi-locus (A) and single locus (B) VNTR genotyping.

for radioactive work are needed. It typically takes several days or even weeks to obtain a VNTR profile. The technology also relies on starting with a big volume of biological material and on good quality DNA. Both these requirements are rarely met by samples collected at crime scenes.

While effective at producing highly discriminatory patterns, VNTR genotyping technology is slow, cumbersome, manual and could not be automated. All this prompted a shift towards PCR-based DNA markers, like STR, which enables automating of DNA profiling. Although traditional VNTR genotyping is not used any more for DNA profiling by leading UK, US and European forensic laboratories, results obtained by this system before the advent of STR genotyping are occasionally presented by the prosecution in cases when a link between a defendant and a crime committed before 1994 or 1995 is alleged.

1.6.2 STR

STR are also called microsatellites or Simple Sequence Repeats (SSR) in scientific literature. The nature of microsatellite repeats is very similar to that of minisatellites. Microsatellite sequences are randomly scattered throughout the genome and are simple repeats which, in contrast to VNTR, have the repeat unit of only 1–7 bases long, repeated 5–100 times (Figure 1.5). This is a very polymorphic marker system with multiple alleles for a single STR locus, which differ by a single repeat unit or sometimes by just a fraction of a single repeat unit.

Among the various types of STR markers, those with the repeat unit of four nucleotides (tetra-nucleotide repeats) are predominantly used in forensic DNA analysis. The use of tetra-nucleotide STR reduces such DNA profiling artefacts like peak stutter (see below) and improves electrophoretic separation, thus increasing the quality of data obtained. The SGM and new SGM Plus DNA profiling systems used for forensic DNA analysis in the UK are composed exclusively of tetra-nucleotide STR markers.

Current methods of STR analysis are based on the process called Polymerase Chain Reaction (PCR). The PCR is a widely used technique for the selective amplification of a DNA sequence of interest. PCR can amplify a desired DNA sequence hundreds of millions of times in a matter of hours which makes it an indispensable tool in cases when the amount of biological material is minute (e.g., droplet of blood, a single strand of hair etc.) or where rapid and high throughput screening is required. PCR is a highly specific and easily automated technique. At its core is a specialised DNA polymerase enzyme, which can synthesise a complementary strand to a given DNA strand in a mixture containing the four nucleotides (A, T, C and G) and two synthetic DNA fragments called primers (small DNA fragments, approximately 20 bp in length, which flank the sequence of interest on both sides). The DNA sequence to be amplified by PCR is called the 'amplicon'. The reaction occurs in three major steps – (1) separation of two DNA strands at a high temperature, (2) annealing the primers to the target area at a lower temperature and (3) extending the primers using DNA polymerase at an intermediate temperature. Repeated heating and cooling cycles multiply the target DNA exponentially, since each newly synthesised double strand separates to become two templates for further synthesis. Every PCR cycle increases

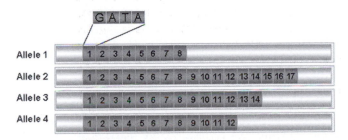

Figure 1.5 The structure of an STR locus.

the amount of amplified product two-fold. Theoretically after 28 cycles of PCR the amount of starting DNA in the reaction is increased by a factor of 268,435,456.

Before the advent of automated DNA sequencers, the products of the PCR reaction were separated on a gel by electrophoresis and made visible using UV light. This approach was very labour consuming and did not allow high throughput screening. It is still occasionally being used by researchers when a small number of STR needs to be investigated, however, in recent years this method of detection has been superseded by automated DNA analysis (see below).

There are simple and compound STR markers. Simple markers contain a core repeat unit like AGAA (e.g., locus D18S51) repeated a number of times. Compound markers contain more than one type of repeat. For example, the locus vWA contains units TCTA and TCTG repeated various numbers of times. This leads to the appearance of microvariants – fragments of the same length but different composition. As an example, allele 15 of vWA has two microvariants of 172 bp in length. The first variant has a core repeat sequence TCTA[TCTG]$_4$[TCTA]$_{10}$ while the second one has a composition of TCTA[TCTG]$_3$[TCTA]$_{11}$ (Brinkman et al, 1996). Microvariants exist for most STR loci but are most commonly found in more polymorphic loci, like FGA and D21S11 (Butler, 2005).

STR loci are named in two ways. If a locus is a part of a protein-coding gene the name of the locus contains the abbreviation of this gene. For example, vWA and FGA are named after von Willebrand Factor and human α-fibrinogen gene respectively. The nomenclature of STR loci with no connection to known function genes is based on the chromosomal position and the order in which they were discovered. The name of these loci always starts with 'D' for 'DNA sequence' followed by the chromosome name and the letter 'S' for 'sequence number'. Thus, D18S51 is a DNA marker located on chromosome 18 and was the 51st sequence identified on this chromosome.

The allelic nomenclature of STR loci is based on the number of repeat sequences present in an allele. For example, allele 18 at D18S51 indicates that it contains 18 repeat units. Sometimes an allele has a partial repeat sequence present. In such cases, the size of the partial repeat is given in bases after a decimal point; for example, the allele 18.2 at D18S51 consists of 18 full repeats and a partial repeat of two bases.

1.6.3 SNP

Recently, a new class of DNA markers, known as single nucleotide polymorphisms (SNPs) has been generating a lot of interest among forensic scientists. A SNP exists in a population when there are two alleles that differ by one nucleotide base (Figure 1.6). Typically SNP markers are bi-allelic, i.e., there are only two alleles at a given locus. The most common type of SNP is a C/T

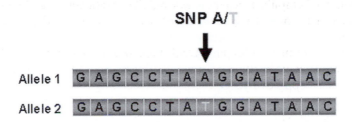

Figure 1.6 The structure of a SNP locus.

polymorphism although other combinations like A/G, C/G etc have also been identified.

SNP markers account for 90 per cent of all inherited human variation and are found every 500–1,000 bases in the human genome. They have several properties that make them particularly attractive for genetic and forensic studies. SNPs are more frequent than microsatellites. There are more than 3,000,000 known SNP markers evenly spread throughout the genome and the total number of SNPs in the human genome is estimated to exceed 10,000,000. SNPs have a very low mutation rate, which is advantageous in such applications as paternity testing and identifying of victims of mass disasters.

Because of their nature, PCR amplicons for SNP detection can be significantly smaller than those used for STR genotyping thus enabling analysis of highly degraded DNA samples when STR genotyping would normally fail to produce results. SNPs are also cheaper to analyse than STR and are especially suitable for high throughput automation (Sobrino et al, 2005).

There are various approaches for SNP genotyping. Most methods include PCR amplification of a DNA fragment containing SNP with subsequent determination of the allelic state using a number of different technologies like mass spectrometry and DNA arrays. The scope of this book does not allow discussing these technologies in detail. Suffice it to say that current SNP genotyping approaches allow rapid and simultaneous detection of thousands of SNPs.

SNPs have two major disadvantages when compared to STR markers. Most SNP markers have only two alleles per locus while for STRs, their number averages five (Butler, 2005). To obtain the discrimination power similar to STR 5–10 times more SNP markers need to be analysed. However, because SNP genotyping per locus is potentially cheaper, it is not anticipated that this will present a big problem when SNPs eventually replace STRs as the method of choice for forensic DNA analysis. The other disadvantage of SNP markers is poor performance when working with mixed DNA samples, the type of samples often obtained from a scene of crime. STR genotyping is more reliable in mixture discrimination and more research is required to develop a SNP system which can rival STR in mixture analysis.

At this moment of writing, it is unlikely that SNP genotyping will completely replace STR profiling as a preferred method of testing of forensic and database samples in the foreseeable future (Gill et al, 2004). However, it is anticipated that SNP genotyping of mtDNA and Y chromosome, as well as for identification of victims of mass disasters, may enter the courtroom within the next couple of years.

1.7 The DNA testing process

DNA evidence presented in the UK and other countries is predominantly produced by STR genotyping. Obtaining this type of evidence involves five major steps:

1.   DNA extraction and purification
2.   PCR amplification of extracted DNA
3.   Separation of PCR products
4.   Detection of alleles
5.   Data analysis and interpretation.

Biological samples are found at the scene of crime in many different forms such as semen, blood and saliva. The samples could be visible and invisible and be present in liquid or dried state. Forensic samples could be found everywhere – on the ground, on plaster walls and metallic door handles, on clothing and glass among other places – which often causes them to be contaminated by various chemical and biological agents, many of which interfere with the DNA testing process. This means that extracting pure and good quality DNA is the main prerequisite for obtaining good quality results.

The process of DNA isolation from biological material must successfully separate DNA from cellular material as well as from substances which contaminated the biological samples, while trying at the same time to preserve its integrity by reducing degradation. Several methodologies have been developed that allow isolation of good quality DNA including extraction of samples with organic solvents (phenol and chloroform) and using specific resins, like Chelex® 100, which bind to DNA and then release it into solution under certain conditions. Depending on the source of a sample, DNA extraction can take anything from one to several hours. After extraction, the quality of DNA is assessed and the amount of DNA recovered from the sample can be measured.

Next, extracted DNA is amplified by PCR, which allows the targeting of particular loci and creating millions of exact copies of them to facilitate the detection process. PCR is performed in special DNA thermal cyclers and usually takes 1.5–2.5 hours. After amplification, PCR products are purified and prepared for the separation step.

Most biological molecules are electrically charged. In DNA, this charge is negative, which means that in an electric field, it will migrate away from the negative electrode towards the positive one. This is the principle of electrophoresis – the process used for separating DNA molecules. PCR products must be separated in a way which allows unambiguous identification of their size. This is achieved by placing the DNA sample into a polymer gel-based separation medium and applying electric current. Small molecules will migrate faster than big ones and after a period of time, size separation is achieved. Old generation automated DNA analysers use slab gels which allowed analysis of 48–96 samples in a single run (two to three hours). New generation instruments employ capillary electrophoresis for DNA analysis (Figure 1.7). These instruments allow separation of DNA within 10–20 minutes and analysis of several thousand DNA samples per day.

The main advantage of automated DNA detection is its precision. Apart from the size, it also allows detecting the amount of each product, which is important for applications such as resolving mixture and low copy number DNA testing (see below). PCR primers used for STR analysis contain fluorescent labels of different colours depending on the locus (see Chapter 3 for more details). During electrophoresis, DNA fragments migrate past a laser detector, which excites the fluorescent label and collects the information about their size and the intensity of the fluorescent signal, which is proportional to the number of copies. The data are then fed into genotyping software which determines the exact size and amount of each fragment.

After the information about allelic states of the loci tested is produced, the

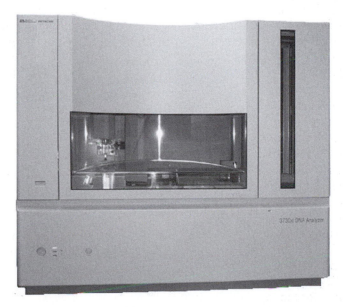

Figure 1.7 ABI 3730x genetic analyser.

results are analysed to determine whether the obtained DNA profile is male or female, whether it belongs to one individual or is a mixture of several contributors, and various other pieces of information important for describing the nature of the evidence. Data analysis and interpretation is discussed in detail in the following chapters.

Chapter 2

Forensic DNA testing

In legal practice, examination of DNA has two major applications – non-criminal and forensic applications. The main difference between forensic and non-criminal DNA analysis is the purpose of testing. The purpose of forensic DNA testing is to identify whether a crime scene sample matches a DNA sample from the suspect. In non-criminal legal practice DNA testing is used to reveal a relationship between two (or more) individuals and also the nature of this relationship.

In non-criminal legal practice, DNA analysis is used when the identity of an individual needs to be determined or relationships between individuals resolved. This mainly applies to cases dealing with wills and probate, child support and immigration. Forensic DNA testing is used to solve crimes. In the UK, forensic testing is predominantly used in rape (70 per cent of all criminal DNA use) and murder cases, and volume crimes, such as burglary. Other applications of criminal DNA testing are used to support charges in cases of concealed births, abandoned children or infanticide, as well as proscribed (incestuous) sexual relationships. Identification of bodies for legal purposes and victims of mass disasters are also major applications of forensic DNA testing.

The first time DNA analysis was used for forensic purposes was in 1986 in solving the Enderby murder case. Two schoolgirls, Lynda Mann and Dawn Ashworth were raped and strangled in 1983 and 1986 respectively. Similarities between the two murders led the police to believe that the same man had committed both crimes. A major investigation quickly resulted in the apprehension of the main suspect, a young kitchen porter, Richard Buckland, who confessed to the rape and murder of Dawn Ashworth. However, his confession was immediately problematic for the police. Serological testing of seminal fluid recovered from the first victim matched that from the second one but did not match the prime suspect. In addition, he denied any involvement in the murder of Lynda Mann. In an attempt to solve the case, the investigating officers approached Professor Sir Alec Jeffreys, who had recently developed DNA fingerprinting, to analyse forensic samples – semen from both crime scenes and a blood sample from the suspect. Surprisingly, DNA fingerprints between both crime scenes were identical; however they did not match Richard Buckland. On 21 November 1986, in the Leicester Crown Court, Richard Buckland made legal history by becoming the first man exonerated by DNA evidence. There is little doubt that without DNA evidence he would have been convicted for a crime he did not commit.

Because circumstantial evidence indicated that the murderer was a local man the police initiated the first DNA-based manhunt in history, which included more than 4,500 serological and 500 DNA samples. One sample the police collected was from Ian Kelly, who gave his name as Colin Pitchfork and used Pitchfork's passport with an altered photograph for identification. After analysing all the DNA samples no match was found and it was not until several months later that Ian Kelly voluntarily admitted the fact of deception. When police received this admission, both men were arrested and on arrest, Colin Pitchfork quickly confessed to the murders of both Lynda Mann and Dawn Ashworth. Subsequent analysis showed a conclusive match between his DNA and the DNA from the samples recovered from both crime scenes. Colin Pitchfork was convicted and sentenced to life imprisonment in 1988. After this, DNA testing rapidly spread throughout the world to become the method of choice in forensic identification.

In solving the Enderby murder case, Jeffreys used multi-locus VNTR genotyping, which was soon adopted by the Forensic Science Services (FSS) for forensic casework. Within the next five years PCR-based DNA testing was developed. Early PCR-based systems targeted SNPs in the HLA-DQ1 gene. Later polymorphic STR loci were discovered and the first commercial STR profiling kits appeared on the market in 1992, which looked at only four microsatellite markers. Development of genotyping instrumentation and technology soon allowed automation of forensic genotyping. In 1996, the six-locus STR system known as 'second-generation multiplex' (SGM) completely superseded VNTR genotyping in the UK. This system was expanded in 1999 to include 11 loci with the introduction of SGM Plus (also referred to as SGM+) and is the current method of choice for forensic genotyping in the UK and many other countries.

2.1 Forensic samples

The aim of forensic DNA investigation is to reveal the source of biological evidence collected at the scene of crime. This involves comparing a DNA profile from a crime stain to that of a suspect or to the profiles contained in a criminal DNA database.

There is an important difference between the types of samples collected at scenes of crime and the samples obtained from suspects. At the crime scene, biological samples can be in any form of biological tissue, bodily fluids or any other material which was in contact with, or could be handled by, the perpetrator. Although DNA could survive for a long time in various forensic samples, crime scene samples can sometimes be far from ideal for DNA analysis. They are often in various states of degradation, having been exposed to lengthy periods of harsh environment such as sunlight or humidity. In some cases biological material could be subjected to caustic chemicals or extreme temperatures. All this affects the integrity of DNA negatively and complicates forensic DNA examination. Of no less importance is the fact that the amount of rescued biological material may be very small, requiring the use of sensitive assays (e.g., LCN DNA testing, see below) and the undertaking of special precautions to minimise laboratory based contamination. In many cases, forensic scientists have only one attempt at obtaining DNA evidence, leaving no margin for error.

In contrast, biological samples from suspects are usually of one type, collected under controlled conditions and properly stored. The amount of biological material is enough to obtain good quality DNA and re-collection of samples is easily possible if required.

2.1.1 Crime scene samples

Blood, semen, saliva and other types of bodily fluid or tissue are the most common types of biological evidence collected at crime scenes. In addition, non-biological items which come into contact with people can be used to obtain DNA evidence. These commonly include items of clothing, bed sheets and blankets, various weapons, cups and glasses, cigarette butts, discarded condoms and chewing gum.

2.1.1.1 Blood

Blood is a human tissue that contains three major types of cells – erythrocytes (red blood cells), leukocytes (white blood cells) and platelets (thrombocytes). DNA is present only in leukocytes, cells which constitute approximately 3 per cent of the total blood cells and are part of body's immune system.

At the scene of crime, blood can be found in liquid or in dry form. Often, blood stains can be invisible to the naked eye due to the effect of the environment, the size of blood spots (e.g., microscopic blood spots) or their location being complicated by the state of the evidential object (e.g., soiled items of clothing).

If a blood stain is suspected, forensic evidence is subjected to one of several available presumptive tests for the presence of blood, such as the luminol or benzidine test, prior to undertaking DNA work. Most presumptive tests detect blood by the presence or absence of the oxygen-transporting molecule haemoglobin which is found in erythrocytes. Results of presumptive testing being negative indicate that no blood in detectable quantities is found on an item but a positive result does not automatically mean that a blood stain is present. There are a number of substances like bleach and other household chemicals that can produce false positive results; to confirm whether the blood is really present, the sample is taken for a specific serological or DNA analysis. When the blood stain is to be taken further for DNA analysis, the choice of presumptive tests is very important as the test must not compromise the integrity of the DNA nor interfere with subsequent DNA testing.

2.1.1.2 Semen

Semen or sperm is fluid produced by the testes, seminal vesicles and prostate. Semen consists of seminal plasma and sperm cells or spermatozoa, which contain DNA. A mature spermatozoon has an oval-shaped head, the basal body and the tail. The head contains a haploid number of chromosomes while a single spiral mitochondrion is present in the basal body. The number of spermatozoa in ejaculate normally varies from 200,000 to 500,000, which make up about two to five per cent of the volume of seminal fluid.

The presence of sperm is usually detected either by direct observation of spermatozoa under a microscope or by presumptive testing. Finding spermatozoa under microscopic examination indicates the presence of sperm in an evidential sample. However there are cases when it is not possible to find spermatozoa in seminal fluid. Semen of vasectomised and azoospermic (aspermic) men have no spermatozoa present. In addition, oligospermic men may have a very low sperm count.

When no spermatozoa are observed during microscopic examination of a potential semen stain it is necessary to be able to identify semen by other methods. Several presumptive tests for semen are currently used by forensic scientists. At the crime scene the presence of a semen stain can be detected by a hand-held UV source. Under UV light, a semen stain will fluoresce brightly. A more accurate presumptive test looks for the presence of acid phosphatase, the enzyme secreted by the prostate gland and found in abundance in seminal fluid.

2.1.1.3 Saliva

Saliva can be found on various items including bite-marks, drinking cups and glasses, cigarette butts, envelope flaps and stamps. DNA in saliva comes mainly from cells shed from the mouth lining and also from blood. The presence of saliva is usually confirmed by a presumptive test for amylase, the enzyme involved in starch metabolism, which is abundant in saliva. However, because amylase is also present in semen and vaginal secretions, this test is not specific for saliva and a positive result may not necessarily indicate the presence of saliva on an evidentiary sample.

2.1.1.4 Hair

Hair is one of the most common types of evidence found at crime scenes. Hair consists of the shaft and the root (or hair follicle). Only the root, and a section of the hair below the scalp leading from it, is alive and growing. The shaft of the hair is made of proteins and does not contain living cells. The root is bedded in a sheath, consisting of a number of layers of living tissue, which nourishes and supports the hair through its root.

Genomic DNA suitable for STR genotyping is found exclusively in the hair root and sheath because the biochemical processes which lead to formation of the hair shaft cause disintegration of nuclear DNA. The hair shafts though contain a large number of mitochondria making hair a good source of mtDNA. At the same time, genomic DNA can in some cases be found on hair shafts. There is substantial evidence indicating that people could deposit DNA on hair by touching, and occasionally STR profile can be obtained from hair shafts recovered from the scene of a crime (obviously, DNA in this case is located on the outside of the shaft and not inside). The propensity of people to deposit DNA by touching is donor-dependant and the probability of finding genomic DNA on hair shafts is highly dependant on the time since last washing.

Before the advent of DNA testing, hair analysis was performed by microscopic examination, studying hair pigmentation, cross-sectional shape, diameter and other parameters related to hair morphology. In recent years, DNA testing has superseded microscopic examination especially when hairs recovered from different crime scenes have to be compared or the identity of the donor has to be resolved unambiguously. Comparison of conventional and molecular hair analysis showed that microscopic and mtDNA examinations of hair are highly correlated, thus making these two approaches complementary (Houck and Budowle, 2002).

Current DNA technology allows a full STR profile to be obtained from a single hair follicle. In practice though, the hair root may often be damaged and several hairs are usually required to accomplish this task. A single hair may also be enough to obtain a full mtDNA profile. The ability to obtain a full or partial mtDNA profile largely depends on the hair age, diameter and intensity of hair pigmentation. With increasing age of the hair the likelihood of obtaining the full profile decreases. The more intense is the pigmentation and the bigger the hair diameter, the higher are the chances of obtaining a good mtDNA profile (Melton et al, 2005). Colouring and shampoo washing of hair is thought not to affect the success rate of mtDNA extraction and analysis.

2.1.1.5 Skeletal remains

Genetic identification of human remains is usually done by analysing DNA extracted from bone or tooth material. Bone matrix and tooth pulp are rich sources of mtDNA while genomic DNA can also be isolated from them. Because DNA in bones is encapsulated within a hardened calcified matrix it can withstand severe environmental injury and be preserved for a very long time. mtDNA was successfully extracted from bones and teeth several hundred years old, and partial mtDNA profiles were obtained from hominoid samples estimated to be more than 200,000 years old. In forensic practice, analysis of skeletal remains is widely used for identification of missing people, victims of mass disasters and bodies from mass graves. Two recent examples involve identification of the victims of the 9/11 act of terrorism in the USA and bodies from the mass graves in Srebrenica (Bosnia-Herzegovina).

2.1.1.6 DNA profiling of non-biological samples and fingerprints

DNA profiles can be obtained from items that have been worn or handled, due to the presence of transferred DNA derived from skin cells. The amount of DNA deposited on contact depends on the donor. The ability of a person to be a good or bad 'shedder' of DNA is thought to be genetically controlled and even sex dependant.

The introduction of PCR in early 1990s allowed the obtaining of profiles from minute amounts of DNA. In forensic casework good quality DNA profiles are routinely obtained from weapon handles, insides of gloves, items of clothing and jewellery, shoes and other objects. A single skin contact with an object is often enough to deposit DNA in amounts sufficient for profiling. The success rate of obtaining DNA of sufficient quality and quantity for profiling depends on a number of factors such as the state of the evidential object, environmental factors, how intensively the object was handled, the type of bodily fluid deposited on the object and so on. The typical success rate of isolating DNA from various samples achieved by the FSS is presented in Table 2.1.

Developments in DNA technology, especially low copy number DNA analysis (LCN, see below), made it possible to produce a DNA profile from a fingerprint left on an object even if it is smeared or not visible (van Oorschot and Jones, 1998). DNA profiling from archived fingerprints is also possible (Schulz and Reichert, 2002). When fingerprints found at a crime scene cannot be classically analysed, they can still be used as a possible DNA source for forensic investigation especially when no other DNA sources are found.

2.1.2 Criminal justice samples and samples from suspects

As there are three different jurisdictions within the UK – England and Wales, Scotland, and Northern Ireland – the legislation governing the way DNA samples can be collected by police from individuals varies depending on

Table 2.1 Current success rates for obtaining DNA evidence from various samples achieved by the FSS (ACPO, 2005)

Evidence type	Success rate, %
Blood	87
Semen	90
Saliva	40
Hair with roots	50
Hair without visible roots	40
Fingernail clippings	69
Chewing gum	78
Cigarette butts	75
Cigarette lighter	10
Comb	53
Razor	53
Watch strap	8

where the crime is committed. Because of the scope of this book, I only describe the legal aspect of collecting DNA samples under English law in this section. The legal provisions governing DNA sample collection for the purpose of criminal investigation in Scotland and Northern Ireland are discussed in detail by Laurie (2005).

Under s 63A of Police and Criminal Evidence Act 1984 (PACE) supplemented by the Code D of the statute, DNA samples for profiling are taken from a person arrested on suspicion of being involved in a recordable offence, or charged with such an offence, or informed they will be reported for such an offence. PACE makes a distinction between 'intimate' and 'non-intimate' samples although DNA evidence can be derived from either.

2.1.2.1 Intimate samples

Intimate samples as defined by s 65 of PACE as amended by s 58 of Criminal Justice and Public Order Act 1994 (CJPOA) are:

(a) a sample of blood, semen or any other tissue fluid, urine or pubic hair,
(b) a dental impression, or
(c) a swab taken from a person's body orifice other than the mouth.

As governed by s 62 of PACE amended by the Criminal Justice and Police Act 2001 an intimate sample may be taken from a person in police detention or from a person who is not in police detention but from whom, in the course of the investigation of an offence, two or more non-intimate samples have been taken which have proved insufficient, only:

(a) if a police officer of at least the rank of inspector authorises it to be taken; and

(b) if the appropriate consent is given.

An intimate sample, except in the case of a sample of urine, may be taken from a person only by a registered medical practitioner or a registered health care professional.

If consent for obtaining an intimate sample is not given by the person, the sample cannot be taken forcefully, as opposed to non-intimate samples (see below), however the court or jury can draw an adverse inference from a refusal to provide the sample without good cause.

2.1.2.2 Non-intimate samples

Under s 65 of PACE as amended a non-intimate sample is:

(a) a sample of hair other than pubic hair;

(b) a sample taken from a nail or from under a nail;

(c) a swab taken from any part of a person's body including the mouth but not any other body orifice; or

(d) a footprint or a similar impression of any part of a person's body other than a part of his or her hand.

As governed by s 63 of PACE as amended non-intimate samples may not be taken from a person without the appropriate consent. In the case of a juvenile person, an appropriate adult must consent on his or her behalf. At the same time, a non-intimate sample may be taken without the appropriate consent (a) if the person is in police detention in consequence of their arrest for a recordable offence or is being held in custody by the police on the authority of a court and (b) s/he has not had a non-intimate sample of the same type and from the same part of the body taken in the course of the investigation of the offence by the police or such a sample taken before proved insufficient. Independent of whether a person is in police detention or not, a non-intimate sample may be taken without the appropriate consent if the person has been charged with a recordable offence or informed that s/he will be reported for such an offence or s/he has been convicted of a recordable offence.

An officer of at least the rank of inspector must authorise a non-intimate sample to be taken from a person without the appropriate consent. The officer may only give the authorisation if s/he has reasonable grounds (a) for suspecting the involvement of the person from whom the sample is to be taken, of a recordable offence and (b) for believing that the sample will tend to confirm or disprove their involvement. The authorisation may be given orally or in writing but if given orally it has to be confirmed in writing as soon as is practicable.

A person who refuses to give the appropriate consent for providing a non-intimate sample shall be told the reason before the sample is taken which should be recorded as soon as practicable after the sample is taken. Reasonable force may be used, if necessary, to take a non-intimate sample from a person without their consent.

The most common non-intimate sample taken for the purpose of DNA analysis is a mouth (buccal) swab. A sample of mouth cells is taken using a swab with a sterile tip made of synthetic fibre such as Dacron® by rubbing it 10–15 times against the inside of the cheek. Usually, two buccal swabs are taken from a person – one is used for obtaining a DNA profile, while the second swab is analysed only when profiling of DNA extracted from the first swab is unsuccessful. If it is not used, the second swab is stored by the testing laboratory until informed by the police that it is to be destroyed.

Alternatively, the person may opt for a hair sample to be taken instead of a mouth swab. In this case, at least 10 hairs with the roots are individually plucked from the part of the body chosen by the suspect (but not pubic hair).

A hair plucked with the roots always contains cells which make up the sheath. Although the hair and the hair sheath, which contain the source of DNA for STR profiling are two different entities they are interpreted as a single entity by s 65 of PACE. This was recognised in *R v Cooke* [1995] 1 Cr. App. R. 318 where it was argued by the defence, *inter alia*, that because hair sheath as an entity is different from the hair, plucked hair samples are not 'non-intimate' samples as defined by ss 63 and 65 of PACE. The defence argued that when complete hairs are extracted from a scalp in order to extract part of the sheath for DNA testing, this is not 'a sample of hair'. Such a sample is a sample of the sheath around the hair, and the hair itself is the means by which the sheath is extracted. Being a different entity from the hair the sheath is not a 'non-intimate' sample and evidence obtained from profiling DNA extracted from the hair sheath must not be admitted. Dismissing the appeal the Court of Appeal upheld the ruling of the original trial judge and his conclusion that the word 'hair' in s 65 '. . . must be taken to include those inner sheaths which are inevitably withdrawn with the hair as it is pulled from the head.'

Police casework distinguishes three types of samples used for criminal investigation purposes – criminal justice samples, evidential (casework) samples and samples from victims, witnesses etc. used for elimination purposes. It is important to understand the distinction between these types of samples as only one of them is usually used for obtaining DNA evidence.

Criminal justice samples are non-intimate samples taken under PACE from a suspect arrested for, charged with, reported for or convicted of a recordable offence, primarily for intelligence purposes only. These samples are used to interrogate the National DNA Database to identify a match between the suspect and a crime stain profile on the database. Criminal justice samples are not to be used for evidential purposes although in exceptional circumstances the authority for such use can be given by the National DNA Database Board.

The Database is not intended to be used for prosecution purposes so when a match has been found, an evidential sample is taken from the suspect and this is the sample which is used to obtain the DNA evidence. Evidential samples are intimate or non-intimate DNA samples taken from a suspect under PACE in relation to a recordable offence for use in evidence.

Samples for elimination purposes are collected by normal case-working methods such as mouth swabs or hair samples.

2.2 Autosomal marker systems

Forensic DNA analysis is currently done using STR multiplex systems which allow testing several loci in a single-tube PCR reaction. The STR loci chosen to be included in a multiplex have to be highly variable. The length of alleles should be within the optimal range for detection (usually 90–500 bp) and they should ideally be located on different chromosomes to eliminate the effect of linkage on the results. Forensic multiplexes employ tetra-nucleotide STRs which improves the efficiency of PCR amplification and minimises the appearance of spurious DNA peaks (peak stuttering) which complicate the interpretation of DNA profiles.

There are many commercially available STR multiplex systems used for forensic casework and other types of DNA analysis such as paternity testing. The number of loci included in each multiplex vary from 7 (SGM) to 15 (CODIS). Multiplexes with even more loci are also available on the market. Some of the most popular forensic STR systems and the DNA markers included in each of them are listed in Table 2.2.

The first STR multiplex used in forensic casework ('first generation multiplex') included only four loci and was developed by the FSS in early 1990s. It provided a match probability of approximately 1 in 10,000 and was not able to give information as to the sex of the DNA donor. Subsequent improvement led to development of 'second generation multiplex' (SGM) in 1995 by addition of two highly polymorphic STR markers and a gender identification marker. SGM genotyping allowed achieving the match probability of about 1 in 50,000,000 and it was this system which was initially used for genotyping samples for the UK National DNA Database (NDNAD).

In 2000 SGM was modified by introducing four additional loci. The new system, called SGM Plus, minimised the possibility of a chanced match several fold. The estimated probability of a match between two unrelated individuals using SGM Plus is less than 1 in 10 billion, vastly exceeding the entire human population. When reporting match probabilities in court, however, prosecution laboratories take a conservative approach. Thus, when a complete 10 locus match between a crime scene and a suspect is obtained, the current practice is to report a match as 'less then 1 in 1 billion' although the

Table 2.2 STR loci used in most popular forensic STR multiplexes (after Gill and Buckleton, 2005)

Locus	Chromosomal location	STR multiplexes			
		CODIS	ISSOL	SGM	SGM+
D2S1338	2				*
TPOX	2 (2p13)	*			
D3S1358	3	*	*		*
FGA	4	*	*	*	*
CSF1PO	5 (5q33.3–34)	*			
D5S818	5 (5q21–31)	*			
D8S1179	8	*	*	*	*
TH01	11	*	*	*	*
vWA	12	*	*	*	*
D13S317	13	*			
D16S539	16	*			*
D7S820	17	*			
D18S51	18	*	*	*	*
D19S433	19				*
D21S11	21	*	*	*	*
Amel	X,Y		*	*	*

p – short arm of the chromosome, q – long arm of the chromosome

exact match probability is most likely to be several times smaller. The rationale for this is that the probability of this sort of match is too small to be calculated with any degree of accuracy and the 'less then 1 in 1 billion' approach is reasonable, fair and does not overstate the weight of DNA evidence. Currently SGM Plus is the system used in the UK for profiling all casework samples as well as the system of choice for profiling samples for the NDNAD.

Various criminal justice systems use different STR multiplexes for casework. SGM Plus was adopted in the UK, The Netherlands, Austria and many European countries, and New Zealand, and CODIS (Combined DNA Index System) was adopted by the USA, Canada and several other countries. In some countries like Spain several commercially available kits are used for forensic casework (Romeo-Casabona et al, 2005).

The marker systems used by police forces in different countries vary in the number of loci and their type. To harmonise STR loci used in forensic work and facilitate DNA data exchange between countries and police forces, Interpol has introduced the Interpol Standard Set of Loci (ISSOL) containing the seven loci (six informative loci, one optional gender marker) which are common between major forensic DNA profiling systems. The European Network of Forensic Science Institutions coordinates a European Community funded initiative to validate commercially available multiplexes for use within the EC in order to ensure that all STR systems used by police forces of the member countries contain the seven ISSOL loci and possibly have more STR loci in common.

2.2.1 Conventional SGM Plus DNA profiling

The SGM Plus multiplex system contains 10 autosomal loci and one gender identification locus, amelogenin (Amel) located on the X and Y chromosomes (Table 2.2). Genetic information used for calculating the match probability is obtained from the 10 autosomal loci while Amel allows the determination of whether the donor of the DNA sample was male or female.

Loci included in the SGM Plus multiplex are labelled with four different fluorescent pigments to enable automated genotyping. This is done by attaching a fluorescent dye of a certain colour to a PCR primer which, during the process of amplification, is incorporated into the target DNA sequence. SGM Plus employs three different fluorescent dyes for labelling STR loci:

5-FAM (Blue) – loci D3S1358, vWA, D16S539 and D2S1338;
JOE (Green) – loci Amel, D8S1179, D21S11 and D18S51; and
NED (Yellow) – loci D19S433, TH01 and FGA.

SGM Plus genotyping is used to profile all casework samples as well as criminal justice samples. When results obtained indicate that the amount of DNA in a sample is very small, the sample may be analysed by LCN (Low Copy Number) DNA analysis, which is described below.

SGM Plus profiling involves PCR amplification of the target DNA for 28 cycles. Following amplification, DNA fragments are resolved on a capillary electrophoresis instrument; the DNA fragments are represented by peaks of certain height and position, which correspond to alleles for each locus tested (Figure 2.1A). The determination of DNA fragment sizes and designation of alleles at specific loci is done by comparing the fragments to standard size and allelic markers which is done in several steps using special software. Initially, DNA peaks are identified and sized for each colour channel. Then the peaks are assigned to alleles by comparing with allelic ladders for each locus. This is followed by examination of the data by two independent examiners and signing off the results.

Once a DNA sample is analysed, a DNA profile is produced (Figure 2.1B). A DNA profile is a computerised alpha–numeric code obtained from the output of the DNA analytical process. A DNA profile of a sample is the combination of genotypes for all STR loci tested. It includes the names of STR loci and alleles detected for each of them. (With the exception of Amel, vWA, FGA and TH01, an abbreviated name for each locus, indicating the chromosomal location of the marker, is usually given in a DNA

A

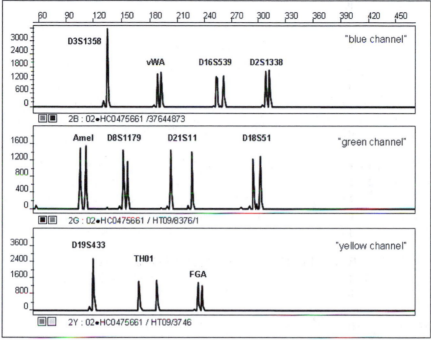

Horizontal scale: size of DNA fragments in nucleotides; vertical scale: signal intensity (relative fluorescence units)

B

Full name	D3S1358	vWA	D16S539	D2S1338	Amel	D8S1179	D21S11	D18S51	D19S433	TH01	FGA
Shortened name	D3	vWA	D16	D2	Amel	D8	D21	D18	D19	TH01	FGA
Genotype	17, 17	18, 19	10, 12	20, 21	X, Y	14, 15	28, 32.2	15, 17	13, 13	5, 9.3	21, 22

Figure 2.1 Results of SGM Plus genotyping. A – Electrophoregram, B – DNA profile.

report. Thus, the locus D8S1179 is designated as D8, D21S11 as D21 and so on.)

2.2.1.1 Interpretation of STR profiles

After an STR profile is obtained it is subjected to initial analysis to determine whether the source of DNA is from a single person or from more than one person. This is usually accomplished by examination of the number of alleles at each locus and by analysing peak area and ratios between allelic peaks.

2.2.1.1.1 DNA PROFILES WITH SINGLE CONTRIBUTOR

Barring some genetic abnormalities discussed below, when DNA in a sample comes from a single contributor it is expected to see no more than two alleles at each locus (Figure 2.1A). The height and the shape of the peaks are extremely important when determining whether the source of DNA is from a single or multiple contributors. Because the peak area depends on the relative amount of DNA in the sample, when a locus is heterozygous both peaks should be of the same size and the ratio between the peak areas approximately 1:1 (e.g., Fig.2.1A, locus vWA). Within a single colour channel, peaks for all alleles are expected to be of similar height, although in practice STR loci of larger sizes have peaks somewhat smaller than those for smaller loci (compare, for example, loci Amel, D8D1179, D21S11 and D18S51 on Fig. 2.1A). When a sample is homozygous for a particular locus, only one peak is observed but the area of this peak is approximately twice the area of individual peaks for this allele (loci D3S1358 and D19S433 on Fig. 2.1A). This is important to remember in order to discriminate between a homozygous case and a case when one of the alleles is not detected due to allele dropout or heterozygote imbalance (these phenomena are discussed in more detail below) or when a sample profile consists of partial profiles from two or more contributors.

Peak area is also important for determining whether the contributor of DNA to the sample was male or female. Women are homozygous for amelogenin locus and a single large peak corresponding to the allelic variant on X chromosome will be observed when analysing female DNA. In contrast, two smaller peaks for X and Y chromosomes, as in Fig. 2.1A, will be seen on a sample containing DNA from a male contributor. In this sample, the ratio between the peaks corresponding to X and Y chromosomes will be 1:1. In vary rare cases the donor of the DNA sample may have sex chromosome abnormalities such as karyotype 47, XXY. In the case of a 47, XXY, the ratio between the peaks corresponding to X and Y chromosome will be 2:1 indicating the double dose of the X chromosome.

Peak areas can also be used to identify other chromosomal abnormalities of the donor of a DNA sample. SGM Plus contains a locus D21S11 which is located on chromosome 21. DNA of people with Down's syndrome, contain three chromosomes 21 in their genome. In individuals with Down's syndrome who are heterozygote for D21S11 the ratio between the allelic peaks will be approximately 2:1 while in homozygote individuals the peak will be almost three times the area of an allele at D8S1179 or D18S51 which are located close to this locus in the same colour channel and could be used as a reference.

2.2.1.1.2 DNA PROFILES WITH MORE THAN ONE CONTRIBUTOR

When a sample contains a mixture of DNA from two or more contributors, its DNA profile is markedly different from that of a single contributor

(Fig. 2.2). The decision as to whether a sample contains DNA from more than one individual is made after evaluation of all loci. This involves analysis of the number of observed alleles per locus and of the morphology of the allelic peaks.

It is common for samples with multiple contributors to contain more than two alleles at one or several loci and this is the fist indicator of a mixed sample. When the number of alleles is four or three, the sample is presumed to contain DNA from two contributors if nothing indicates otherwise. When more than four alleles are present this usually indicates that the number of contributors is higher than two. Most mixtures encountered in forensic casework contain DNA from two individuals. This type of mixture is termed a 'simple' mixture. Mixtures with more than two contributors are referred to as 'higher-order' mixtures. There are three major types of mixtures – mixtures containing DNA from a major and (a) minor contributor(s), mixtures with a known contributor and mixtures with indistinguishable contributors.

When a sample contains a mixture of major and minor contributors a

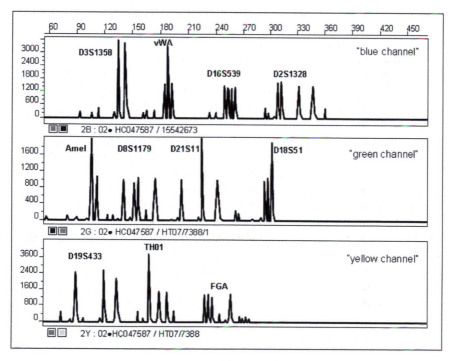

Figure 2.2 An electrophoregram of a mixed DNA sample.

Horizontal scale: size of DNA fragments in nucleotides; vertical scale: signal intensity (relative fluorescence units)

distinct contrast in peak areas between the alleles is observed. If it is possible to identify unambiguously the profile of one contributor, it is referred to as the 'major component' or 'major profile' and the remaining components are called 'minor components' or 'minor profile'. The probability of finding major and minor profiles depends on the proportion of DNA from each of the contributors in the mixture. This parameter, called 'mixture proportion', takes any value within a range between 0 and 1 in a two-person mixture. When the mixture proportion is 0.5, individuals have contributed equal amounts of DNA to the mix.

When contributors to the mixture share the same allele it may be difficult to deduce the genotypes of the donors. This phenomenon is called 'allele masking'. Allele masking can often be distinguished by examining alleles at other loci that have unshared alleles and estimating the mixture proportion between the donors.

The sex of the contributors to the mixture is determined by the genotype at the Amel locus. In cases where a single major contributor can be identified, it is possible to determine whether they were male or female or whether the mixture contains DNA from several contributors, one of whom was male. In discerning the sex of the contributors it is important to estimate the mixture proportion by analysing other loci and then use this information for comparing X and Y peaks. For example, in a mixture with equal contribution from a male and a female, the ratio of X to Y peak area will be 3:1, while that for a mixture with male contributing twice as much DNA as female, will be 2:1.

When the DNA profile of one of the contributors is known, the profile of the unknown donor may be inferred. This can usually be accomplished by subtracting the contribution of the known donor from the mixed profile while taking into account peak areas of the alleles. In samples in which the identity of contributors is unknown individuals may be included or excluded as possible contributors using special statistical approaches. Evaluation of mixtures is one of the most difficult areas of forensic DNA analysis and is beyond the scope of this book. Interpretation of DNA results from mixed profiles is briefly discussed in the following chapter. Readers who want to know more about this complicated but exciting subject I would refer to the excellent discussion by Clayton and Buckleton (2005).

2.2.1.1.3 PARTIAL DNA PROFILES

In some cases, when genomic DNA in a sample is present in very small quantities or is degraded, or the efficiency of PCR amplification is reduced by the presence of inhibitors, a partial DNA profile may be obtained instead of a full one. In this case the smaller the STR loci, the better the chances for them to be detected. Usually, in partial profiles, loci with PCR products of larger sizes, such as D8S1179 or D21S11 amplify less efficiently when small quantities of DNA are present in the sample, or the amplification fails when DNA is degraded. The same rule also applies to amplification of alleles of different sizes within a particular STR locus – alleles of smaller sizes usually amplify more efficiently than those of larger sizes.

Partial profiles can be identified by the absence of allelic peaks at one or several loci as well as by analysing the total number of alleles in the profile. Mixed samples often contain a major profile and (a) partial minor profile(s). The value of matching statistics obtained between a partial and a full profile depends on how many alleles are included in the partial profile. The more alleles present in the partial profile, the more reliable the match. When the partial profile is thought to be due to the limited amount of DNA, the sample is usually further analysed by LCN DNA testing which, in most cases, allows obtaining a more complete partial profile or even a full profile.

Interpretation of DNA profiles could be complicated by various factors including possible PCR artefacts, some genetic anomalies, the level of degradation of DNA samples and the number of contributors. This topic is discussed in detail in Chapter 5.

2.2.2 LCN DNA testing

The amount of DNA recovered from a crime stain may often not be enough to obtain a full profile using conventional SGM Plus profiling. In many cases, areas on objects believed to have been touched by a perpetrator have to be analysed. These areas may have no visible biological stain present and the number of cells left by the donor on the object on contact is usually very small. Indeed, there can be as little as a single cell left on the object. When dealing with such samples the sensitivity of SGM Plus genotyping is often not enough to produce results of sufficient quality to reveal the full or even partial profile of the donor or be adduced as evidence. In the late 1990s, forensic scientists in the UK and Australia developed Low Copy Number (LCN) DNA testing specifically for applications when the amount of DNA in a sample is extremely small and launched it into casework in the UK in early 1999.

LCN DNA testing is a modification of the routine SGM Plus profiling technique for cases where the amount of recovered DNA is less than the minimum required for conventional SGM Plus genotyping. The threshold sensitivity of SGM Plus profiling, which involves PCR amplification of target DNA for 28 cycles, is 250 pg of DNA, roughly equivalent to 40 individual cells. LCN testing is conducted using the SGM Plus multiplex with 34 amplification step cycles (as opposed to 28) to enhance the sensitivity of DNA analysis. The addition of 6 extra cycles into the PCR stage increases the number of target DNA molecules by a factor of 64 making it possible to analyse DNA from as little as a single cell.

The introduction of LCN into casework allowed forensic scientists to analyse a new range of evidence types which previously could not be examined because of the low amounts of recovered DNA. At the same time, the increased sensitivity of DNA testing achieved by the use of LCN comes at a price. LCN DNA profiling is very sensitive to the starting amount of DNA template present in the reaction and often partial profiles are generated because of various artefacts of this technology.

Because LCN testing is capable of detecting DNA present as a single copy in the PCR reaction there is a greater need for quality control to reduce the chances of contamination of both biological samples and the plasticware used for performing the analysis. The increased number of PCR cycles may negatively affect morphology of a DNA profile. This has made it necessary for forensic scientists to develop a specific interpretation framework for LCN profiles that is different from the one for the SGM Plus profile. A completely different set of rules is also required for determining the number of potential contributors to a mixed sample. Because of stochastic effects, the number of alleles per locus in a two-way mixture observed on an LCN profile can be anything from 0 to 4 and standard genetic theory is not applicable here when determining the number of individuals who contributed their DNA to the sample. All this effectively decreases the robustness of LCN DNA testing results compared to conventional SGM Plus profiling, thus making it possible to challenge them successfully in the courtroom.

2.3 Non-autosomal markers

The source and conditions of forensic samples sometimes make it impossible to use autosomal markers for obtaining DNA evidence. A hair shaft does not contain any chromosomal DNA. However, mtDNA is present there in abundance and can be used to link a suspect to a crime scene when a rootless hair strand is found at the scene. In rape cases, a high level of female DNA can complicate interpretation of DNA extracted from a vaginal swab especially when the rapist is a relative of the victim. In such cases, the use of non-autosomal DNA markers, like those located on the Y chromosome is the only way reliable DNA information could be obtained from an evidential sample.

2.3.1 Y chromosome testing

More than 93 per cent of violent crimes against the person and more than 99 per cent of sexual assaults in England and Wales are committed by men (Home Office, 1995). As the Y chromosome is found only in males, DNA analysis of the male component can be of high informative value in solving these crimes.

The main forensic application of Y chromosome testing is sexual assault cases. Vaginal swabs usually contain a mixture of DNA from the victim and the perpetrator(s). It is important to be able to differentiate the perpetrator's

DNA from that of the victim, especially when the perpetrator could be related to the victim. Forensic scientists use a specific technique called differential lysis to accomplish this task. This technique allows removal of the female DNA from the sample leaving male DNA. In practice, however, differential lysis fails to remove completely the female fraction and the sample will still contain significant amounts of victim's DNA. When this sample is analysed a mixed profile will be obtained and often alleles of the assailant will be masked by the alleles of the victim. In such a case, Y chromosome testing can be an effective tool for obtaining genetic information about the perpetrator. Because females lack the Y chromosome, DNA from the victim will not interfere with the testing process and only markers specific to the Y chromosome will be detected. Even in cases of several assailants, Y chromosome testing is efficient in identification of those responsible. Because only one copy of the Y chromosome is present in the male genome, many complications associated with the diploid nature of autosomal loci are not encountered when analysing Y chromosome mixtures.

Other important forensic applications of Y chromosome testing are identification of missing persons, victims of mass disasters and paternity testing. Because of its unique mode of inheritance, analysis of the Y chromosome allows patrilineal male relatives of the victim to be used as reference samples. In paternity testing, analysis of the Y chromosome allows exclusion of the alleged father in motherless paternity cases, and, when the alleged father is unavailable, the testing can be performed using his patrilineal male relative.

The Y chromosome is one of the smallest human chromosomes and is thought to have evolved from a severe degenerate X chromosome (Ohno, 1967). The majority of the Y chromosome (95 per cent) does not undergo recombination during meiosis and is always in haploid state. This area is called the non-recombinant region of Y chromosome (NRY). DNA markers used for forensic Y chromosome analysis are located within this area. Distal portions of the Y chromosome, termed pseudo-autosomal regions 1 and 2 (PAR1 and PAR2), are homologous to the X chromosome and may exchange regions with it. The lack of ability to recombine means that all markers located on the Y chromosome are transmitted from generation to generation virtually unchanged. Mutations are the only way to accumulate diversity of the Y chromosome.

SNP, VNTR and STR markers have been identified on the Y chromosome. At present STR are the markers of choice for forensic Y chromosome testing. Several commercially available multiplex kits for forensic Y chromosome applications are currently available. Some of them allow simultaneous analysis of up to 21 Y-STRs. The nomenclature and allele designation of Y-STR markers is identical to that described above for autosomal STRs.

As DNA markers on the Y chromosome are linked and no recombination happens when the chromosome is transmitted from father to son, the markers on the chromosome are treated as a whole unit, termed haplotype. If, for autosomal markers, the frequencies of each allele are needed to calculate the uniqueness of the STR profile, how common or rare a particular haplotype is, is estimated by assessing its frequency in a database. A number of Y-STR haplotype databases have been established for this purpose. The size of the database is extremely important in finding how unusual a particular profile is. A European database extensively used by forensic scientists contains more than 14,000 Y-STR profiles from 94 European populations (Roewer et al, 2001). Similar databases exist for other world populations.

When a Y-STR match between a suspect and a crime stain is obtained, it does not carry as much significance or weight in the courtroom as an autosomal STR match. This is due to the fact that Y-STR databases do not provide reliable frequencies of haplotypes of the population at large, which means the match should be treated as qualitative rather than quantitative (Butler, 2005). When a Y-STR profile is observed with a specific frequency in a database, it does not mean that it will be found with the same frequency in the general population. Certain sampling strategies will lead to over-representation of rare variants in the database while combining multiple populations into a single database will adversely affect the frequency estimation. In addition, barring mutations, all male patrilineal relatives of the suspect will have identical Y-STR profiles. Therefore when a Y-STR match is found it is only possible to say that the suspect cannot be excluded from the number of potential donors. This is because patrilineal male relatives of the suspect as well as an unknown number of unrelated males will have the same Y-STR profile.

At the same time, it may be important to express the significance of the match to the jury by providing a statistical value and confidence limits. This can be achieved by implementing the 'counting method' which expresses the rarity of a particular haplotype in a database, or likelihood ratio approaches. Statistical approaches for evaluating Y chromosome evidence are discussed below.

Y chromosomal haplotypes show a remarkable degree of population specificity (Jobling et al, 1997) thus making Y-STR profiling a useful tool in determining the population origin of the donor (see below). In addition, Y chromosomes are co-inherited with surnames in many societies and in some cases a Y haplotype could give the police the surname of the person who left his DNA at the crime scene (Jobling et al, 1997).

2.3.2 mtDNA testing

When analysis of genomic DNA fails to provide acceptable results, examination of mtDNA is often the only way to obtain DNA evidence. This is usually the case when biological material to be examined has been subjected to severe environmental injury (heat, moisture, caustic chemicals), been buried for a long time or, because of its origin, does not contain any nuclear DNA (e.g., hair shafts). The main forensic application of mtDNA testing is identification of victims of mass disasters and missing persons. In recent years mtDNA testing was successfully used for identification of the members of the Russian Tsar's family murdered in 1918 near Yekaterinburg and for identification of victims of the 9/11 act of terrorism in the USA.

The mitochondrial genome was first sequenced in Cambridge in 1981 by Anderson and colleagues (1981) and the sequence was refined in 1999 (Andrews et al, 1999). The Anderson sequence is also referred to as the Cambridge Reference Sequence (CRS) and currently, the refined version of this sequence (sometimes referred to as 'rCRS' where 'r' means 'refined') is used by forensic laboratories worldwide for producing mtDNA evidence. Because mtDNA is very small and in most parts shows low variability, any mtDNA sequence can be described in terms of the differences from the CRS, the approach used in reporting forensic mtDNA data.

As we have seen earlier, the mitochondrial genome has two regions, HV1 (342 bp) and HV2 (268 bp), which were found to be highly variable between individuals. To obtain mtDNA evidence HV1 and HV2 regions are independently amplified by PCR and the nucleotide sequence of each region is determined. The resulting sequences are then compared to the corresponding sequences in the CRS and any differences from the reference sequence are recorded. Because there is no recombination in mtDNA it is inherited as a haplotype in a fashion similar to the Y chromosome. mtDNA haplotype is often called a 'mitotype' in forensic and genetic literature.

Results of mtDNA testing are reported as differences from the CRS at a particular nucleotide in the following way. When a difference between the evidential sample and the CRS is reported, the position of the nucleotide which is changed is indicated, followed by the nucleotide observed in the evidential sample. For example, 16,240G indicates that at the position 16,240 the evidential sample contains 'G' instead of the nucleotide published in the CRS. Nucleotides that cannot be unambiguously identified are designated as N. More specific codes have been developed for designating ambiguous nucleotides depending on the nature of ambiguity. For example, when sequence heteroplasmy (see below) is present at a particular position, two or even three different nucleotides can be detected there. Depending on the observed nucleotides this situation is designated by a standard code which is specific to a particular nucleotide combination. Thus, when A and T are present at the position 81, this will be reported as 81W, although notation 81A/T can also be used.

In cases when insertion of a nucleotide is observed in the sample in comparison to the CRS, this is reported as the number of inserted nucleotides and their type after the position on the CRS. For example, 210.2T indicates that there are two extra T nucleotides after the nucleotide 210. When deletion of a nucleotide is observed, this is designated by 'del', 'd', 'D' or '-' following the nucleotide position where the deletion occurred. For example, 280- or 280D indicates that nucleotide 280 is missing in the evidential sample.

Extensive guidelines on interpreting mtDNA profiles have been developed by the European DNA profiling group (EDNAP) and they are followed by the FSS for analysis and reporting mtDNA results (Tully et al, 2001). The aim of mtDNA profiling is to determine whether the evidential sample originates from the suspect or from someone else. Based on a set of rules, mtDNA results can indicate exclusion, be inconclusive or fail to exclude the suspect from being the donor of DNA. The mtDNA results of the evidential sample and a suspect's sample can either be concordant (i.e., can match) or not. However, due to heteroplasmy and mutations the interpretation of the results is not always straightforward.

Because mtDNA is inherited as a haplotype, the same set of rules for assessing the strength of mtDNA match in cases of non-exclusion as those for Y chromosome testing are applied. Currently, most laboratories use the frequency of a particular mitotype in a population database for estimating the strength of the match even though this method suffers from the same problems of interpretation as Y chromosome results. Recently, approaches for assessing the strength of mtDNA evidence based on likelihood ratios have been developed. These are discussed below.

Mitochondrial DNA has a matrilineal mode of inheritance: offspring inherit mtDNA from their mother. In recent years it has been shown that in some extremely rare cases, offspring can inherit mitochondria from their father. This results in the presence of two populations of mitochondria (and consequently two different types of mtDNA) in the organism, the pheno-menon known as heteroplasmy. Usually, when an egg is fertilised, the head of the spermatozoon is disconnected from the basal body thus insuring that no male mtDNA enters the ovum. However, in extremely rare cases, the basal body may be in contact with the ovum long enough for the male mito-chondrion to enter the egg and as a result the zygote will have two different types of mitochondria – maternal and paternal. This happens in about 1 in 10,000 fertilisation events.

Heteroplasmy can also originate in a different way. Mitochondrial DNA has a high rate of mutation. Somatic mutations in mtDNA can cause the appearance of different populations of mitochondria in a single cell. Because of the increased rate of mutation it is highly unlikely that all mtDNA in the human body will be identical. It is possible to observe differences in mtDNA analysis between samples taken from different tissue types from the same individual. It is thought that heteroplasmy is present in every individual to some extent.

There are two types of heteroplasmy – sequence or point heteroplasmy, when the length of mtDNA between mitochondria is identical but the nucleotide composition is different, and length heteroplasmy – when the length of mtDNA from one mitochondrion is different from that of another. Sequence and length heteroplasmy are often observed together.

Heteroplasmy may be observed in two major ways – several types of mitochondria may be present in the same tissue, and different tissues may have different mtDNA types. In addition, an individual may be heteroplasmic in one tissue type and homoplasmic in the other one. Heteroplasmy is typically described by the ratio between nucleotides at a particular position, for example, 16,169T/C heteroplasmy with the ratio 35:65. The ratio of nucleotides may vary depending on the tissue type and even within the same tissue type. The fact that different hair can have different nucleotide ratio has been documented (Sekiguchi et al, 2003) and analysis of multiple hair samples is usually required to confirm heteroplasmy.

Although heteroplasmy complicates mtDNA analysis, it sometimes increases the strength of evidence when the same degree of heteroplasmy is observed between the evidentiary sample and the suspect. The presence of a particular heteroplasmy was used to positively identify the bones of the last Russian Tsar Nicolas II when his DNA was compared to that of his brother Gerogij (Ivanov et al, 1996).

2.4 Parentage and relatedness testing for forensic purposes

In many instances in criminal practice it is important to establish relatedness between people in order to solve a particular crime. DNA testing is the most reliable tool for accomplishing this task. In the criminal context, relatedness testing is used for three major purposes – sexual assault cases, identification of missing persons, and identification of victims of mass disasters and acts of terrorism (Buckleton et al, 2005b). Both autosomal and non-autosomal genotyping are used for these purposes but the choice of genetic markers depends on particularities of a specific case. Whereas the purpose of forensic DNA identification is to determine whether the suspect can be the donor of the crime stain, the aim of forensic DNA relatedness testing is to establish whether two individuals are related and, in some cases, identify the nature of this relationship.

2.4.1 Parentage testing

The great majority of parentage analysis performed for forensic purposes is paternity analysis. In criminal contexts parentage testing can be required when the identity of the father of a child conceived as a result of a sexual assault needs to be determined; in cases of child abandonment and abduction; when investigating incestuous sexual relationships; and in non-criminal contexts, for identification of missing persons and of victims of mass disasters.

The purpose of parentage testing is to establish whether the alleged parent can be a biological parent of the child. The most appropriate markers for this analysis are STR markers although in some cases, when the alleged father or mother is missing, Y chromosome and mtDNA testing can be used for these purposes. Various commercial multiplexes for paternity have been developed such as AmpF/STR Indentifiler (Applied Biosystems) or Power-Plex 16 (Promega). Multiplexes with 16 STR markers are currently the systems of choice for parentage testing.

In the majority of cases, samples used for parentage testing are mouth swabs or blood samples. These samples provide good quality DNA and do not cause complication of the analysis and interpretation of the results. However, in some cases, samples from decomposed bodies, histological samples or pregnancy termination products are used for DNA analysis. These samples are not ideal and can pose considerable technical challenges. Histological samples may present the problem of obtaining DNA of sufficient quality for analysis, as the fixation process used for preparation of many histological samples as well as subsequent storage of the samples often compromise the integrity of DNA. Pregnancy termination products present a problem of another nature. Procedures used for pregnancy termination cause fragmentation of the embryo and mixing embryonic and maternal tissues. When pregnancy is terminated at an early stage, it is sometimes impossible to separate foetal and maternal tissue and resulting DNA profiles are mixed profiles containing alleles from both the mother and the foetus. In some cases, only the maternal profile may be observed when forensic scientists fail to identify foetal tissue correctly. This complicates the analysis of the results, as the mixture needs to be resolved prior to using the data for parentage determination.

The use of DNA testing for establishing paternity (as well as other relationships) is based on two fundamental laws of genetics, discovered by Gregor Mendel in the middle of the nineteenth century – the law of segregation and the law of independent assortment. As we have seen in the previous chapter, people inherit one copy of DNA from the father and the other one from the mother. According to the law of segregation a parent passes a copy of each genetic factor to the child in a random fashion. This means that when a parent is heterozygous for a genetic locus there is a 50 per cent chance that the child will inherit one of the two parental alleles. Barring genetic linkage, the phenomenon when loci are located in close proximity on the same chromosome, each allele is transmitted to the offspring independently of any other. This is the law of independent assortment.

Assuming for simplicity no mutations, the rules for parentage testing can be inferred from the laws of Mendelian inheritance (Primorac et al, 2000):

- The child cannot have a genetic marker that is absent in both parents.
- The child must inherit one of each pair of genetic markers from each parent.

- The child cannot have a pair of identical genetic markers unless both parents have the marker.
- The child must have any genetic marker that is present as an identical pair independently in both parents.

Parentage testing can be performed using DNA samples from both parents and the child (parentage trio test) or only a single parent and the child (parentage duo test). The conclusion as to whether an alleged parent is the true biological parent is based on the Combined Parentage Index (CPI), which takes the form of the Combined Paternity Index (also, unfortunately, CPI) or the Combined Maternity Index (CMI) in corresponding tests. The alleged parent can either be excluded or not excluded from being the biological parent of the child. In cases of exclusion, the child has alleles, which are absent from the genome of the alleged parent (although they may or may not be present in the genome of the second parent). Parentage exclusions are always 100 per cent accurate (barring genotyping errors). When the alleged parent and the child have alleles in common for all the loci analysed, biological parentage is possible. No matter how many loci are analysed, DNA testing does not give a 100 per cent probability of confirming parentage. When biological parentage is possible, its likelihood is estimated by the CPI. The value of the CPI indicates how many more times the alleged parent is likely to be the true biological parent of the child in comparison to an untested unrelated individual from the same population. In some rare cases, mutation events in germ cells can cause the child to have a genetic variant which is absent from the parent, so mutations have to be taken into account when calculating parentage indices. Interpretation of DNA evidence in parentage cases is presented in the next chapter.

2.4.2 Relatedness testing

In forensic practice, relatedness testing is predominantly used for identification of missing persons and victims of mass disasters. A DNA sample from a first degree (or in some cases second degree) relative is used as a reference sample for comparing with the sample from the victim. In non-criminal practice, relatedness testing is used predominantly in immigration and probate cases. When a DNA sample from a first degree relative is available, the testing is usually done using autosomal STR markers. Only when, due to the condition of the body, it is impossible to obtain good quality nuclear DNA from the remains, mtDNA testing is used for this purpose. mtDNA and Y chromosome markers can also be the markers of choice when a DNA sample of a distant relative has to be used for reference, sometimes in conjunction with autosomal STR genotyping.

Apart from parentage testing, the most common relatedness tests used for forensic purposes is the siblingship test, which determines whether two or more individuals have one or both biological parents in common, although cousinship, grandparentage and avuncular (this type of test determines whether one individual is an uncle or an aunt of another individual) tests are sometimes used. Conclusions as to whether individuals are full or half siblings or are otherwise related are based on the Combined Relatedness Index (which, for a siblingship test, for example, takes the form of the Combined Siblingship Index). As with parentage testing, this index is calculated as products of the individual relatedness indices for each marker tested. Individual indices for the markers in relationship testing are calculated as the chances of the allele shared by two individuals being identical by descent (i.e., inherited by the parties to the test from the same ancestor) as opposed to not (i.e., coming from different ancestors). The subject of statistical interpretation of relatedness testing data is comprehensively treated by Buckleton and colleagues (2005c).

2.5 Novel approaches in forensic DNA testing

When a DNA profile from a crime scene has been obtained and no suspect is available, it is used to interrogate a criminal DNA database in search of a match to a subject sample stored in it. If the search does not produce any results and no eye witness account of who the perpetrator might be is available, any information about the possible donor of the biological stain is extremely important for solving the crime. DNA is a rich source of such information.

Currently, gender is the only physical information about the identity of the contributor which is routinely obtained by forensic DNA testing. At the same time, recent developments in forensic DNA analysis can provide much more personal information about the donor. Besides the conventional DNA profile, it is possible to determine the ethnic origin of someone who left a biological stain at the scene of a crime, his/her hair, eye and skin colour, predisposition to certain diseases and even biological age.

2.5.1 Determination of ethnicity

In spite of the fact that more than 95 per cent of DNA is identical between all people on the planet, various ethnic groups are very different from each other. Individuals from different populations are on average genetically more different from one another than individuals from the same population.

When analysing individuals from ethnically different populations, one of the important disadvantages of STR markers is that they exhibit very low inter-population variation and thus are not suitable for deducing the ethnic origin of the donor. Recently, potential forensic applications of SNP markers have generated significant interest among specialists. SNPs are extremely abundant in the human genome and it has been shown that some SNP markers are specific for one population and not another.

In recent years, autosomal SNP markers specific to various ethnic groups have been identified. Most or even all members of these groups will have them in common but individuals belonging to other groups will be easily distinguished. This type of marker is known as an 'Ancestry Informative Marker' or AIM. The latest tests have shown that by analysing as few as 175 AIMs it is possible to obtain information about the ethnic origin of an individual who left his/her DNA at the scene of crime (Shriver and Kittles, 2004). This analysis also allows identifying whether the donor is of mixed ethnicity and even estimate the proportion of ancestors from each ethnic group this individual has. For example, results of DNA ethnicity testing can indicate that the donor is 60 per cent European, 15 per cent Afro-Caribbean and 25 per cent Asian. (Afro-Caribbean is the term which is used in forensic reports and throughout this book to indicate that the person may be from Africa directly *or* via the Caribbean.) It is also possible to tell which part of Europe ancestors of the donor came from, whether it was Southern Europe, Northern Europe or even the Middle East. Research into AIM markers for various European, African and Asian populations is currently under way.

Analysis of AIMs is not the only way of deducing information about ethnicity of the donor of a crime stain. Analysis of Y chromosome and mtDNA can also reveal similar information. Markers on Y chromosome and mtDNA show strong geographic differences and contain information on ethnic and population origin of the donor. The major difference between these markers and AIMs is that AIMs are located on autosomes, chromosomes which are passed via both the maternal and paternal lines, whereas Y chromosome and mtDNA markers are inherited only via paternal (former) or maternal (latter) lines. In addition, the Y chromosome is only present in males and Y chromosome analysis is of no use when the donor of the crime stain is female.

Because Y chromosome and mtDNA are passed from generation to generation virtually unchanged, there may be situation when a Caucasian male whose great-great-grandfather was an African slave has a Y chromosome typical for someone of Afro-Caribbean ethnicity. The same is also true for mtDNA when an individual might have mtDNA from his/her ancestor who was of completely different ethnicity. This highlights the main disadvantage of using Y chromosome and mtDNA for deducing ethnicity of the crime stain donor – instead of information about ethnicity, Y chromosome and mtDNA give information about the ethnic origin of the paternal and maternal ancestors of the donor, who lived many generations ago. Their ethnicity could be the same as that of the donor but in some cases, is completely different and this possibility has to be kept in mind when construing ethnicity by Y chromosome and mtDNA analysis. A more robust approach for determining ethnicity is to combine AIM genotyping with analysis of Y chromosome and mtDNA.

2.5.2 Determination of phenotypic characteristics

Human phenotypic traits, such as skin and iris pigmentation, stature, and facial characteristics, have a strong genetic component. At the same time many of these traits are controlled by a large number of genes, which makes the study of these traits complicated. Forensic scientists have therefore turned their attention to the traits which are controlled by a single gene or by a small number of genes.

Genetic markers associated with skin and hair pigmentation have been identified and extensively studied (Valverde et al, 1995). SNP markers for eye (iris) colour have also been found (Sturm and Frudakis, 2004) and successfully used to predict the eye colour of individuals by analysing their DNA. Skin, hair and iris pigmentation in combination with AIMs can produce remarkable results in obtaining information about the physical description of the crime stain donor.

2.5.3 Estimating biological age

Information about the age of the perpetrator is among the most crucial in correctly identifying the suspect. In recent years it has been shown that because of a remarkable ability of DNA within cells to change with time it is possible to use these changes for determining an individual's age.

Human chromosomes have specialised DNA sequences at their ends, termed telomeres, which shorten every time a cell divides. Because a cell has a finite number of divisions it is possible to deduce the age of the cell by analysing the length of the telomeres and consequently the age of the individual this cell came from. Although the length of telomeres depends on both environmental and genetic factors, it correlates highly with human age. Currently, the error of age determination by telomere shortening analysis exceeds five years but with improvement of the methodology, it will soon be possible to estimate the age with a very small margin of error (Tsuji et al, 2002).

Another method of determining biological age relies on the fact that with age, various mutations accumulate in DNA and analysis of these mutations can give information about the age of the individual (Michikawa et al, 1999). This approach has been developed for mtDNA and produces promising results. However, it often gives erroneous estimates when individuals are of an advanced age and have heart disease or other disorders (Meissner et al, 1999).

Although initial applications of the above-mentioned approaches show very promising results, the use of DNA analysis for determining physical characteristics is still in its infancy and is not yet developed enough to be widely used by the forensic community. One of the first cases when DNA testing was used for determining physical characteristics of the perpetrator was in the

USA in 2003, when ethnicity testing was used to apprehend a suspect in a murder and aggravated rape case. The eye witness testimony described the perpetrator as Caucasian but by DNA analysis it was established that he was 85 per cent African American and 15 per cent Native American. Based upon these findings, police altered the focus of their investigation and included as a person of interest Derrick Todd Lee, who was later convicted for these crimes. Police admitted that without this sophisticated DNA testing, the perpetrator could still be at large.

With development of new technologies and constantly increasing knowledge about the mechanism of the functioning of human genes, the scope of parameters about an individual that can be obtained by DNA analysis can only expand. No other type of evidence is capable of producing so much information about an individual as DNA. Novel forensic approaches transform DNA from being the source of genetic information to being the source of physical information about the individual. However, the introduction of novel forensic technologies needs to be regulated, as together with obvious benefits come ethical and human rights issues. One of the major concerns is that the information obtained by DNA testing (especially information about age and ethnic origin) could make police concentrate on a population of particular ethnic origin or age group during a crime investigation, which could lead to discrimination or to mass collections of DNA samples. Considering that currently, DNA samples from Afro-Caribbean and other minority groups are more likely to go to the UK National DNA Database than DNA data from Caucasians, proper legislation needs to be put in place prior to adoption of this new and exciting technology.

2.6 Non-human DNA testing

Human DNA is not the only type of DNA found at the crime scene. DNA from animals, plants and micro-organisms is also used in some cases to prove or disprove the guilt of the suspect. Forensic animal DNA testing is used in cases dealing with illegal trade of animal and animal products, animal abuse and theft as well as an animal attack on a person. It can also be used for linking a suspect to the crime scene by comparing animal hair collected at the scene and from the suspect.

Analysis of cat DNA was successful used in Canada to convict Douglas Leo Beamish of second degree murder of his former wife, Shirley Douglas, in 1996. Shirley Douglas disappeared in October 1994 and her battered and decomposed body was discovered in a shallow grave in May 1995. A blood-stained jacket which contained white cat hair was found at the crime scene. DNA analysis proved that the cat hair came from a white cat Snowball who lived at the same premises as Douglas Leo Beamish, while the blood stains on the jacket contained the DNA from the victim. This case gave rise to an unsuccessful appeal on the ground of admissibility of DNA evidence pertaining to the identity of the cat hair found on the jacket (*Beamish v The Queen* (1999) (Crim.)(P.E.I.), 27545)

Analysis of plant DNA can give vital information linking a suspect or a victim to a particular location where the crime was committed. In forensic drug investigation, plant DNA analysis is used to identify the source of cannabis samples. In commercial disputes, the identity of commercially valuable cultivars and species can be determined by DNA analysis.

Bio-terrorism has spurred the development of analytical DNA methodology for identifying fungal, bacterial and viral pathogens which are potential bacteriological weapons. After the anthrax terror mail campaign in the USA in 2001, a lot of effort was put into studying the genomes of *Bacillus anthracis* (anthrax) and other organisms which could be used for causing deaths and epidemics on a mass scale.

Another application of non-human DNA testing is testing for *Chlamydia trachomatis* (Chlamydia) infection in cases of child sexual abuse. When no assailant DNA could be recovered from the victim, the presence of Chlamydia infection in the child can be of high probative value if it was also detected in the suspect. DNA analysis can not only confirm whether the infection is present but also give information about the identity of a particular strain of Chlamydia and whether it matches the alleged offender.

Non-human DNA testing is a relatively recent development in forensic DNA analysis. Presenting non-human DNA test data in court is associated with various issues relating, in particular, to admissibility of technology and statistical interpretation of the results.

Chapter 3

Interpretation and statistical evaluation of DNA evidence

Because DNA evidence is relatively new, there is a misconception among many legal practitioners that there is something special about it and that it has to be treated in a different way from other types of evidence. The idea that DNA is unique for each individual (but, crucially, not DNA profile!) and the fact that interpretation of DNA evidence relies heavily on the use of statistics gives DNA evidence an aura of impregnability often leading to the belief that DNA evidence adduced against the accused is an unassailable proof of his/her guilt. This is far from what DNA evidence really is. There is nothing 'special' about DNA evidence to make it different from other types of evidence. It may also be surprising to many to find out that DNA evidence, besides being one of the best studied, is much simpler than many other types of evidence, such as glass or handwriting evidence. The fact that in most cases DNA evidence is easily quantifiable makes it clearly and intelligibly presentable to the jury while the statistical parameters provide quantitative information on the probative value of a particular DNA profile.

Interpretation of forensic evidence is typically performed within a framework appropriate for both scientific analysis and presentation in the courtroom. For some types of evidence, including DNA, the concepts best fitted for interpreting the evidence are not the best for presenting the evidence in court and explaining it to the jury. This contradiction often means that when there are several ways of analysing the evidence (e.g., calculating frequency of a particular DNA profile, and Bayesian analysis of DNA evidence), the best method for analysis (the Bayesian approach) is beyond the comprehension of someone who does not have strong statistical background and, thus, cannot be clearly explained to the jury. Attempts at presenting the most appropriate but mathematically challenging approaches for the interpretation of DNA evidence have led to several important court rulings, in particular that of *R v Adams (Denis)* [1996] 2 Cr. App. R. 467, *R v Doheny and Adams* [1997] 1 Cr. App. R. 369 and *R v Adams (Denis) No.2* [1998] 1 Cr. App. R. 377 which, despite providing logical and structured guidelines for the presentation of DNA evidence in court, limits, in the opinion of many specialists in the field, what a DNA expert may comment on.

In this chapter I examine the logic of forensic DNA inference and the approaches employed for analysis of DNA evidence by forensic scientists (some of them, not necessarily used when presenting DNA testing in court) and then explain various statistical parameters used for interpreting DNA results and presenting the evidence to a jury.

3.1 Initial assessment of DNA evidence

When a scientist is first assessing DNA evidence s/he formulates different propositions representing both prosecution and defence hypotheses in order to evaluate the evidence correctly. Here I follow Aitken and Taroni (2004) and also Buckleton (2005) in describing different propositions available to the scientist for setting DNA evidence into the framework acceptable for scientific evaluation and presentation in court.

The framing of the propositions is based on three key principles (Evett and Weir, 1998):

- Evaluation of DNA evidence is only meaningful when at least one of the two (or in some cases more) competing propositions is addressed. Usually these are the prosecution hypothesis (H_p) and the defence hypothesis (H_d).
- Evaluation of DNA evidence considers the probability of evidence under the two competing propositions.
- Evaluation of evidence is carried out within a framework of circumstances and is conditioned not only by the competing propositions but also by the structure and content of the framework.

The propositions or hypotheses must be mutually exclusive (Robertson and Vignaux, 1995) and are formulated so that they represent the prosecution and defence views (although because of the presumption of innocence, the defence is not required to put forward any proposition whatsoever), for example:

H_p: The DNA comes from the suspect
H_d: The DNA comes from a male other than the suspect

Commonly, there are only two propositions which are analysed in pairs but because the hypotheses do not need to be exhaustive there may be three or more propositions although, in most cases, they can be reduced to just two alternatives. For example, the following propositions:

H_p: The DNA comes from the suspect
H_{d1}: The DNA comes from the father of the suspect
H_{d2}: The DNA comes from the brother of the suspect

can be reduced to:

H_p: The DNA comes from the suspect
H_d: The DNA comes from a male related to the suspect

The choice of the propositions to be addressed depends on the circumstances of the case, the observations that have been made and the available background information (Aitken and Taroni, 2004). Setting appropriate alternative propositions is crucial for correct evaluation of DNA evidence as the inappropriate choice of proposition can make the evidence irrelevant in the circumstances of a particular case, leading to its dismissal.

There will be various propositions considered by various parties involved in the case and ultimately the trial. Aitken and Taroni (2004) classify the hierarchy of the propositions into three levels:

• Offence (crime) Level
• Activity Level
• Source Level

The Offence Level proposition is at the top of the hierarchy and deals with the ultimate issue such as 'the defendant is guilty of raping the victim'. This proposition is solely the domain of the jury and is above the level of forensic scientist. All evidence adduced at the trial (and DNA evidence may be one of many types of evidence) must be taken into account to assess the guilt or innocence of the defendant. At this level, the jury evaluates whether both *mens rea* and *actus reus* in relation to the defendant have been proved by the prosecution to the required standard.

The second level of hierarchy, the Activity Level, deals with activity in question, for example 'the defendant had intercourse with the victim'. This level of proposition can be addressed by the scientist but, because of various other evidence not accessible to the scientist, this activity level should also be left for the jury to consider. As an example, semen of the defendant can be found on a vaginal swab from the victim but it does not necessarily mean that the defendant had intercourse with the victim. Semen obtained from the defendant in a way other then vaginal intercourse (e.g., oral sex or masturbation) could have been planted inside the vagina by the victim who had a grudge against him and then accused him of raping her. The evidence related to the possibility of oral sex or masturbation may not (and should not) be available to the scientist, making his/her conclusion on the possibility of the intercourse between the defendant and the victim groundless.

The Source Level is the lowest level of the hierarchy. This level is an exclusive prerogative of the forensic scientist who considers questions such as 'did semen from the vaginal swab originate from the suspect' using available background information for the case. Recently, an extra level below the source level termed 'sublevel I' was introduced into the hierarchy. This was done because of the sensitivity of DNA technology – there may be uncertainty regarding which body fluid the DNA could came from and an extra level was required to answer this question. The typical proposition considered at this level is 'DNA came from the suspect'.

Framing the propositions is the first stage of the analysis. Next, the scientist has to choose the appropriate analytical approach for the evaluation of DNA evidence. Depending on how much background information is available to the scientist and also on the type of evidence that s/he is expected to obtain, the scientist can choose to treat the evidence using the 'frequentist', 'logical' (also called 'Bayesian') or the 'full Bayesian' approach (Buckleton, 2005). An excellent treatment of these approaches can be found in Buckleton (2005). I follow him in discussing them here.

3.1.1   The frequentist approach

The frequentist approach takes its name after the frequentist definition of probability. According to the adherents of this school of thought, the probability of a particular event is defined over a number of observations by the frequency of the event out of all possible events. The alternative, subjective definition is that probability is a measure of personal belief in the occurrence of the event, which is conditional on the amount of background information available, the amount of new information obtained during the process of the evaluation and the person making the assessment (Aitken and Taroni, 2004). The subjective interpretation of probability lies in the foundation of interpreting the evidence using the logical or full Bayesian approaches.

Under the frequentist approach, DNA evidence can be treated in terms of coincident probabilities or exclusion probabilities. The approach of coincident probabilities is somewhat similar to the logical *reductio ad absurdum* approach used in philosophy and mathematics. In broad terms, the approach states that given a proposition, the evidence is unsound if the proposition is true. Hence, it supports the alternative proposition. Under this approach, alternative propositions are that the evidence came from the suspect and that the evidence is coincidental and the observed match is due to chance. The less likely this chance is under the proposition the more weight is given to the alternative.

The process of interpreting DNA evidence using the coincident probabilities approach starts with formulating the null hypothesis:

H_0: DNA came from a man other than the suspect

The alternative hypothesis will be:

H_1: DNA came from the suspect

To estimate the probability of the evidence under H_0, the scientist needs to compare the evidentiary DNA profile and the profile from the suspect. If the profiles are identical, s/he needs to calculate the frequency of occurrence of this DNA profile in general population. If the chances of finding the crime stain profile are, say, 1 in 10,000,000, the probability of H_0 (DNA came from a man other than the suspect) will be very small and the null hypothesis can be rejected in favour of the alternative.

Under the exclusion probability approach the probability that a random man or a contributor to the mix (if a mixed DNA profile was obtained) will be excluded as the donor of the DNA from the crime scene is calculated. According to this approach, if a random man is excluded it is unlikely that the suspect is a random man and hence, the null hypothesis is rejected in favour of the alternative. The smaller the exclusion probability, the stronger the support for the alternative hypothesis. The advantage of the exclusion probability approach is that, as opposed to coincidence probability, it is applicable to mixtures and paternity testing.

The coincidence and exclusion probability approaches are easily understood by lay people and can be clearly explained to a jury. However, they have several drawbacks which can become the subject of hot deliberations in the courtroom. Under these approaches, the propositions have to be very carefully drawn, which sometimes is not straightforward. These approaches fall short when several types of DNA evidence have been recovered from the same crime scene or when three or more hypotheses can be put forward as to the origin of DNA from the crime stain. The other drawback is the threshold value for rejecting the null hypothesis. In the above scenario, besides the suspect, about five other people living in the UK (assuming the total UK population of 60 million) may have an identical DNA profile to that from the crime stain. Is it justifiable to reject the null hypothesis under such circumstances? And what if the chances of finding this profile were higher? The decision on when exactly the null hypothesis is to be rejected is very subjective and depends not only on the population size but also on other evidence. Other disadvantages of using exclusion probabilities in relation to DNA evidence interpretation are discussed in Chapter 7.

Under the frequentist approach only one hypothesis is analysed and should it be rejected the alternative hypothesis is taken to be true. In the courtroom, though, the situation is markedly different. The prosecution and the defence present their alternative hypotheses, which have both strengths and weaknesses. In reaching its conclusion as to the most likely course of events, the jury weighs the strengths and the weaknesses of each hypothesis. Using the frequentist approach, this type of analysis in relation to DNA evidence cannot be accomplished. It becomes possible only when the evidence is evaluated under the logical approach.

3.1.2 The logical (Bayesian) approach

As in forensic science, there is a real paucity of numerical data the subjectivist approach allows to overcome this problem. The subjectivist approach defines probability as a measure of belief that a particular event is more likely to have occurred than an alternative; it enables the combining of objective probabilities, based on data, and subjective probabilities, for which the knowledge and experience of the forensic scientist may assist in provision of estimates (Aitken and Taroni, 2004). When the jury evaluates the prosecution and the defence hypotheses as to the fact at issue, it does so by weighing which of the alternative explanations of the fact at issue is most probable, considering all the evidence adduced. This is exactly what the logical approach does – determining the most probable origin or the likelihood of DNA evidence (evidentiary fact) and weighing both prosecution and defence hypotheses using evidence available to the scientist.

Central to the logical approach is Bayes' theorem formulated by Reverend Thomas Bayes and published posthumously in 1763 in *An Essay towards solving a Problem in the Doctrine of Chances*. Applied to DNA evidence, Bayes' theorem deals with the likelihood of the fact at issue under two alternative propositions (the prosecution and defence hypotheses) before and after DNA evidence is adduced.

Let:

H_p be the hypothesis advanced by the prosecution,
H_d be the hypothesis advanced by the defence,
E be the event that defendant's DNA profile matches the DNA profile from the crime stain, and
I be all background (other) evidence in the case.

Then we can formulate probability Pr of the hypotheses advanced by the prosecution H_p and the defence H_d, given DNA evidence E and other evidence I as: $\Pr(H_p \mid E, I)$ and $\Pr(H_d \mid E, I)$ respectively (the sign '|' reads as 'given').

Using laws of probability it is possible to compare the two alternative probabilities as:

$$\frac{\Pr(H_p \mid E, I)}{\Pr(H_d \mid E, I)} = \frac{\Pr(E \mid H_p, I)}{\Pr(E \mid H_d, I)} \times \frac{\Pr(H_p \mid I)}{\Pr(H_d \mid I)}$$

The expression:

$$\frac{\Pr(H_p \mid I)}{\Pr(H_d \mid I)}$$

termed 'prior odds', represents the view of the alternative hypotheses which is formed by the jury before DNA evidence was adduced. This is something which is not expressed numerically and does not need to be, as the opinion on the fact at issue is formed in the minds of the jury based on the evidence adduced *prior* to DNA evidence. Being the exclusive realm of the jury, 'prior odds' are beyond the scope of the forensic scientist who must not express his/her opinion on this matter.

The expression:

$$\frac{\Pr(H_p \mid E, I)}{\Pr(H_d \mid E, I)}$$

called 'posterior odds', represents the view of the jury on the alternative hypotheses of events *after* DNA evidence was adduced.

The expression:

$$\frac{\Pr(E \mid H_p, I)}{\Pr(E \mid H_d, I)} \tag{1}$$

called 'likelihood ratio' (LR) describes whether the DNA evidence is more likely under the prosecution (numerator) or defence (denominator) hypotheses and is the numerical measure of the weight of DNA evidence. When a forensic scientist evaluates the evidence using the logical approach s/he typically reports only the LR, which is then used by the jury to weigh the prosecution and defence hypothesis against each other. If the LR is greater than 1, DNA evidence supports the prosecution hypothesis on the origin of DNA in the crime sample. The higher is the LR the more weight is put on the prosecution hypothesis. Alternatively, the smaller the LR, the more weight is put on H_d. When the likelihood ratio is close to 1, both prosecution and defence hypotheses are likely and the probative value of DNA evidence is very small.

To illustrate how the likelihood ratio is calculated let us look at the following simple example. Assume that a crime was committed. Let c be the stain recovered at the scene. Suppose DNA analysis revealed that the profile of the stain is G_c. Later a suspect s was arrested whose DNA profile G_s is identical to G_c. The prosecution alleges that DNA in the crime stain comes from the suspect s who is the perpetrator of the crime. The defence's case is that it was not the suspect s but the real criminal x who is the donor of the DNA found in the crime sample and that the suspect s and the real criminal x have identical DNA profiles due to chance. In this case, the prosecution and defence hypotheses will be:

H_p: The DNA in the crime stain c came from the suspect s.
H_d: The DNA in the crime stain c came from the real criminal x.

In order to estimate the weight of DNA evidence, let us calculate the probability Pr of DNA evidence under H_p and H_d. This probability for H_p will be $\Pr(G_c \mid G_s, H_p)$ which is read as 'the probability of finding the DNA profile G_c in the crime stain c, given that the suspect s has the DNA profile G_s'. As under H_p it was the suspect who had committed the crime and nobody else, $\Pr(G_c \mid G_s, H_p) = 1$.

According to H_d the suspect s and the real criminal x have identical DNA profiles. Let us write the probability of finding this profile as $\Pr(G_c \mid G_s, H_d)$. This probability can be estimated by the frequency f of suspect's DNA profile G_s in the population. Hence, we can write that $\Pr(G_c \mid G_s, H_d) = f$. Then, we can write the likelihood ratio (1) as follows:

$$LR = \frac{\Pr(G_c \mid G_s, H_p)}{\Pr(G_c \mid G_s, H_d)} = \frac{1}{f}$$

If f is very small, the LR would favour H_p; when f is relatively large, the weight of H_p will be less.

When the same DNA evidence is analysed using the frequentist approach, the probability of a coincidental match between the suspect's profile G_s and the crime stain profile G_c will be equal to the frequency f of finding G_s in the population. When f is very small the defence hypothesis of a chanced match will be rejected in favour of the prosecution theory of events. However, using the logical approach, the defence hypothesis is not rejected! The likelihood ratio simply indicates how many times more likely is the prosecution hypothesis in comparison to that of the defence based, on DNA evidence and the background information available to the scientist, leaving the decision of rejecting it up to the jury. Using this information the jury then puts it in the context of *other* evidence adduced at the trial in reaching the conclusion as to the guilt or innocence of the suspect s. This presents a clear advantage of the logical approach in comparison to the frequentist one, as it is the jury and not the scientist who makes a decision as to acceptance or rejection of a particular hypothesis.

The likelihood ratio is an objective estimation of the weight of DNA evidence because it is based on parameters and statistics that are obtained experimentally (for example, allelic frequencies, or the coefficient of co-ancestry). However, forensic scientists usually accompany the likelihood ratio with a qualitative verbal explanation of the support that should be given, in their view, to one of the competing hypotheses (usually the prosecution hypothesis). This is typically done by assigning a non-numerical weight to LR using one of several verbal scales proposed for this purpose. An example of such a scale is given in Table 3.1. The idea behind the verbal explanation is to assist the jury in understanding how much weight should be given to the hypothesis that the accused is the donor of the DNA in the crime stain. By

Table 3.1 Verbal scale used for reporting weight of DNA evidence (Buckleton, 2005)

LR value	Verbal scale	Hypothesis supported
1,000,000	Extremely strong support	
100,000	Very strong support	
10,000	Strong support	H_p
1,000	Moderately strong support	
100	Moderate support	
10	Limited support	
1	Inconclusive	Neither
0.1	Limited support	
0.01	Moderate support	
0.001	Moderately strong support	H_d
0.0001	Strong support	
0.00001	Very strong support	
0.000001	Extremely strong support	

admittance of forensic scientists this scale is arbitrary and hence subjective (Buckleton, 2005).

When presenting results using the verbal scale, the wording expresses either the personal opinion of the scientist who wrote the DNA report about the strength of support for one of the hypotheses, or the personal opinion of the scientist who developed this verbal scale. The description of the strength of evidence attached to the LR values in Table 3.1 will vary, depending on the size of the population in question, the discriminating power of the technique used and also on the personal opinion of the author of the scale. If the crime happened on an island with a population of, say, 500 people the LR of 1,000 will be a very strong indication that it was the defendant who is the donor of the DNA from the crime sample, thus making the phrasing 'moderately strong support' in Table 3.1 (should it be used) an underestimation of the weight of DNA evidence. Wording for the same LR in the verbal scale published by Evett (1991) would be 'strong'.

Robertson and Vignaux (1995) discuss the issue of relying on a verbal scale to explain likelihood ratios to a jury. They put forward several objections to using a verbal scale for this purpose. The scale is designed to be used when dealing with high likelihood ratios, however, most of the 'ordinary' evidence which courts accept as 'strong' have LRs of only 10–50, which, if Table 3.1 were used, would be somewhere between 'limited' and 'moderate' support.

Then, the meaning of the expression 'moderate support' or 'limited support' has to be explained to the jury and the defence. The jury will have to have a table, like Table 3.1, explaining the meaning of the words together with the LR values, which raises the problem of standardisation of the scale. In a situation when the LR of one piece of evidence is, say, 1,100 and of another,

9,900, the verbal scale does not allow discriminating between them. When evidence is stronger than 'very strong' but less than certainty, words become inadequate to express the strength of evidence. It is also impossible to express the strength of evidence by words when two different types of evidence have to be evaluated together (e.g., results of SGM Plus genotyping and Y chromosome testing). When the strength of evidence is expressed by numbers, it is possible to perform mathematical manipulations with them to evaluate the strength of combined evidence. In all these instances, the weight of evidence would be better expressed by using numbers.

When a scientist expresses the strength of the scientific support to one of the alternative hypotheses, s/he appears to be commenting on the ultimate issue which in most cases is whether or not the accused is the source of the crime stain. In English courts it is the prerogative of the jury to decide this issue. The jury is guided in this decision by the statistical information provided by the forensic scientist and should not be affected by his/her personal opinion as to the source of DNA evidence. This point was decided in *R v Doheny and Adams* [1997] 1 Cr. App. R. 369:

> The expert should not be asked his opinion on the likelihood that it was the defendant who left the crime stain, nor when giving (p. 370) evidence should he use terminology which may lead the jury to believe that he is expressing such an opinion.

It is regrettable that in contravention of this ruling, almost every DNA report submitted to courts does contain the verbal expression of how much support is to be given to the prosecution hypothesis and in most cases this is allowed to be admitted and aired in front of the jury.

3.1.3 The full Bayesian approach

Using the frequentist or logical approaches, it is only possible to accommodate two alternative hypotheses. But what about cases when more than two hypotheses are put forward? While the prosecution hypothesis may be something like this:

H_p: The DNA comes from the suspect.

The defence may have several hypotheses, for example:

H_d: The DNA comes from a male unrelated to the defendant.
$H_{d(1)}$: The DNA comes from the brother of the defendant.
. . .
. . .
$H_{d(n)}$: The DNA comes from a male n, related in some way to the suspect.

To accommodate this scenario we need to have a formula which will be able to compare the prosecution hypothesis to all possible defence hypotheses. This is provided by the general form of Bayes' theorem (Buckleton, 2005):

$$Pr(H_1 \mid G_c, G_s) = \frac{Pr(H_1)}{\sum_{i=1}^{N} Pr(G_c \mid G_s, H_i)Pr(H_i)}$$

where $Pr(H_1 \mid G_c, G_s)$ is the probability of hypothesis 1, given DNA evidence from the crime stain and the suspect's DNA profile; $Pr(H_1)$ is the probability of hypothesis 1 (the probability that person 1 is the offender); $Pr(G_c \mid G_s, H_i)$ is the probability of DNA evidence given the suspect's DNA profile under hypothesis i and $Pr(H_i)$ is the probability of the hypothesis i (the probability of person i being the offender).

The major disadvantage of this formula is that it cannot be applied in the courtroom because the terms $Pr(H_i)$ relate to the prior probability of the ith individual being the source of DNA (Buckleton, 2005). It is not up to the forensic scientist to assign a prior probability of being the source of DNA to a particular individual but rather the decision on this lies with the jury. One of the solutions to the problem is for the court to supply its view on the prior odds in terms of referring to a forensically relevant population or, when it is known that the culprit comes from a particular area, thus eliminating people from outside it (i.e., setting the prior probability for members of this population to 0). In a very simple case, considering no other evidence except DNA, if the perpetrator comes from a village of 5,000 people, the prior odds for each individual will be 1/5,000). But even in a case when such information is provided to the scientist, the equation is far too complex to be useful for the jury.

3.1.4 Legal issues related to DNA interpretation approaches

Generally speaking, forensic DNA evidence can be interpreted using either the frequentist or the full Bayesian approach since the logical approach is a special case of the full Bayesian approach for two alternative hypotheses. Despite being the method of choice for analysis of DNA evidence among forensic scientists, it is difficult for approaches based on Bayes' theorem to find acceptance in court. The only exception is parentage testing where results are presented using a likelihood ratio like the CPI.

The first time that the presentation of DNA results in court was put under scrutiny was in *R v Deen* TLR 1994 Jan 10. In presenting DNA evidence, the prosecution confused the probability that defendant's DNA matched the crime sample given that s/he was innocent, i.e., the random match probability, with the probability of the defendant being innocent given that his/her sample matched the crime sample. This is known as 'the prosecutor's fallacy' and will be discussed in detail below. For now, this case illustrates that the concepts of probability and likelihood ratio are sometimes difficult to grasp even for prosecution scientists who have specific training in the statistical interpretation of DNA results.

The difficulties of using Bayes' theorem in court are related to the fact that it combines evidence expressed in both numerical and non-numerical ways in the same formula, and some of this evidence, as well as the prior odds, is not available to the scientist. Even if this evidence were available, s/he does not possess the means of finding out whether or not this evidence is true and how much weight should be given to each piece of evidence in the context of a particular case. The responsibility for deciding the truthfulness of evidence is that of the jury, thus making it impossible for the scientist to apply Bayes' theorem in full to estimate the weight of DNA evidence. However, in order to calculate the likelihood ratio, the scientist only needs minimum background information on the case, if any at all, and the use of the likelihood ratio for such purposes can be completely justified.

The reluctance to accept Bayes' theorem for evaluating DNA evidence has a valid basis. Understanding the theorem requires good knowledge of statistics and even many university students find it difficult to get to grips with it. A jury is very unlikely to have sufficient statistical background to understand the theorem and its applications. Trying to explain it in lay terms typically ends in confusion of the jury and the judge (see *R v Adams (Denis)* [1996] 2 Cr. App. R. 467 and *R v Adams (Denis) No.2* [1998] 1 Cr. App. R. 377). This is especially true for the full Bayesian approach, which, as many forensic scientists admit, cannot be used in court. These problems prompted the ruling of the Court of Appeal in the case of *R v Adams (Denis)* [1996] 2 Cr. App. R. 467 at p. 482 which made Bayes' theorem inadmissible as part of DNA evidence.

The way DNA evidence is to be presented in court was outlined in *R v Doheny and Adams* [1997] 1 Cr. App. R. 369 (discussed in more detail later). The ruling describing the guidelines on procedure in relation to DNA evidence and advises that all DNA evidence should be presented using the frequentist approach:

> The expert will, on the basis of empirical statistical data, give the jury the random occurrence ratio – the frequency with which the matching DNA characteristics are likely to be found in the population at large.

In relation to the use of Bayes' theorem, the ruling agreed with the earlier ruling in *R v Adams (Denis)* [1996] 2 Cr. App. R. 467 at p. 482 that:

> To introduce Bayes' Theorem, or any similar method, into a criminal trial plunges the jury into inappropriate and unnecessary realms of theory and complexity deflecting them from their proper task.

and then specifically advised against the use of likelihood ratios when presenting DNA evidence (p. 370):

> It is inappropriate for an expert to expound a statistical approach to evaluating the likelihood that the defendant left the crime stain, since unnecessary theory and complexity deflect the jury from their proper task.

The debate as to whether, in the words of David Balding (2005), rational reasoning, exemplified by Bayes' theorem, was officially prohibited from UK courtroom by the rulings in these two cases is still going on but there are many important cases in which likelihood estimation is the only logical approach to evaluating DNA evidence. This is especially true for parentage and relationship testing, identification of missing people and interpretation of mixed profiles. As we will see later, the concept of random match probability, which is a likelihood ratio, more accurately describes the nature of a match between two DNA profiles than a frequency of this DNA profile in a population.

3.2 Introduction to population genetics

Interpretation of DNA evidence requires assigning a probability to a match between a crime sample and a suspect. When calculating this probability, various population genetic parameters related to the frequency of alleles and genotypes in a relevant population, as well as to the structure of the population itself, have to be taken into consideration. Before we look at the indices used for presenting the results of DNA analysis in court, I would like to introduce key concepts of population genetics in order to provide necessary background to how these indices are calculated.

Genetic loci in a population can be either monomorphic or polymorphic. When a locus is polymorphic there will be more than one genetic variant (allele) present in the population. Each of these variants will be present in the population with a specific frequency reflecting the probability of finding a particular allele in a randomly picked member of the population.

When investigating a particular population, one of the key questions is whether allele frequencies stay the same from generation to generation or change. If they change, what are the causative factors of this process and is it possible to account for them when calculating a probability of a match between a crime stain and a suspect?

The other set of questions which are of paramount importance for forensic DNA profiling deals with the probability of finding a particular genotype (a combination of two alleles at an individual locus) in a population. What are the chances of finding a particular genotype in a population given frequencies of alleles which make it up? When DNA is analysed for more than one locus, what are the factors affecting the chances of finding a particular combination of genotypes? Will the chances of finding this combination in one individual affect the chances of finding the same combination in another individual? These questions ultimately lead to the concept of a random match, which I discuss below.

The behaviour of alleles in a population is governed by the Hardy-Weinberg law which states that in an infinitely large population with random mating and assuming no selection, migration or mutation, the frequencies of alleles at a specific locus will remain constant from generation to generation. One of the outcomes of this law is that the probability of finding a particular genotype in a population can be derived from allelic frequencies. When only two alleles, A and a, are present in a population at a specific locus i with the probabilities of p_A and p_a respectively, the probability Pr of finding the homozygote genotypes AA or aa or the heterozygote genotype Aa can be calculated as follows:

$$\text{Pr}_{AA} = p_A^2, \text{Pr}_{aa} = p_a^2, \text{and Pr}_{Aa} = p_A \times p_a \tag{2}$$

The Hardy-Weinberg law is idealised. Most human populations are governed by a set of state laws, religious customs and cultural habits that regulate migration and marriage. Human populations have a finite size and the choice of a spouse is not random. People use various types of selection to find a mate – physical, cultural and economic features make people prefer one individual over the other, causing deviation from the random mating requirement. Human populations undergo admixtures from other populations due to migrations. In the twentieth century, the decrease in the cost of travel, and changes in political and economic situations on a global scale caused levels of human migrations never seen before. Mutation processes can produce novel DNA variants as well as change the frequencies of the alleles present in the population. All this can limit the applicability of genetic frequencies calculated on the basis of the Hardy-Weinberg law to everyday situations.

To estimate a frequency of alleles at a particular locus, DNA from a large number of individuals is genotyped, alleles identified and their frequency determined by dividing the number of incidents of a particular allele by the total number of alleles observed. For example, when 100 people are genotyped for a locus A the total number of alleles observed at this locus will be 200 (assuming no missing data or genetic abnormalities). If out of these 200 alleles allele a_1 was observed 52 times the frequency fa_1 of this allele will be fa_1 = 52 ÷ 200 = 0.26. Typically, about 100–120 genotypes are required to obtain reliable data as to the number and types of alleles present in the population and also to estimate their frequencies (Evett and Gill, 1991), however, forensic laboratories use a bigger population for this purpose.

Besides allelic frequencies the structure of human population also affects the frequency of occurrence of a particular genotype. The population, which may seem homogenous, is, at a closer look, more likely to be heterogeneous and consequently should be treated as such. Racial groups which are called 'Caucasian', 'Afro-Caribbean' or 'Asian' are in reality made up of ethnic groups that have not really mixed their genes. The majority of the UK's population can be considered to be Caucasian, however, it is represented by English, Scots, Irishmen, Jews, Italians, Poles and other ethnic groups which form sub-populations with unique genetic features. Because of different patterns of migration and intermarriage, such groups are not very well defined and simple population-genetic models do not exactly apply in this case (Balding, 2005).

Within sub-populations the probability of finding a particular allelic variant may be different from that for the general population and this has to be taken into account when calculating a match probability. After a number of generations, because of random genetic processes (called 'genetic drift'), the frequency of alleles in sub-populations may change and a particular allele may even become fixed, meaning that it is the only allele which is found at a particular locus in this sub-population.

Let us have a second look at the numerical example above. Let assume further that the population of 100 people is made of two sub-populations split by different religious beliefs with almost no inter-sub-population marriages (a real-life example is the Caucasian population of Belfast which is made of the Catholic and the Protestant sub-populations). At the locus A four alleles are present in the total population – a_1, a_2, a_3 and a_4 with the frequencies 0.26, 0.24, 0.30 and 0.20 respectively. Alleles a_1 and a_2 are found exclusively in the sub-population 1 while alleles a_3 and a_4 in sub-population 2. If we were to calculate the probability $\mathrm{Pr}a_2a_3$ of the genotype a_2a_3 using the allelic frequencies we would obtain the value of $\mathrm{Pr}a_2a_3 = 0.24 \times 0.30 = 0.072$. The real probability, however, of finding this genotype will be 0 as the two sub-populations never mix.

To account for genetic differences between sub-populations and to measure their relative progress towards fixation, Sewell Wright (1951) introduced the parameter θ (theta), also called F_{ST} in forensic literature. This parameter deals with the structure of sub-populations and is known as the 'sub-population correction'. Because members of a specific sub-population are more related to each other than to members of other sub-populations, θ may also be considered to be a measure of relatedness between the members of the sub-population. Hence, θ is also known as the 'between-person co-ancestry coefficient'. θ takes the values from 0 to 1. When θ is 1 it means that all sub-populations have reached fixation at the locus. When θ is 0 the allele frequencies are the same in all sub-populations meaning that for this locus the population is homogenous. Published estimates of θ at STR loci for sub-populations within the major human racial groups are often small, typically less than 1 per cent (Balding, 2005) although θ values of up to 5 per cent are used in forensic practice. In practice, forensic scientists tend to use relatively large values for θ (2–4 per cent) thus giving a conservative estimate of a match probability which usually tends to favour the defendant. In the UK, the FSS guidelines recommend the use of $\theta = 3$ per cent with the Caucasian and Afro-Caribbean populations and 5 per cent with the Asian (Indo–Pakistani) populations (Foreman and Lambert, 2000).

3.3 Random match probability

David Balding (2005) presents an elegant and simple explanation of the concept of random match probability. Let us assume that a crime was committed and a DNA profile D was obtained from the crime scene. Then, a suspect s was arrested and his/her profile was found to match that obtained from the crime scene (i.e., $s \equiv D$; this is read as the suspect s has a profile D). The probability of this match R_i is known as 'random match probability' or 'match probability', and the i denotes an individual randomly taken from a relevant population.

Under the prosecution hypothesis, the suspect s is the real criminal C (i.e., $C \equiv s \equiv D$), while under the defence hypothesis the real criminal C is an unknown individual i. Now, we can write the likelihood ratio (1) in the form:

$$R_i = \frac{\Pr(C \equiv s \equiv D \mid C = s, I)}{\Pr(C \equiv s \equiv D \mid C = i, I)}$$

where I denotes all background evidence.

This equation can be simplified to give a formula for random match probability:

$$= \frac{\Pr(s \equiv D \mid I)}{\Pr(i \equiv s \equiv D \mid I)} = \frac{1}{\Pr(i \equiv D \mid s \equiv D, I)}$$

The random match probability indicates the chances that a randomly selected unrelated man will share the same DNA profile as the one observed in the accused. Note that this is not the measure of (a) the probability that the accused has committed the crime in question, nor of (b) the probability that someone other than the accused has committed the crime, nor of (c) the probability that someone other than the accused is the source of DNA in the crime stain (Koehler, 1997).

It is important to distinguish between the probability of finding a particular DNA profile in the population and the random match probability. While the probability of a DNA profile represents the chances of finding this profile in the population, the random match probability is the chance of finding another person with the DNA profile in question, assuming the accused has this profile, since the concept of a match involves two individuals. This is discussed further in Chapter 7.

As we have seen in the previous section, the probability of finding a particular genotype in the population is a function of the frequencies of the relevant alleles. For a single locus it will be the probability of the observed genotype (for simplicity I assume completely homogenous populations). To account for the level of co-ancestry between apparently unrelated individuals, the match probability needs to be conditioned on the sub-population correction θ.

A single locus can be either heterozygous or homozygous for a particular allele. Balding (2005) gives the following formulae for calculating single locus match probabilities for homozygous and heterozygous cases accounting for the population sub-structure:

heterozygous case:

$$R_i = 2\frac{(\theta + (1 - \theta)p_A)(\theta + (1 - \theta)p_B)}{(1 + \theta)(1 + 2\theta)}$$

homozygous case:

$$R_i = \frac{(2\theta + (1 - \theta)p_A)(3\theta + (1 - \theta)p_A)}{(1 + \theta)(1 + 2\theta)}$$

where p_A and p_B are the frequencies of alleles A and B respectively and θ is the between-person co-ancestry coefficient.

However, in forensic investigation, DNA is analysed for several loci; in the case of SGM Plus, the number of loci used for calculating random match probability is 10. A random match probability R_D of a multi-locus genotype D may be estimated by multiplying genotype probabilities for individual loci (the so called 'product rule') as follows:

$$R_D = Pr_1 \times Pr_2 \times \ldots \times Pr_i \tag{3}$$

where $Pr_1 \ldots Pr_i$ are random match probabilities for loci 1 to i

For equation (3) to hold, the loci should be inherited completely independent of each other, i.e., the alleles have to be in linkage equilibrium. The concept of linkage equilibrium describes a state of independence between alleles at different loci and largely depends on whether or not the loci are located on the same chromosome. When loci are located on the same chromosome, the alleles may be physically linked and thus inherited together. The probability of two alleles on the same chromosome being inherited together is in reverse proportion to the distance between them – the closer the alleles, the more likely they will be passed on together. All loci in SGM Plus are located on different chromosomes and thus are inherited independent of each other.

However, even when loci are on different chromosomes, it is not necessarily true that they are in a state of linkage equilibrium. Population effects such as sub-division or admixtures can cause alleles at loci on different chromosomes to be inherited together. To account for such effects, calculations of the random match probability have to include θ.

3.4 Non-autosomal markers

Because of uniparental inheritance, the above approach for calculating the random match probability is not applicable to non-autosomal DNA markers. Instead, a method based on the frequency of a particular haplotype in the population is used to evaluate the strength of non-autosomal DNA evidence.

3.4.1 mtDNA

When a suspect is identified and his/her DNA is obtained, mtDNA analysis can determine whether or not s/he could be the donor of the DNA recovered from the crime scene sample. When it is impossible to obtain a DNA sample from the suspect, mtDNA analysis can determine whether s/he could be the donor of the DNA from the evidentiary sample by analysing DNA from his/her maternal relative.

The interpretation of mtDNA evidence can be done within either the frequentist or the logical approach. Under the frequentist approach, the suspect can be either included or excluded from being the donor of the DNA from the crime stain. Inclusion is usually defined by specifying the maximum number of bases at which two samples may differ and yet be deemed to match (Buckleton et al, 2005c). When the differences between the two samples are greater than the pre-defined requirement, the suspect is excluded. The Scientific Working Group on DNA Analysis Methods (SWGDAM) recommends the following criteria for inclusion or exclusion (SWGDAM, 2003):

- Exclusion. If there are two or more nucleotide differences between the questioned and known samples, the samples can be excluded as originating from the same person or maternal lineage.
- Inconclusive. If there is one nucleotide difference between the questioned and known samples, the result will be inconclusive.
- Cannot Exclude. If the sequences from questioned and known samples under comparison have a common base at each position or a common length variant in the HV2 C-stretch, the samples cannot be excluded as originating from the same person or maternal lineage.

In case of inclusion, the frequency p of a particular mitotype can be calculated according to the following formula:

$$p = X/N$$

where X is the number of times a particular mitotype is found in the database containing N profiles.

Because various laboratories may have different criteria under which a sample will be included or excluded it would be helpful for the defence team to ask the forensic laboratory to provide the criteria used for evaluating mtDNA evidence together with the expert statement.

Interpretation of mtDNA evidence could be complicated by the presence of heteroplasmy, which can be tissue specific. To deal with heteroplasmy, Budowle and colleagues (2002) suggest the following approach:

- Failure to exclude. If the two sequences are the same at all sites either both heteroplasmic or both homoplasmic or if one sequence shows heteroplasmy and the other is homoplasmic sharing bases.
- Inconclusive. If both sequences are homoplasmic but differ by one nucleotide.

Under the logical approach a likelihood ratio for the two alternative hypotheses is calculated in a fashion similar to that described for STR loci. As an example, let us assume that a hair allegedly from the perpetrator of the crime c has been found at the scene and the mtDNA profile G_C of the hair matches the mtDNA profile G_S from the suspect s. According to the prosecution hypothesis H_p the suspect is the perpetrator of the crime; the defence alleges that the hair comes not from the suspect but from a different person. We can now construct the following likelihood ratio:

$$LR = \frac{\Pr(G_C \mid G_S, H_p)}{\Pr(G_C \mid G_S, H_d)}$$

Since, in the view of the prosecution, the suspect and the perpetrator are one and the same person, the probability of H_p is 1 and the likelihood ratio can be re-written as:

$$LR = \frac{1}{\Pr(G_C \mid G_S, H_d)}$$

When G_S is unknown but it is possible to obtain an mtDNA profile G_K from the material relative K of the suspect s, G_S should be substituted by G_K in the above formulae. In addition, the likelihood ratios have to be conditioned on the background information, I, which should include, in particular, the information about the relationship between the suspect s and the relative K.

To estimate the denominator we need to assess the frequency of the mitotype in question. I will follow Balding (2005) in explaining how this index is calculated.

Because of population heterogeneity and sampling variation the frequency p of a mitotype is uncertain. To account for these factors, both mtDNA profiles from the defendant and the evidentiary samples have to be included with those of the population database. In this case we use not the frequency p of a mitotype but rather the estimator of the frequency, $\hat{p}$. For a database containing N profiles where a particular mitotype is encountered x times the estimator of the frequency will be:

$$\hat{p} = \frac{x + 2}{N + 2} \tag{4}$$

Taking into account the effect of population sub-structures and after some modifications, the match probability R_i for a mtDNA profile will be:

$$R_i = \theta + (1 - \theta)\hat{p} = \theta + (1 - \theta)\frac{x + 2}{N + 2} \tag{5}$$

When matching heteroplasmic profiles between the crime stain and the suspect are observed, the estimate $\hat{p}$ should be calculated on the basis of the population proportion of the profiles in the database displaying the same heteroplasmy.

Because of the statistical uncertainty of the mitotype frequency, accompanying it with 95 per cent confidence intervals is recommended. This confidence interval gives an estimated range of values that will contain the real value of the mitotype frequency with a probability of 0.95.

These can be calculated as follows (Buckleton et al, 2005c):

$$p \pm 1.96\sqrt{\frac{(p)(1 - p)}{N}} \tag{6}$$

where p denotes the proportion of a particular mitotype in the database containing N profiles.

In some cases a previously unseen mitotype could be obtained from the suspect and the crime scene. As it is not in the database, the formula (4) for calculating the probability of a particular mitotype is not applicable. Although in this situation it will be impossible to estimate the frequency of this mitotype, it is possible to give a confidence interval within which the frequency could be found with necessary probability (Buckleton et al, 2005c). This confidence interval can be calculated as:

$$\hat{p} = 1 - \alpha^{1/N} \tag{7}$$

where α is the confidence coefficient (for 95 per cent, α is set to 0.05). Using this formula it is possible to estimate the upper bound of the frequency $\hat{p}$ of a novel mitotype.

3.4.2 Y chromosome

Examination of the Y chromosome is done by STR genotyping. It should be remembered that as all the markers analysed are located on the same chromosome and, barring extremely rare cases, are inherited together as a haplotype the product rule cannot be used for estimating the probability of a Y chromosome match. The logic and approaches for statistical interpretation of mtDNA matches can be applied to the Y chromosome with some minor modifications related to using θ estimated for the Y chromosome instead of that for mtDNA and appropriate population databases. The probability of a Y chromosome match and the confidence interval for the estimate can be calculated using formulae (5–7).

3.5 Mixtures

Crime samples often contain bodily fluids from several individuals. A DNA profile obtained from such stains will be a mixture of profiles from those who contributed their biological material to them. When evaluating mixtures, the aim of the forensic scientist is to determine whether or not a suspect is one of the contributors and give a numerical estimate of the probability. Mixtures can be genotyped using both autosomal and non-autosomal markers. In this section I will discuss the approaches of evaluating mixed profiles using results of STR genotyping. The approaches to interpretation of mtDNA and Y chromosome mixtures have been described elsewhere (Buckleton et al, 2005c; Fukshansky and Bär, 2005).

The evidential value of a mixed DNA profile is in reverse proportion to the number of contributors to the mix – the higher is the number, the less is the cogency of DNA evidence (Evett and Weir, 1998). Evaluation of mixtures can be made using the frequentist or the logical approach. In the first, the probability of excluding the suspect from being one of the contributors is calculated. The second approach is based on evaluating the likelihood ratio of the two alternative hypotheses.

3.5.1 Frequentist approach to mixture evaluation

I have briefly discussed exclusion probabilities for the evaluation of DNA evidence at the beginning of this chapter. In the context of mixture analysis, the exclusion probability is defined as the probability that a random person would be excluded as a contributor to the observed DNA mixture (Clayton and Buckleton, 2005). This probability is known as random man exclusion probability and this approach of mixture evaluation is often referred to as the Random Man Not Excluded (RMNE) approach as it determines the proportion of the population that could not be excluded from the set of potential contributors to the mixture.

For calculation of the RMNE index, two pieces of information are required – the genotype of the crime stain and the frequency of the alleles that make it up. Knowledge of the suspect's genotype is not required to compute the RMNE statistic as it is solely based on the alleles identified in the crime stain. When a DNA mixture has, at a locus A, alleles $a_1, a_2 \ldots a_n$, the RMNE index at this locus will be calculated as the squared sum of allelic probabilities:

$$\text{RMNE}_A = \left(\sum_{i=1}^{n} p(a_i) \right)^2$$

Then, the random man exclusion probability, PE, for the locus A will be:

$$\text{PE}_A = 1 - \text{RMNE}_A$$

If the forensic stain is analysed for n loci, then the combined exclusion probability CPE_n will be:

$$\text{CPE}_n = \text{PE}_1 \times \text{PE}_2 \times \ldots \times \text{PE}_n$$

The RMNE approach has a distinct advantage over other approaches – it does not assume the number of contributors to the mixed profile, which is often difficult to establish especially when the number of contributors exceeds two. Thus, it allows the estimating of the probative value of the evidence without reference to a suspect's DNA profile, which is important for cases where there are several possible perpetrators of the crime or where there is no suspect.

Another advantage of the RMNE approach is that it does not require the defence (or by the same token the prosecution) hypothesis to determine whether or not the suspect could have contributed to the mixture. There can be many scenarios determining who the potential contributors to the mixture are. There is a danger that the forensic scientist could present scenarios with very high likelihood ratios and omit those with lower likelihood ratios. For example, the forensic scientist can report a likelihood ratio for the scenarios such as 'the suspect and another individual unrelated to the suspect are the donors of the DNA in the mixed profile, as opposed to two individuals unrelated to the suspect' which can be extremely high, but not report the ratio for the scenario 'the suspect and another individual unrelated to the suspect are the donors of the DNA in the mixed profile, as opposed to the cousin of the suspect and another individual unrelated to the suspect' which could be significantly less. The forensic scientist may have only a limited amount of background information about the cousin's involvement in the crime, if any. The defence may put forward this hypothesis after the scientist has produced the report, when s/he could not have a chance to evaluate it. As the knowledge of both the prosecution and defence hypotheses is not required to compute the RMNE statistic, this approach may be more favourable to the defendant, considering also the fact that, for the same data, the RMNE value can be significantly less than LR values for some of the propositions. The other obvious advantage is that the concept of RMNE is easier to explain to a jury than the likelihood ratio.

The main disadvantage of RMNE is significant loss of information due to inability of the approach to take into account the genotype of the suspect and hence, it reduces the probative value of DNA evidence. This significantly limits applications of the RMNE approach in mixture analysis.

3.5.2 Logical approach to mixture evaluation

Depending on whether only qualitative (information about the number and type of alleles present in the mixture) or both qualitative and quantitative data (quantitative information about allelic peak parameters, such as area) are used for determining the origin of DNA in the mixture, several methods exist for mixture evaluation. Among them the quantitative and the semi-quantitative (binary) approaches are the most popular within the forensic community.

Under the qualitative approach of mixture evaluation, alternative hypotheses are compared using a likelihood ratio. Let us assume a stain M was found at the crime scene and, following genotyping, a mixed profile G_M was obtained. The profile G_M contained alleles also found in the DNA profiles G_v and G_s, which belong to the victim v and the suspect s respectively. The prosecution alleges that, besides the victim v, the suspect s is a contributor to the mixture, while the defence's hypothesis is that it is the victim v and the real perpetrator of the crime C who are the two contributors. Using this information we can build a likelihood ratio to compare the two propositions:

$$LR = \frac{Pr(G_M \mid G_s, G_v, H_p)}{Pr(G_M \mid G_C, G_v, H_d)}$$

As the probability of the prosecution hypothesis in the numerator is equal to 1, and, assuming that no genotyping error occurred, the genotypes are in Hardy-Weinberg equilibrium and that contributors to the mixture are unrelated, this formula can be simplified to:

$$LR = \frac{1}{\Pr(G_M \mid G_C, H_d)}$$

It is interesting that this formula does not take into account the suspect's and victim's genotypes. Only information about the allelic composition of these profiles is used to deduce possible genotype(s) of the real perpetrator.

This point can be illustrated by the following example. A vaginal swab from a rape victim was genotyped for the locus A and a mixed DNA profile G_M containing three alleles a_1, a_2 and a_3 was obtained. The genotype of the victim G_v was a_1a_2 and the genotype of the suspect G_s was a_2a_3. The prosecution alleges that the suspect is the rapist and that both the victim and the suspect have contributed their DNA to the G_M. According to the defence, the suspect has nothing to do with the rape and the crime was committed by another man, C; as the genotype of the victim G_v is a_1a_2 and the genotype of the mixed profile G_M is $a_1a_2a_3$ the allele a_3 must have come from the criminal C. In such a case, the criminal can have three potential genotypes: a_1a_3, a_2a_3 (the same as G_s), and a_3a_3. The likelihood ratio can be evaluated as:

$$LR = \frac{1}{\Pr(a_1a_3) + \Pr(a_2a_3) + \Pr(a_3a_3)}$$

If the population is in Hardy-Weinberg equilibrium, the probabilities of these genotypes can easily be deduced using genotype probability values from equation (2). Then the likelihood ratio will take the form:

$$LR = \frac{1}{2p_{a_1a_3} + 2p_{a_2a_3} + p^2_{a_3a_3}}$$

where $2p_{a_1a_3}$, $2p_{a_2a_3}$, and $p^2_{a_3a_3}$ are the probabilities of the genotypes a_1a_3, a_2a_3, and a_3a_3 respectively.

For evaluating DNA evidence under the qualitative model it is not important to know the number of potential contributors. In any case, the judgement on this matter lies with the jury. At the same time, information on how many individuals have contributed their DNA to the mixture is important for choosing correct alternative propositions and for correctly calculating the likelihood ratio. We have seen above that the number of potential contributors to the mixture can be determined not only by the allelic composition but also by studying the morphology of the identified allelic peaks. The latter however is disregarded in the quantitative model. The reason for this is that the quantitative approach was developed at the beginning of forensic DNA era, when it was difficult or even impossible to do a qualitative assessment of each individual peak and then use this information for evaluating mixed profiles. Since then, advances in DNA analysis instrumentation have allowed scientists to obtain precise information about the amount of DNA in each particular peak, thus enabling them to estimate the copy number of alleles. This in turn has led to the development of the binary model for mixture interpretation, which utilises both quantitative and qualitative data.

The binary or semi-quantitative approach (Clayton et al, 1998) involves a series of steps aimed at establishing the number of potential contributors to the mixture by determining the mixture ratio of individual contributors using information on morphology of allelic peaks (peak area and peak height). This is done manually using a set of special rules for interpreting the quantitative output of the genotyping instrument. Once the number of potential contributors has been identified, all possible genotype combinations can be considered and those which are most likely under the propositions chosen by the scientist, and also possible under the data interpretation criteria, are used for comparing with the genotypes of the suspect. The genotype of the suspect matching one of the selected allelic combinations is consistent with the hypothesis of his/her being one of the contributors to the mixture and a likelihood ratio can be calculated to determine the weight of evidence. If however no match is found, his/her contribution can be excluded.

The binary approach is widely used by UK forensic laboratories. Although reliable, this model has some important limitations that restrict its application. When the number of contributors to the mixture is more than two, the statistical evaluation of all possibilities becomes so complex that it will be theoretically impossible to exclude a great proportion of the general population from being among the contributors! The binary model also assumes that the mixture proportion is constant across all loci and that the peak area is proportional to the copy number of a particular allele. Because of PCR artefacts, the assumption that the mixture proportion will be the same across all loci analysed can break down, leading to an incorrect conclusion as to the number of possible contributors and also affecting the decision as to which genotype configuration is possible under the chosen rules for data interpretation.

Because of the limitations of the approaches currently in use for mixture evaluation, there are efforts to develop alternative methods based on sophisticated statistical algorithms like Monte Carlo models and Markov Chains. We will have to wait and see whether they will be more reliable than the qualitative and binary models and whether, due to their extreme complexity, they will be accepted for presenting the DNA evidence in court.

3.6 Paternity testing

In legal practice parentage testing is mostly used for determining paternity; in only a few cases does it take the form of maternity testing. As the reasoning in parentage testing is very similar, whether it is paternity or maternity that needs to be determined, I will use paternity testing as an example of how the data of parentage testing are analysed and interpreted.

Evaluation of paternity testing data usually proceeds by calculating the Paternity Index (PI) and the probability of paternity. The PI is computed via a likelihood ratio which weighs two probabilities – the probability that the alleged father s is the true biological father of the child c under the prosecution hypothesis H_p and the probability of another man i and not the alleged father s being the true biological father of the child c under H_d. Typically, DNA profiles from the alleged father, biological mother and the child are required for calculating the PI, although it can also be estimated without the mother's profile. Let E denote all DNA evidence in a particular parentage case (i.e., DNA profiles from the child, mother and the alleged father). Then, by applying Bayes' theorem to DNA evidence as described at the beginning of this chapter, we will have (Buckleton et al, 2005a):

$$\frac{Pr(H_p \mid E)}{Pr(H_d \mid E)} = \frac{Pr(E \mid H_p)}{Pr(E \mid H_d)} \times \frac{Pr(H_p)}{Pr(H_d)}$$

This formula is virtually identical to that used for evaluation the prosecution and defence hypotheses under the logical model of evaluation of forensic evidence (section 3.1.2). The likelihood ratio:

$$\frac{Pr(E \mid H_p)}{Pr(E \mid H_d)}$$

in terms of parentage testing is called Paternity Index; it shows how many times more plausible the prosecution hypothesis is, given the DNA evidence. Usually, the numerator of this fraction, and consequently the probability of paternity under the prosecution hypothesis, will be equal to 1, while the denominator depends on the genotypes of the participants, which alleles are common between the alleged father, the child and the mother (if the mother's sample is analysed) and their frequencies in the population.

When the alleged father is not excluded from being the true biological father, the weight of the evidence toward this is the relative chance that he has transmitted the obligate allele (i.e., the allele which has to come from the alleged father if he is the biological father) to the child, when compared to an unrelated individual from the same population. Thus, PI for a particular locus expresses the relative chance of the alleged father transmitting the obligate allele versus an unrelated individual in the population. Buckleton and colleagues (2005a) and Balding (2005) present the formulae used for calculating PI in duo and trio paternity cases taking into account various population genetic parameters as well as mutation events. Typically, PI is calculated for each locus tested and the CPI for the total number of loci N is calculated as a product of the individual PI:

$$CPI_N = PI_1 \times PI_2 \times \ldots \times PI_N$$

The probability of paternity Pr(P) is another representation of the CPI and is the probability of the alleged father being the true biological parent of the child. This index is calculated as follows:

$$Pr(P) = \frac{CPI}{1 + CPI}$$

For a reasonable number of markers tested, the value of CPI usually exceeds 1,000. In non-criminal cases, a CPI of at least 100 (which corresponds to the probability of paternity of 99 per cent) is required for proving paternity in UK courts.

The prior probability expression:

$$\frac{Pr(H_p)}{Pr(H_d)}$$

evaluates the probability of paternity based on non-genetic evidence. Typically, in paternity disputes, the probability of both prosecution and defence hypotheses are considered to be equal to one-half. This practice is considered to be unfortunate by many eminent authors (for commentary see Balding, 2005). The alleged father may have had a sexual intercourse with the mother (possibly on more than one occasion) which increases his chances of paternity. If the alleged father had unprotected sexual intercourse with the mother around the time when the baby was conceived, the chances of him being the father will be even higher. Surely, if such evidence is available, the practice of assigning equal probabilities for H_p and H_d is misguided and even erroneous. However, no matter what the facts are, it is very difficult and even impossible for the jury to put a numerical value to non-scientific evidence. This is one of the pragmatic reasons for assigning equal prior probabilities to the alternative hypotheses.

Chapter 4

Criminal DNA databases

Once DNA analysis on evidentiary samples or samples from suspects is complete, there are several rationales for keeping the results as well as the samples on record in a database. The profile of the suspect can be used for comparison with profiles from other crime scenes, especially from unsolved crimes. The crime scene profiles can be used for linking various crimes to a particular known or unknown perpetrator. Keeping DNA samples and information on record could help to exonerate wrongfully convicted people when new, more powerful DNA testing technology enters the courtroom. DNA databases can be interrogated by profiles from other countries and jurisdictions in order to track fugitives from justice or link crimes committed elsewhere.

Overall, the idea behind DNA databases is to make criminal intelligence more proactive, efficient and organised on the one hand and to reduce miscarriages of justice on the other hand. This fact has been recognised by the House of Commons Home Affairs Committee which, in the late 1980s, advocated the creation of such a database in the UK, intended to assist in both the prevention and detection of crime and also, to provide robust authority to forensic science (HC Paper 26-I, 1989). This eventually led to the establishing of the National DNA Database in the UK in 1995, which was the first of its kind in the world. It was soon followed by other European countries and the USA. Currently, police DNA databases have been established in all EC member states, as well as in the USA, Canada, Australia, New Zealand, Argentina and other countries. Chalmers (2005) and Williams and Johnson (2005) provide a comprehensive review of the situation with national databases in Europe and some other countries and I would like to refer those who are interested in the subject to these excellent reports. The situation with national and state DNA databases in the USA is outlined by Herkenham (2002).

4.1 The National DNA Database

The National DNA Database (NDNAD) was established on 10 April 1995. The setting up of the NDNAD was preceded by the introduction of the legislation which gave the police powers to obtain DNA samples from individuals (even those who had not been charged with an offence) and retain the information derived from them, as well as allowing the use of profiles obtained for cross-checking against profiles from unsolved crimes (speculative searching). This was established under the Police and Criminal Evidence Act 1984, as amended by the Criminal Justice and Public Order Act 1994 and Criminal Justice and Police Act 2001. The latter amendment also allows the use of NDNAD for crime investigation on a UK-wide basis.

The legal foundation for the creation of the NDNAD was the Home Office Circular (HOC) 16/1995 as amended by HOC 47/1996, HOC 27/1997 and HOC 58/2004 which provided guidance on its operation and conditions regarding the taking and submitting of samples, database access and data security issues. This legislation ensured that the information derived from the samples could be crosschecked against records held by or on behalf of police forces in England and Wales, Scotland, Northern Ireland, Jersey, Guernsey and the Isle of Man as well as the DNA databases maintained by, or on behalf of, Scottish forces and the Police Service of Northern Ireland (formerly the Royal Ulster Constabulary) (see section 4.2).

The NDNAD, including the DNA samples and the information derived from them, is owned by the Association of Chief Police Officers of England, Wales and Northern Ireland (ACPO). The custodian of the NDNAD is the FSS which is also the main provider of DNA profiling services to the police. The database is governed by the NDNAD Board which as of 2005 was composed of representatives from ACPO, FSS, the Home Office and the Human Genetics Commission (ACPO, 2006). The NDNAD Board is accountable for how the database is used and for improving the way it works.

The NDNAD was intended as an intelligence database only; results of any analysis carried out solely for the database, or found after a speculative search, were not intended to be used for prosecution purposes. This, however, was changed by HOC 58/2004 which amended s 23 of HOC 16/95 allowing the charging of suspects on the basis of a match between a crime scene DNA profile and a profile on the National DNA Database from an individual, so long as there was further supporting evidence.

The Database contains four types of samples:

- scene of crime (SOC) samples;
- casework samples taken from suspects for comparison with a SOC sample in a specific case;
- criminal Justice (CJ) samples, taken for intelligence purposes only; and
- volunteer samples.

DNA profiles from volunteers are used only for elimination purposes in a specific case. They are not checked against SOC sample profiles from other crimes or against the subject sample profiles, and are not entered onto the database unless a written consent from the volunteer is produced. Once the consent is given it cannot be withdrawn.

Together with the DNA profile, the CJ/PACE (subject) Sample Record includes the sample identification number, the Arrest/Summons Report Number, the subject's full name, gender, date of birth, ethnic appearance, the force/station code, the name of the officer who took the sample, sample type, the test type and the laboratory which performed the analysis. The information about SOC samples, besides the DNA profile, includes the sample identification number, information about the crime, the force/station code, the name of the officer who took the sample, sample type, the test type and the laboratory which performed the analysis.

The FSS is the main supplier of subject and SOC samples to the NDNAD. In addition to FSS, in England and Wales, the analysis of subject and SOC samples is performed by LGC Ltd and Orchid Cellmark. A number of UK laboratories are in the process of negotiation with the NDNAD Custodian in order to get accreditation for submitting DNA profiles to the database.

The NDNAD contains the largest number of DNA profiles in absolute numbers and in terms of the proportion of the population represented on the database (5.2 per cent in the UK compared to 1.13 per cent in the European Union and 0.5 per cent in the USA) in the world (Parliamentary Office of Science and Technology, 2006). On 31 March 2005, there were 3,072,041 CJ/PACE sample profiles (some of them are duplicates though; the number of unique profiles in the NDNAD is approximately 2.7 million) and 12,095 volunteer sample profiles on the National DNA Database (ACPO, 2006). In addition, the database contains 232,343 crime scene sample profiles. It is estimated that currently, the NDNAD contains DNA samples from virtually the entire UK criminally active population, which is estimated by the Home Office to be in the region of 3 million people (Home Office, 2000).

At its inception, DNA profiles uploaded to the NDNAD were obtained using SGM genotyping. Since 2000 all new DNA profiles in the database are SGM Plus profiles. Pre-2000 SGM profiles are being upgraded to SGM Plus profiles although this process is hindered by high costs. Currently, approximately 23 per cent of the subject sample profiles and 17 per cent of the crime scene sample profiles on the NDNAD are still SGM profiles.

The minimum age at which an individual can be put on the database is 10. Almost 85 per cent of DNA profiles stored belong to people younger than 45. More than 80 per cent of all subject samples in the NDNAD have been obtained from males. With respect to ethnic origin, more than 20 per cent of DNA samples belong to ethnic minorities. People who are classified by the police as black based on their appearance are clearly represented in greater proportion on the NDNAD than those whom they classify as white skinned European. This pattern is similar for all ages and both sexes (ACPO, 2006). It was recently estimated that NDNAD contains DNA profiles from nearly one-third of UK's black adult men, compared to only 8 per cent of white adult men (*New Scientist*, 2005). This raises some important ethical issues which will be discussed later.

The NDNAD does not keep records of offences for which DNA samples from subjects were taken (this information is kept separately on the Police National Computer). However, the information of the type of offences for which DNA samples are taken from subjects can be deduced from the crime scene sample records. About 88 per cent of the crime scene sample records on the database are related to volume crime offences and 8 per cent to serious crime offences with the type of offence for the remainder not recorded.

The NDNAD is an important tool for crime detection although DNA detection is featured only in 0.8 per cent of all crime investigation. When used, it increases the detection rate by 40 per cent with initial detection resulting in a further 0.8 crimes being solved (ACPO, 2006). Such a small percentage can be attributed to the fact that there are a relatively small number of crime scenes from which DNA samples can be recovered, and even then, DNA evidence may have very little value, for example, in cases where the identity of the perpetrator is not in question. Because the main purpose of DNA evidence is identification, the database is most helpful in detecting crimes where the identity of the perpetrator is unknown. The identity of the perpetrator is a particular problem in volume crimes such as burglary and theft, when the use of the NDNAD increases the chances of detection 3–8 fold compared to cases where no DNA was loaded on the database.

4.2 Databases in Scotland and Northern Ireland

Although the NDNAD is a UK-wide criminal investigation tool, only samples collected in England and Wales are deposited to it directly. Scotland and Northern Ireland have their own DNA databases which contain samples collected by Scottish Police Service and the Scottish Division of the MoD Police, and by the Police Service of Northern Ireland respectively.

The Scottish DNA Database was founded in 1997 and is supervised by the Tayside Police Laboratory. DNA profiles from all subject samples taken in Scotland are added to the Scottish DNA Database and then exported to the NDNAD on a daily basis. As of 2005 the NDNAD contained 169,651 Scottish samples. The Tayside Police Laboratory and the Strathclyde Police Forensic Science Laboratories have been accredited for submitting subject and SOC profiles (the former) and only SOC profiles (the latter) to the Scottish DNA Database and NDNAD.

The Northern Ireland DNA Database, which was set up in 1996, is operated by Forensic Science Northern Ireland in Belfast which is also the sole provider of both subject and SOC samples to the Database. Initially, there was no exchange of data between the Northern Ireland DNA Database and the NDNAD but since 2005 all new subject profiles from Northern Ireland are routinely uploaded to the NDNAD.

4.3 The Police Elimination Database

The Police Elimination Database (PED) was established in February 2000 in order to eliminate police officers from the investigative process when a senior investigating officer genuinely believes that innocent contamination of a crime scene by a police officer may have occurred. In accordance with HOC 41/2001 all newly recruited police officers must provide a DNA sample as a condition of appointment. Accordingly, the Police Regulations 1995 (as amended by the Police (Amendment) Regulations 2002) make the provision by inserting reg 20A which stipulates that every member of a police force, except members appointed following their transfer from another police force must provide a sample of hair or saliva for DNA profiling purposes upon appointment. These samples and the information derived thereof are to be kept separate from the samples taken under s 63 of PACE and should be destroyed when the police officer ceases to be a member of the particular force otherwise than on transfer to another police force. The PED is serviced by the FSS.

4.4 The NDNAD and the process of DNA identification

Every new SOC or subject sample profile loaded onto the NDNAD is checked against all other SOC and subject sample profiles already on the database. This process of crosschecking is called 'speculative searching'. Depending on whether the DNA profile is from a subject or an SOC sample, several types of comparison are possible. When a new subject profile is loaded and compared to the profiles in the Database, the following types of matches may be detected:

- A match to a subject sample profile already on the database, indicating that the person is already on the database (possibly under a different name).
- A match to a SOC sample profile from an unsolved crime, identifying a suspect and possibly leading to solving old crimes.

When a new SOC profile is loaded and compared to the profiles in the database there may be the following types of matches detected:

- A match to a subject sample profile already on the database. This match can identify a potential suspect for the offence; or
- A match to (an)other SOC sample profile(s) from unsolved crimes. This can assist in finding an association between different crimes although the identity of the perpetrator in this case will not be revealed.

Following a match, the information from the database, together with any identification made relating to other offences, is passed to a point nominated in each force for receiving it. The information derived from analysing casework samples is passed in the normal way to the investigating officer submitting the case sample.

To be loaded on the NDNAD, a crime scene sample must meet the minimum criteria set by the Custodian. When the profile is of inferior quality it will not be loaded on the database but it can still be searched against it on a one-off basis (one-off speculative search). Such searches are only usually requested by the police for profiles from serious crimes where they may be prepared to deal with the large numbers of potential suspects that could be generated.

The database is very useful in identifying possible suspects by matching subject and crime scene samples. Since May 2001, 195,779 SOC sample profiles have been matched with 157,096 separate individuals. For more than 65 per cent of the crime scene profiles, a single suspect was reported while for the remainder, a list of potential suspects was produced. It is estimated that, on average, 50 match reports linking suspects to violent crimes are generated daily by the database (ACPO, 2006).

Surprisingly, the NDNAD does not allow searching SOC profiles from solved crimes with new subject profiles. Once a crime is successfully prosecuted, SOC profiles from this crime are erased from the Database. This practice is opposed by many criminal solicitors and barristers as it may preclude re-opening the case should new evidence come to light and it assumes that no miscarriage of justice is ever committed in the courtroom. The success of the Innocence Projects in the USA, which was specifically set up to deal with post-convictional DNA testing of evidence, proved that even following a successful prosecution, post-convictional DNA testing can exonerate those who were wrongfully convicted. The issue of deleting SOC profiles from solved crimes and the Innocence Project are discussed below.

The other controversial issue of NDNAD is familial searches, which are used to identify offenders through their possible close relatives whose profiles are on the database. The search produces a list of individuals who theoretically might have a relative whose DNA profile was obtained from the SOC sample. Although such use of the database is compliant with PACE, the Human Rights Act 1998 and Data Protection Act 1998 it clearly represents a major intrusion into family life (GeneWatch UK, 2005) as it has the potential to reveal information that may relate to sensitive family issues, such as paternity, that are unrelated to crime prevention.

4.5 Retention and removal of samples and genetic information derived from them

Pursuant to what used to be s 64(3B)(b) of PACE, fingerprints and samples taken from an individual had to be destroyed under what was s 64(1) if that individual was later acquitted of the offence in respect of which they were taken, or where a decision was later made not to prosecute the individual for that offence. The information derived from the samples that had to be destroyed should not have been used in evidence against the person or for the purposes of any investigation of an offence. (At the same time, there was no requirement to destroy this information.) HOC 16/1995 also required that samples should be retained only for the same period as the person's criminal record on Phoenix and that the samples should be destroyed when the associated database record is weeded. This requirement was removed by s 82 of Criminal Justice and Police Act 2001 which amended s 64 of PACE allowing retention of samples providing that they not be used by any person except for the purposes related to the prevention or detection of crime, the investigation of an offence or the conduct of a prosecution.

The main reason for retaining samples after a DNA profile has been obtained is cited by the NDNAD Board as 'for re-analysis, should new technologies for DNA analysis be introduced' (ACPO, 2006). Other reasons for keeping samples on archive are for facilitating international DNA data exchange, quality control, error checking, possible miscarriage of justice, and research. The last point falls under criticism of many Human Rights organisations and will be addressed separately in the final chapter.

The idea of storing DNA samples has powerful advocates among the forensic community. DNA technology is changing fast. During the short history of the NDNAD, a change in genotyping technology had already happened once, in 1999, when SGM Plus replaced SGM as the profiling system. Although to date no adventitious matches (i.e., due to chance) between two full SGM Plus profiles have been observed, the increasing size of the database may require profiling to be performed with a bigger number of markers. Using current SGM Plus profiling, a match probability of 1 in 1 billion or more is achieved, which is enough to discriminate between full DNA profiles belonging to two unrelated individuals. However, when relatives, especially close relatives, are to be compared, SGM Plus may not be adequate to discriminate between them, especially when the SOC sample profile is a mixture or partial. Addition of new markers would help to avoid these problems. Being able to re-test samples using additional DNA markers would also enable more efficient cross-searching between international DNA databases. This is particularly important for data exchange with the countries, such as the USA and Canada, which are using a DNA profiling system different from SGM Plus.

According to the agreement between the ACPO and the FSS (ACPO, 2003) all items submitted by the police to the FSS will be returned to the police, normally as soon as possible after the laboratory examination is complete unless the samples present potential health hazard risk (samples which constitute body fluids such as blood, semen or saliva) in which case they are destroyed in accordance with HOC 40/1973, HOC 41/1973, HOC 125/1976,

HOC 55/1980, HOC 74/1982 and HOC 25/1987. The FSS has the right, in the event of an agreement between it and a relevant police force/organisation having been reached, to retain samples, or part of them, under specialised storage conditions, for reference purposes or for possible future re-examination using improved techniques. The samples can be retained for the period of three, seven, or 30 years depending on the severity of crime, after which, in the absence of written instruction to the contrary, the samples will be destroyed.

The defence can request the FSS not to destroy the samples. As required by HOC 40/1973 and HOC 74/1982 the police must notify the defence with regards to the destruction of samples at which point, to prevent the samples from being destroyed, the defence must give a written notice to the laboratory within 21 days of receiving the notification from the police.

One of the main reasons for destroying samples is limited special storage capability. But even when biological samples are destroyed or returned to the police, the policy of the FSS is to keep in perpetuity DNA extracted from them. This requires considerably less storage space and provides the defence with an opportunity to re-test the samples some time in the future.

Under current practice, SOC profiles are removed from the database by the Custodian after receiving notification of a successful prosecution from the police. The rationale for destroying SOC profiles cited by the NDNAD is to prevent further redundant match reports being issued for the same offence if the convicted individual is subsequently arrested as a suspect for another offence and another profile for that individual is used to interrogate the database (ACPO, 2006). However, this practice automatically precludes alternative potential suspects from being identified at some time in the future. The NDNAD justifies this practice by the fact that when a full SGM Plus profile has been obtained from the crime scene sample, the profile of the matched subject will often suffice as a proxy reference for the SOC sample profile, to allow identification of any subject sample profile added to the NDNAD later that also matches the deleted crime scene sample profile. However, not all SOC profiles are full profiles. If a disputed conviction has occurred in a case when the SOC sample profile was a partial one, the profile of any new entrant to the database could match the crime scene partial profile but not the full profile of the person convicted. This is also true in cases of mixed SOC sample profiles. Acknowledging these possibilities, the NDNAD board is currently reviewing the policy of removing SOC sample profiles following successful conviction (ACPO, 2006).

All subject samples and profiles which fall under what used to be to be s 64(3B)(b) of PACE had to be removed from the NDNAD prior to the change in legislation in 2001. However, an alarmingly big number of subject records remained on the database. As at 31 March 2005, there were roughly 186,900 DNA profiles from different individuals illegally kept on the database which should have been removed prior to the legislative change in 2001. Out of all the individuals whose records were illegally kept on the database, only 4 per cent have been subsequently linked to one or more offences, 95 per cent of which are volume crimes (ACPO, 2006). Section 82(6) of the Criminal Justice and Police Act 2001 explicitly allows the police to retain and use samples that should have been destroyed under what was s 64 of PACE, but were not, as well as any information derived from them.

Even prior to the changes made to s 64 of PACE by s 82 of Criminal Justice and Police Act 2001 the practice of retaining the profiles from individuals who were not prosecuted or were acquitted, was hotly debated by human rights groups and was the subject of several court cases. The matter was finally resolved by the decision of the House of Lords in *Attorney-General's Reference (No.3 of 1999)* [2001] 1 Cr. App. R. 34. In this case, the defendant was arrested in January 1998 for burglary. A sample of saliva was lawfully obtained from him and the DNA profile of this sample loaded onto the NDNAD. The defendant was subsequently acquitted of the offence and the sample should have been destroyed under s 64(1) of PACE. This fact that the sample should have been destroyed pursuant to s 64(1) was also conceded by the Attorney-General. In fact, the defendant's sample was not destroyed and in October the same year, a match was found between this sample profile and a SOC sample from an offence committed in early 1997 in relation to the rape, assault and burglary of a 66-year-old woman. The defendant was arrested and charged with these offences. The DNA profile from a sample of hair plucked from the defendant was found to match the SOC sample profile from the rape and burglary offence. The prosecution did not have any other evidence in this case apart from the DNA evidence. At the start of the trial the judge found that as a matter of law the evidence of the DNA profile was not admissible. Directing the acquittal, he ruled that ss 61 to 65 of PACE provided an exhaustive code for the taking, use and destruction of samples and that there was no discretion that would enable the prosecution to use such material because the sample should have been destroyed in accordance with s 64(1) of PACE after the defendant's acquittal in the burglary case. The Attorney-General referred the following question of law for the opinion of the Court of Appeal: 'Where a sample of DNA is lawfully taken from an accused in respect of offence A (of which offence the accused is subsequently acquitted), and information derived from the sample suggests that the accused is guilty of offence B, does a judge have a discretion to permit a prosecution to proceed against the accused for offence B, notwithstanding the terms of section 64(3B) of the Police and Criminal Evidence Act 1984?' (*Attorney-General's Reference (No. 3 of 1999)* [2000] 2 Cr. App. R. 416). The Court of Appeal upheld the trial judge's decision and also quashed a conviction for murder in the conjoined appeal in the case of *R v Weir* [2000] 2 Cr. App. R. 416 (see below). The Attorney-General appealed to the House of Lords who held that the trial judge and the Court of Appeal erred in their interpretation of s 64 of PACE. Reversing the decision of the Court of Appeal, the House of Lords held, that 'although under the imperative terms of section 64(1) of the Police and Criminal Evidence Act 1984 on the acquittal of a defendant, the DNA sample's destruction was mandatory, and section 64(3B)(a) unambiguously spelt out the legal consequences of a breach of an obligation to destroy the DNA sample in question; section 64 (3B)(b) contained no language to the effect that the evidence obtained as a result of a prohibited investigation should be inadmissible; nor did it make provision for the consequences of a breach of the prohibition on investigation'.

In *R v Weir* [2000] 2 Cr. App. R. 416 the defendant had been charged with drugs-related offences and a sample of saliva in the form of a mouth swab was taken from him and submitted for DNA profiling. Later, the charges were dropped and the mouth swab was destroyed in accordance with the provisions of s 64(1) of PACE; however, a DNA sample extracted from them was not and the DNA profile remained on the database. The Crown accepts that the DNA profile should not have remained on the database in a searchable or accessible form. Seven months later the defendant was arrested after a match between his DNA profile in the NDNAD and a DNA profile from samples in a murder investigation. Blood samples from the defendant confirmed the match and he was consequently convicted and sentenced to life imprisonment. The defendant appealed against his convictions arguing that 'not only had he been entitled to the destruction of his first sample under s. 64(1) but that s. 64(3B)(b), as inserted by the Criminal Justice and Public Order Act 1994, excluded the admission of any evidence which had resulted from a link between the first sample, which should have been destroyed, and the second sample and any information derived therefrom'. The appeal was upheld by the decision of the Court of Appeal (see above) however, it was later reversed by the House of Lords in *Attorney-General's Reference (No.3 of 1999)* [2001] 1 Cr. App. R. 34, which specifically referred to this case.

The implications of the new s 64 of PACE as amended by s 82 of the Criminal Justice and Police Act 2001 on the rights of individual guaranteed under the terms of the Human Rights Act 1998 were addressed in *R v Chief Constable of the South Yorkshire Police ex parte S and Marper* [2004] 1 WLR 2196. The claimant in the first case, an 11-year-old boy, was charged with an attempted robbery but was later acquitted. The claimant in the second case was arrested and charged (but not prosecuted) with harassment. In both cases, DNA samples were taken and the police wrote to both claimants informing them that under section 64(1A) of PACE, as amended, the police had the right to retain their fingerprints and DNA samples to aid the investigation of crime and that all such fingerprints and samples would be retained. The claimants sought judicial review on the grounds that the retention of their fingerprints and samples, when they had not been convicted of a criminal offence, was incompatible with their right to privacy under Article 8, and represented discrimination in the protection of their human rights as innocent persons, under Article 14 of the Convention for the Protection of Human Rights and Fundamental Freedoms, as scheduled to the Human Rights Act 1998, and that a general policy of retention was an unlawful fetter on the discretion of the respondent Chief Constable. Unanimously dismissing both appeals the House of Lords admitted that although retention of fingerprints and DNA samples constitutes an interference with private life under Article 8(1) such interference was modest and was objectively justified under Article 8(2) as being necessary for the prevention of crime and the protection of the rights of others. The House of Lords also did not find any breach of Article 14 as the claimants were treated no differently from all other individuals who had provided their DNA samples for the database. Finally the discretion of the Chief Constable to retain, save in exceptional cases, all fingerprints and samples taken from those who have been acquitted of criminal offences or against whom proceedings have not been pursued was lawful. Lord Steyn indicated the aim of the policy 'as directed to the prevention or detection of crime, the investigation of offences, the facilitation of prosecutions, and the speedy exculpation of the innocent as well as the correction of miscarriages of justice'.

In concluding his judgment on the case, Lord Brown of Eaton-Under-Heywood said that 'the cause of human rights generally (including the better protection of society against the scourge of crime which dreadfully afflicts the lives of so many of its victims) would inevitably be better served by the database's expansion than by its proposed contraction. The more complete the database, the better the chance of detecting criminals, both those guilty of crimes past and those whose crimes are yet to be committed. The better chance too of deterring from future crime those whose profiles are already on the database. And these, of course, are not the only benefits. The larger the database, the less call there will be to round up the usual suspects. Instead, those amongst the usual suspects who are innocent will at once be exonerated. Were these appellants to succeed in their challenge, the cause of justice would be seriously impeded'.

Chapter 5

The pitfalls of DNA testing

DNA analysis is the most accurate and reliable method for human identification. However, as with any scientific method, forensic DNA testing has problems and pitfalls that can compromise the integrity of the data and ultimately the cogency of DNA evidence. When analysing the results of STR genotyping the forensic scientist has to answer two crucial questions: (1) does the sample contain DNA from a single donor or is it a mixture of several contributors? and (2) has the genotype at each locus been unambiguously identified? Any mistakes in determining the number of contributors or genotype information drastically affect interpretation of the results.

There are biological and technical factors which affect interpretation of DNA profiles causing appearance of extra peaks or disappearance of true allelic peaks. These spurious peaks can be mistakenly accepted as true ones, affecting the decision on whether the profile is from a single or several contributors. Inability to identify a particular allele in a locus may cause the locus to be interpreted as homozygous instead of heterozygous, leading to false exclusions or inclusions.

The factors affecting the outcome of the DNA testing process can be loosely grouped into five different types: factors related to the donor of the biological sample, factors related to the state of the biological evidence, factors related to DNA testing methodology, human error and contamination.

5.1 Factors related to the donor of the biological sample

Genetic features of the donor as well as past or ongoing medical treatment can in some cases complicate the interpretation of DNA profiles. The genetic factors are associated with the presence of chromosomal abnormalities, somatic mutations and chimerism. Among the non-genetic factors that can cause anomalous DNA results are blood transfusion and specific surgical treatment (such as bone morrow transplantation) due to a number of illnesses (e.g. leukaemia).

Both numerical and structural chromosome abnormalities can cause anomalous DNA profiles. When genotyped with SGM Plus, the profile of a normal individual will have 20 alleles. If a person has numerical or structural chromosome abnormalities the number of observed alleles may deviate from this figure.

Numerical chromosome abnormalities – when affected individuals have different chromosomal complement from 46, XX or XY – have been discovered for various chromosomes. They are rare and are usually associated with severe disorders, both developmental and psychological. DNA profiles from such individuals can have three alleles present in the affected locus, or only one allele in extremely rare cases when the individual lacks a particular chromosome.

The most well-known case of a numerical chromosome abnormality is Down's syndrome, manifested by the trisomy at chromosome 21. If such an individual were tested for D21S111, one of the markers included in the SGM Plus multiplex, the resulting DNA profile may exhibit three alleles at this locus instead of the normal two allele pattern. This may also be manifested as an imbalance between allelic peaks in a heterozygous individual or the appearance of a single abnormally high peak if the individual is homozygous for D21S111.

Structural abnormalities cause deletions, duplications or translocations of DNA fragments within one or between two different chromosomes. Duplications of a DNA segment containing an STR locus can be detected by the presence of imbalance between allelic peaks in a way similar to the one observed in a sample from an individual with a chromosomal abnormality. In some cases the decision as to whether an individual has gene duplication or numerical abnormality can be made only after studying the karyotype using cytological methods.

Three-peak profiles can also be caused by somatic mutations occurring during embryological development. When a new allele appears due to mutation in one cell at the very early stage of embryonic development it will be present in all the cells that originate from this mother cell. Somatic mutations can be identified by studying morphology of the allelic peaks. While, in the above two cases, the areas between allelic peaks would relate as 2:1 (in cases of duplication of an allele of a heterozygous locus) or be approximately three times that of a single allele (in the case of duplication of an allele of a homozygous locus), the ratio between allelic peaks in this sample will depend on the relative proportion of the two types of cells making up the tissue.

When an area on the chromosome harbouring an STR marker of interest is deleted, only a single allelic peak will be observed in a DNA profile. The allele that it was not possible to detect is called the 'null allele'. Most commonly, null alleles are caused by mutations in binding sites of PCR primers used for their detection. The frequency of null alleles depends on the population and the type of allele, and in some cases can be as high as 5 per cent.

Null alleles do not significantly complicate interpretation of DNA profiles.

One important exception is the null allele at the amelogenin locus which is used for determining the sex of the donor of the crime stain sample. Specific mutations in the Y chromosome homologue of the amelogenin gene can cause mistaken identification of a male sample as female, thus affecting the conclusion of the forensic scientist as to the gender of the donor of the crime sample. The frequencies of these mutations are low but in some populations they may be enough to cause significant concern. A recent report indicated that in Indian populations, sex determination by amelogenin genotyping can mistakenly identify males as females in almost 2 per cent of cases (Thangaraj et al, 2002). Null alleles at the amelogenin locus on X chromosome have also been identified and their presence can complicate sex determination of the donor.

Where a possibility of mutation in the amelogenin gene is suspected the sex of the sample donor can easily be determined either by using different PCR primers to amplify the gene or by using Y chromosome-specific STRs. However in some rare cases incorrect sex determination is a possibility and could lead to much confusion especially when the sex of the perpetrator is unknown.

An experienced forensic scientist can often tell whether an unusual DNA profile is caused by a chromosomal abnormality in the donor but sometimes the conclusion is not straightforward. Particularly problematic in such cases are DNA samples of poor quality where the number of loci for which genotypic information is obtainable is low. In a partial DNA profile, the presence of an extra chromosome or an STR duplication may cause the profile to be interpreted as a mixed one. The same can happen when interpreting results of LCN testing, where peak morphology may not be applicable for determining the number of particular alleles present in the sample. At the same time, in some rare cases, the presence of a chromosome abnormality can strengthen the conclusion as to the identity of the crime stain donor.

An interesting and potentially much more difficult situation to deal with is that of a genetically chimeric crime stain donor. Chimerism is the phenomenon whereby an individual has genetically different cell lines. Chimerism can be acquired through bone morrow transplantation and blood transfusion (see below) or it can be congenital. When chimerism is congenital, an individual has cell lines in his/her body that come from different zygotes and because of this, they are genetically different even though the zygotes are produced by the same parents. Individuals with congenital chimerism may have different DNA types in different body tissues (Yu et al, 2002) and when the source of DNA from the crime stain and the subject are different there is a chance that the DNA profiles will not match, which can lead to false exclusions. Alternatively, a profile from a chimeric individual may be mistaken for a mixed profile of two individuals because for some loci this person may have up to four different alleles.

Although the frequency of congenital chimerism is low, recent reports suggest that it may be on the rise because of the increased incidence of *in vitro* fertilisation (Butler, 2005). The implantation of more than one fertilised egg into the uterus in order to increase the chances of pregnancy will also increase the chances of the baby being borne chimeric, even though it will appear both physically and mentally normal. It is estimated that 8 per cent of all non-identical (fraternal) twins and 21 per cent of all non-identical triplets have chimeric blood (van Dijk et al, 1996).

Several non-genetic factors can also be the reason for incorrect interpretation of DNA evidence. People who have undergone successful bone marrow transplantation show a true mixed profile in buccal samples five years after the operation, while in blood, the donor profile completely replaces that of the recipient (Dauber et al, 2004). Interestingly, the hair profile of the individual seems not to be affected by the transplantation and exhibits the true genotype of the recipient.

Recent blood or plasma transfusion (e.g., due to a surgical operation or accident) can also be the reason for observing a mixed profile. In this case, only DNA extracted from a blood sample may exhibit a mixed profile with the mixture proportion depending on the amount of the transfused donor blood. Because of the lifetime of leukocytes, the blood cells which contain the DNA, no mixed profile will be detected in recipient's blood sample three to five weeks after the transfusion.

Owing to congenital and acquired chimerism, a DNA profile from a single individual can be mistakenly identified as a mixed one. Different tissues from the same individual may exhibit different profiles and samples taken at different times from the same individual can also be different. If a DNA sample from a crime stain left by the perpetrator who was chimeric is compared with a sample from the same individual taken some time after the crime was committed, it is not inconceivable that s/he may be excluded by DNA analysis because the tissue samples compared were different or because the chimerism disappeared or the individual became chimeric. The phenomenon of chimerism indicates the importance of obtaining medical information about a suspect who is genuinely believed to be chimeric or to have undergone treatment associated with blood transfusion or bone marrow transplantation. This raises important ethical and human rights issues as well as privacy issues in connection with the Data Protection Act 1998.

5.2 Factors related to the state of biological evidence

When biological evidence recovered from the scene of crime has been subjected to various environmental or chemical insults, or PCR inhibitors are present in the sample, the chances are that some level of degradation will be present in DNA extracted from this sample and/or the efficiency of the PCR reaction will be reduced. In such cases it may only be possible to obtain a partial STR profile from the sample. As the cogency of DNA evidence is directly affected by the number of informative alleles in a DNA profile, any missing genetic information will reduce the random match probability and consequently the probative value of the evidence. Because DNA extracted from evidential samples is often degraded to a certain degree, developing a robust methodology for dealing with degraded samples is important.

In crime investigation, degradation of DNA usually results from natural processes because of exposure of biological evidence to water, heat or various biological agents (e.g., enzymes, bacteria, fungi). The propensity of casework samples to degradation depends on the type of sample, the period since the stain was deposited at the crime scene and the type and harshness of environmental factors. DNA recovered from samples that were found in a dry, dark environment will be of better quality than from those found on wet ground. DNA in soft tissues degrades faster than DNA in bones. The rate of degradation of genomic DNA is faster than that of mtDNA.

Degradation causes random breaks of DNA strands into smaller fragments. A typical amplicon for an STR locus in the SGM Plus multiplex is in the region of 250 to 350 bp. When the average size of DNA fragments in a degraded sample becomes less than 350 bp, the probability of breaks occurring within the PCR amplification region encompassing an allele of interest is very high. When such breaks occur, the reaction cannot proceed and the information on this particular allele will be impossible to obtain. The more degraded the sample, the more broken the DNA and the lower the number of alleles it will be possible to analyse.

Usually, large size alleles are the first affected by sample degradation. Alleles for such loci as D18S51 or FGA will be the first to fail in a degraded DNA sample. When an individual is heterozygous for a particular locus, the chances of obtaining information from a smaller allele are higher in a degraded sample than for a bigger allele.

In the past few years forensic scientists have developed several possible solutions to reducing the effect of DNA degradation on the amount of genetic information obtained from the sample. One of the most promising techniques is miniSTR genotyping, which uses smaller amplicons (approximately 100 bp smaller than in conventional genotyping) for obtaining genetic information from highly degraded samples (Butler, 2005). Reliability of miniSTR genotyping needs to be improved if this method is to be approved for analysis of degraded casework samples but initial results are very promising.

Besides degradation, partial DNA profiles can be caused by the presence of inhibitors during PCR amplification. Soil, leather and textile dyes, wood paint and various household chemicals all contain substances that can interfere with DNA extraction, cause DNA degradation or inhibit activity of the polymerising enzyme. When these substances are present during amplification they may cause the loss of larger alleles in a fashion similar to DNA degradation or even completely inhibit PCR amplification.

To deal with the problem of PCR inhibition several efficient approaches have recently been developed. They are based on reducing the concentration of the inhibitor by increasing the volume of the reaction, using more robust amplification enzymes as well as compounds that protect the enzyme from the effect of inhibitors during amplification.

5.3 Factors related to DNA testing methodology

A problem of a different kind to the one discussed above is the appearance of extra peaks in a DNA profile besides the peaks for the targeted alleles. These extra peaks can arise from the issues related to the technology of detection of fluorescently labelled fragments, biochemistry of genetic analysis and poor operator technique. It is important to discriminate between real and spurious peaks as failure to do so may result in false exclusions. In a mixed sample these artefacts can complicate interpretation of the profile and affect the decision as to the number of potential contributors. In addition, artefacts leading to big changes in peak morphology can cause scientists to draw wrong conclusions as to the genotype of the sample even when no extra peaks are present.

5.3.1 Heterozygote imbalance

Heterozygote imbalance is observed when the peaks for the two alleles at one locus significantly differ in size and area. This phenomenon can be caused by differences in the amount of the two alleles in the reaction, the natural variation in the PCR process, which causes one allele (usually the smaller one) to be more efficiently amplified at the expense of the other one, or by somatic mutations (Gill and Buckleton, 2005). Heterozygote imbalance is easily detected but in some extreme cases the peak for one of the alleles may be interpreted as an artefact and disregarded by the scientist, leading to an incorrect DNA profile for the sample being reported. This usually happens when the amount of DNA in the sample is low or a sample is a mixture of DNA from two or more donors who contributed different amounts of DNA.

5.3.2 Stutter peaks

Appearance of peaks at positions other than the parental allelic position is referred to as stuttering (Gill and Buckleton, 2005). Stutter peaks are the most common source of extra peaks in DNA profiles. These peaks usually appear when a product of amplification is shorter than the expected allelic product. This can happen because of miscopying of the template DNA or polymerase slippage during PCR amplification. The resulting products are typically one repeat unit shorter than the expected allele although loss of two repeat units has also been observed. Stuttering depends on the size of alleles and the length of the repeat unit. Larger alleles tend to stutter more often. The smaller the repeat unit, the higher the stuttering rate. STRs with a three nucleotide repeat unit stutter more than four nucleotide STRs.

When a scientist has to interpret a DNA profile that could be affected by stuttering, s/he has to decide whether a suspect peak is authentic and comes from another contributor to the mixture or is a stutter peak, in which case the sample is derived from a single donor. The decision as to whether a particular peak is a real or a stutter one is done on the basis of its size. Here the scientist needs to discriminate between stuttering and heterozygote imbalance, which can also cause similar peak morphology. Usually stutter peaks are 15 per cent (or less) the size of the parental peak.

5.3.3 Pull-up peaks

Automated STR analysis uses separation of alleles in a multiplexing reaction by length of the amplification product and by colour. Sometimes, because of colour bleeding from one spectral channel to another, a minor peak labelled with one colour can be shown ('pulled-up') among the peaks of a different colour. This causes problems only when the position of the pull-up peak coincides with the position of a 'real' peak. When such a possibility exists, the automated DNA analyser can be re-calibrated, DNA samples diluted and re-analysed, or the locus in question analysed individually.

5.3.4 Allele dropout

As discussed above, there are situations when a particular allele is not seen because of a mutation in a PCR primer binding site. Besides mutations, the other reason why an allele cannot be detected is due to differential amplification of alleles or the low amount of DNA in the sample. This phenomenon is termed 'allele dropout'.

When a particular locus is affected by allele dropout, the DNA profile is very similar to that observed when one of the alleles is a null allele. Because of allele dropout a heterozygous profile may be mistakenly identified as homozygous. When allele dropout at a particular locus is suspected the genotypic information for this allele is reported as 'F' (for 'failed') meaning that any other possible allele could be present at this locus. Allelic dropout is more likely when peak area or height is low. In many laboratories when an apparent homozygous peak is less than 150 relative fluorescence units (rfu) it will be recorded as heterozygous with the second allele designated as 'F'. For example, when genotyping for FGA reveals the presence of a small peak of 145 rfu in height corresponding to the allele 22, the genotype will be recorded as 22,F. Experimental observation suggests that allele dropout does not occur at peak height levels higher that 150 rfu (Gill and Buckleton, 2005).

5.4 Human error

Human error refers to various errors which happen either because of a one-off 'catastrophic' event or when a technician systematically incorrectly performs a certain procedure. The example of a one-off 'catastrophic' error is incorrect labelling of laboratory samples or accidental switching of samples. Kobilinsky and colleagues (2005) give an example in which an analyst working on rape case evidence accidentally switched an evidential sample from the victim and the suspect, which resulted in a report stating that the suspect could have been a potential donor of the seminal stain, while he should have been excluded as the source of evidence. Other examples include pipetting errors, which could result in a sample being loaded incorrectly into the genotyping instrument or placed into a wrong tube or lane.

When a technician performs an operation without following exactly the recommended procedure, it does not necessarily mean that all the samples processed by this individual will be 'erroneous'. Deviation from the recommended protocol will make the chances of an error in the samples processed by this technician more likely. Examples of such errors include persistent incorrect pipetting, tube manipulation errors and errors in setting up PCR reactions.

5.5 Contamination

Contamination is an accidental mixture of forensic samples with foreign substances, which can be of biological or non-biological nature. Various forms of contamination have different effects on DNA analysis. Contamination with non-biological substances like soil or household chemicals can cause failure of DNA analysis while contamination with some biological agents, like bacteria and the products of their metabolism, can affect the integrity of DNA in the sample. Much more serious from the criminal justice point of view is contamination of samples with biological material of human origin. This type of contamination can affect the probative value of DNA evidence, and lead to false conclusions.

There are many ways forensic samples can be contaminated by human DNA. A person who attended the crime scene before, during or after the crime was committed could have inadvertently added his/her DNA to the crime stain. These could be relatives of the victim, members of the public, police officers or members of the criminal investigation team. In the last two cases such contamination could be detected by comparing the DNA profiles from the crime stain against those stored in the PED. At the moment, checks against this database are only made at the behest of a senior police officer and for a particular case against named individuals who inadvertently may have contaminated scene of crime samples. Where such checks are performed, contamination by police personnel has been detected at approximately 10 per cent of scenes (Sullivan et al, 2004). Samples from old crimes committed during the pre-DNA era could be contaminated by the investigative officers because before the advent of DNA testing, evidence handling procedures differed from those adopted to prevent accidental contamination with DNA.

In the forensic laboratory, a sample could be contaminated by samples from the same or different crimes or evidential samples could be contaminated by DNA from a suspect's sample. The laboratory personnel who had access to the sample during the testing process could also have contaminated it with their DNA. People do not need to touch an object to deposit their DNA on it – DNA can easily be transferred through microscopic droplets which are expelled in the air when we breathe, talk, sneeze or cough or by shedding dead skin.

The other source of laboratory contamination is sporadic contamination of tubes and plasticware used in a DNA testing process. Sullivan and colleagues (2004) report a case when, during a murder investigation, an attempt was made to identify the remains of the burnt female victim by analysing DNA from a toothbrush belonging to the suspected victim. The FSS observed a mixed profile comprising both the victim's profile and a minor male profile which by speculatively searching against the National DNA Database was found to match DNA profiles from four unsolved minor offences committed hundreds of miles away from the murder scene. Suspecting contamination, the FSS performed a thorough investigation and discovered that the same profile was observed on nine separate occasions during a three-year period. The source of the profiles was identified as coming from the tubes for PCR amplification and eventually, after analysing 300 blind profiles belonging to the staff of the tube manufacturing plant located several hundred miles from the murder scene, one was found to match those from the murder scene. In addition, checks against records have shown that profiles from 20 of these staff have been observed as sporadic contaminants over a three-year period. During the same time it is estimated that approximately three million units of this type of tube have been utilised in total by the FSS in DNA processing. Of the profiles from these 20 staff, 14 have also been observed to match either partial or full profiles, previously unattributed, in casework samples (Sullivan et al, 2004).

This example indicates that even when a person could not possibly have attended the scene at the time the crime was committed or subsequently have been in contact with DNA samples, his/her DNA can still be found in the sample. Luckily for the individual whose DNA was found contaminating the crime scene samples, the murder was committed far from where he lived and his sample was not on the NDNAD, otherwise the consequences for him could have been much more serious.

As all leading forensic scientists admit, all DNA samples are contaminated with foreign DNA to a certain degree, as it is not possible to avoid laboratory-based contamination completely (Buckleton and Gill, 2005). This means that any crime stain DNA sample is a mixed sample of several contributors. When the amount of 'indigenous' DNA in the crime sample is large, allelic peaks from contaminating DNA will be below the threshold of reporting after conventional 28-cycle PCR STR profiling, and the contaminating DNA will not affect the interpretation of the evidence. However, the introduction of very sensitive DNA testing techniques, such as LCN DNA testing, allows the contaminating peaks to be detected easily, thus making the decision as to whether they belong to contaminating DNA or not much more difficult.

Usually, to control for DNA contamination of reagents and plasticware, scientists perform PCR amplification in a mixture without adding sample DNA. Should one of the components of the reaction be contaminated, a DNA profile will be produced. This is known as negative control (as opposed to positive control, which is done to verify that PCR amplification is working by using good quality control DNA as a template). It is possible to set up a battery of negative controls to check for contamination of each reagent used.

Negative controls are very efficient in detecting contamination of a particular reagent. However, should the actual DNA sample be contaminated, this approach is powerless to detect it. It is also impossible to check every PCR tube or pipette tip prior to DNA analysis because once they have been tested they are discarded. Testing of a sample of components from a batch can help to provide some indication as to the general batch quality. Even so, it will only show whether gross systematic contamination is present and it cannot provide a guarantee that sporadic contamination events have not occurred (Howitt, 2003).

In addition to negative controls, forensic laboratories have measures directed at maintaining general cleanliness which minimise the risk of contamination. These include wearing protective clothing, performing crucial steps of DNA analysis in climate controlled environments, the use of special filter pipette tips to exclude sample-to-sample cross-contamination, and adoption of strict sample handling protocols and automation.

Development of new highly sensitive DNA testing technologies and sporadic contamination of forensic samples has prompted testing laboratories, in particular the FSS, to introduce new improved anti-contamination measures. Besides the general contamination control measures outlined above they include setting up a comprehensive elimination database containing (Sullivan et al, 2004):

• profiles from all laboratory staff (collection of a DNA sample for inclusion on this database is currently a prerequisite of employment of a new member of staff with the FSS);
• profiles of contamination observed when testing consumables for contamination prior to acceptance; and

• profiles of DNA contaminants of unknown origin observed in negative controls and identified during periodic environmental monitoring of the DNA analysis laboratories.

A DNA database of the individuals involved in manufacturing consumables used in forensic DNA testing is also necessary to eliminate any DNA profiles of unknown origin.

To detect any possible contamination, every DNA profile is routinely checked by special contamination-detection software against the DNA database of laboratory staff involved in the analysis (and the PED, if contamination by a police officer is possible) which flags up DNA profiles with suspected contamination.

In spite of these measures contamination of DNA evidence does happen. When the defence team has a genuine reason to believe that a particular evidential sample could have been contaminated, it needs to obtain from the testing laboratory information with regards to the rate of laboratory contamination of samples and the data on quality control of the consumables and chemicals used for analysing evidence. This is especially true when the forensic laboratory in the DNA testing report admits contamination of another sample by a member of staff in the same case. The laboratory reporting officer should be asked for the reasons for how this contamination event came about and about the measures undertaken by the laboratory to prevent this accident from happening again. If the reason for the accident is unknown it is important to emphasise to the jury that because the cause of contamination is unknown it is impossible to introduce measures to prevent it from happening again, which brings more weight to the contamination theory proposed by the defence.

5.6 LCN DNA testing

LCN DNA testing is a modification of the routine SGM Plus profiling technique for cases in which the amount of DNA recovered from a crime sample is insufficient for obtaining reliable results using conventional SGM Plus genotyping. Because of its super-sensitivity, LCN DNA testing is an extremely powerful technique that enables scientists to produce DNA profiles from traces of biological material, sometimes as small as a single cell (more often, 10–15 cells). At the same time there are certain limitations to this technology that are extremely important for correct interpretation of the results. All the artefacts discussed above affect LCN DNA profiles but because of extremely small quantities of DNA template in the sample, their manifestation is exacerbated.

5.6.1 Factors affecting morphology of LCN DNA profiles

The interpretation of LCN DNA profiles suffers from similar problems to normal SGM Plus genotyping which can be traced to stochastic variation due to a combination of the small amount of DNA template and increased number of PCR cycles (34 in LCN DNA testing as opposed to the conventional 28 cycles).

According to Gill (2001), when present in low copy number, a DNA molecule that is amplified by chance during the initial rounds of the PCR is most likely to be preferentially amplified, causing three major unavoidable consequences:

1. allele dropout may occur because one allele of a heterozygote locus can be preferentially amplified;
2. stutters may be preferentially analysed – these are sometimes known as false alleles; and
3. the method is prone to sporadic contamination – amplifying alleles that are not associated with the crime stain, or sample.

When analysing conventional SGM Plus profiles the decision as to whether the peak is real or spurious is made using peak area information as guidance. Peak areas are significantly less useful for interpretation of LCN profiles (Buckleton and Gill, 2005) and are considered to be not informative at all when the area drops below 5,000 rfu (Whitaker et al, 2001). Due to stochastic variation, any apparent homozygote LCN genotype is considered to be a potential heterozygote and the allele that might be present in the sample is designated as 'F' (Gill et al, 2000).

The decision as to whether a peak is real or spurious is much more difficult in LCN testing than in normal SGM Plus profiling. Because of increased sensitivity even slight contamination of the sample with foreign DNA may be picked up by the LCN assay. To control for contamination during LCN testing forensic laboratories use the approaches outlined in the previous section. However, when the events of contamination are sporadic these methods are not very efficient in dealing with the problem because contamination can be specific to individual test tubes.

Sporadic contamination led to developing of the 'drop-in' concept explaining PCR differences between individual test tubes during LCN genotyping. According to this theory, single alleles from degraded or fragmented DNA can randomly affect tubes whether they contain casework samples or are negative control which explains why laboratory-based contamination could affect casework samples only and not negative controls and vice versa (Buckleton and Gill, 2005).

In dealing with the problem of laboratory-based contamination during LCN DNA testing, the method of replication was found to be the most efficient. If the contaminant is truly random the chance of a contaminating allele appearing in two replicated tests is small. Using this approach an allele could only be scored if observed at least twice in replicate samples. If observed only once, the allele should not be reported or taken into consideration when calculating the match probability or making a decision whether or not the suspect should be excluded on the basis of DNA evidence.

5.6.2 Factors affecting interpretation of LCN DNA profiles

The key question in interpretation of LCN DNA profiles is related to estimating the number of contributors to the sample. In standard SGM Plus genotyping the decision as to the number of contributors to a DNA profile obtained is made based on the number of alleles present at a particular locus, the so-called 'biological model'. Assuming a single contributor, two alleles should be present at each locus in standard full SGM Plus. A sample will be considered a mixture when more than two alleles are observed at several loci. This approach however is not applicable to interpretation of LCN DNA profiles.

Because of the factors outlined above, an LCN DNA profile of a sample is obtained as a result of two replications, and the alleles are then scored into a 'consensus' profile. At low concentrations, stochastic processes have a significant effect on the chances of a particular allelic peak being detected. DNA profiles obtained from samples containing small amounts of DNA may exhibit zero, one, two or even more alleles (due to the 'drop-in' phenomenon) at each locus (Buckleton and Gill, 2005). As the peak area at small concentrations is uninformative it is virtually impossible to discriminate between true and spurious peaks. Thus, three alleles may be a result of a contaminant being 'successfully' reproduced in two replications, or indicate a mixture of several true contributors. Conversely, the presence of zero, one or two does not necessarily indicate a single contributor. For example, two alleles may represent two individuals having one allele in common and a single allelic dropout in one of them. That is why the decision as to the potential number of contributors to a LCN DNA profile based on the number of alleles at each locus is very tentative and subjective.

The inadequacy of the 'biological' model for interpretation of LCN DNA profiles has prompted the development of likelihood ratio-based approaches to LCN analysis. This approach is discussed in more detail by Gill and colleagues (2000) and Buckleton and Gill (2005).

LCN DNA testing is a very sensitive technique making it possible to obtain genetic information from exceedingly small amounts of DNA. However, because of the increased sensitivity, LCN is less robust than standard SGM Plus genotyping, with respect to contamination, PCR artefacts etc. This effectively decreases the strength of DNA evidence obtained by LCN comparing to conventional SGM Plus genotyping.

Chapter 6

DNA testing errors

In the above examples I assume that DNA results did not contain any errors. In real life, though, various errors can happen as the sample is being analysed. These errors can be quite common in some laboratories, extremely rare in others, but in any case when evaluating DNA evidence, the possibility of an erroneous result should be kept in mind. When the match probability is very low, the probability of a match due to error may be sufficiently high to be taken seriously and thoroughly investigated. The fact that errors in DNA analysis could happen has been recognised by Phillips LJ who during *R v Doheny and Adams* [1997] 1 Cr. App. R. 369 said:

> (p. 373) The cogency of DNA evidence makes it particularly important that DNA testing is rigorously conducted so as to obviate the risk of error in the laboratory . . .

Errors are intrinsic features of any technical or biological system. Without errors in DNA replication there would be no evolution of life on the planet. Errors are part of our everyday life. Errors happen when we drive our car, write a report or do experiments. Errors happen also during forensic DNA examination. No matter how rigid the system of error prevention, how error-free laboratory procedures are claimed to be, it is only possible to minimise the error rate and impossible to exclude it completely.

Human (and technical) errors can be of two main types – random errors and systematic errors. As it follows from the name, random errors are one-off random events which affect the outcome of the experiment in a random fashion. Systematic errors are inaccuracies which not only affect the result of the experiment but introduce a persistent bias in a particular way. An example of a random error is a typing error due to accidentally pressing the wrong key on the keyboard. A systematic error will be typing a particular word incorrectly all the time.

Both systematic and random errors happen during laboratory examination of DNA evidence. We have seen in the previous chapter that contamination events in LCN DNA analysis are random events, affecting tubes in no particular fashion. If, however, every tube was affected because of poor operator technique this would be a systematic error.

The processes and techniques used for forensic DNA analysis are rigidly controlled but errors do happen during the testing process or when reporting the results. During laboratory examination of biological evidence the results can be wrong because of genotyping errors, laboratory contamination or because they were reported incorrectly. The first two issues relate to laboratory processes, and can be caused by a mixture of human and technical errors, while the last one is solely due to the human error.

6.1 Genotyping errors

A genotyping error occurs when the observed genotype of the DNA sample does not correspond to the true genotype. In the previous chapter we discussed various origins of genotyping errors. It is important to emphasise that it is impossible to disentangle 'method' errors from 'practitioner' errors because in forensic science the method is primarily the judgement of the examiner (Saks and Koehler, 2005). This means that when a particular DNA profile is proved to contain an error it will most likely be due to a combination of human and technical factors.

Genotyping errors can cause either false exclusion of the guilty suspect (false negative error) or false inclusion of an innocent individual (false positive error). In addition to genotyping errors, contaminations, mislabellings, misrecordings, misrepresentations, case mix-ups, and interpretive errors may all lead to false positive errors (Koehler, 1993). The false exclusion rate is thought to be extremely small and is almost irrelevant to evidential weight (Balding, 2005). False inclusions are much more important because innocent individuals may be erroneously linked to and even convicted of crimes they have not committed.

For accurate evaluation of DNA evidence it is important to have information about the probability of a false positive error. Ignorance of, or an underestimation of the potential for, a false positive can lead to serious errors of interpretation, particularly when the other evidence against the accused is weak (Aitken and Taroni, 2004). However, to be able to estimate whether or not the reported match is erroneous, it is important to know not the probability of any error, but the probability of an error leading to a false inclusion. Although it is impossible to say with a hundred per cent certainty, without re-testing, whether a match between the accused and the crime sample is true or false, the probability of error in a specific case can still be estimated when information about the rate of false positives for a particular laboratory is available. This subject is discussed in more detail in the following chapter. Here, it suffices to say that when a forensic laboratory reports a low value for false positive outcomes, it does not follow that the probability of a false inclusion in a particular case will also be low: it may not.

An innocent individual can be linked to a crime scene in two ways – either his/her DNA profile matches that of the real perpetrator, or because of laboratory error. Balding (2005) discusses the effect of false inclusions on the match probability and observes that when the probability of false match (laboratory error) is significantly higher than the match probability, the latter is effectively irrelevant. This means that ignoring the possibility of a laboratory error will be detrimental to the defendant. If laboratory error is a real possibility, the defence team has to explain to the jury that, although very small, the probability of a laboratory error in a particular case has to be weighed against the probability of a random match. For example, when the probability of a laboratory error seems to be extremely low, say only 1 in 1 million, and the prosecution claims a random match probability of less than 1 in 1 billion, the chances of a match due to genotypic error are at least 1,000 times more likely than a random match between a suspect and another unrelated individual of the same ethnicity!

Surprisingly, there are only a few published studies of the rate of genotyping errors in forensics, and in the courtroom, the effect of genotyping errors still remains neglected. Some forensic scientists even think that their results are free of any errors because of the procedures implemented in their laboratories, which aim to minimise the error rate. This thinking is fallacious. Genotyping errors happened in the past, happen now and will happen in the future.

In addition to the reluctance of some forensic scientists to admit the possibility of erroneous results, taking errors into account is complicated by the lack of information about the rate of genotypic errors in a specific laboratory. The error rate of the forensic laboratory which performed DNA analysis in a specific case is a legitimate concern for the defence. In the above example I hypothetically assumed the chances of laboratory error as 1 in 1 million; in real life, though, the chances of genotypic error are much higher. In all studies in which errors were checked in non-forensic research DNA testing laboratories, a non-negligible error rate (from 0.2 per cent to more than 15 per cent per locus) was reported (Pompanon et al, 2005). Rates between 0.5 per cent and 2.5 per cent are common in many laboratories including forensic laboratories (Ewen et al, 2000), while Koehler (1993) suggests an error rate of up to 4 per cent. Even higher error rates are typical of studies that involve DNA of poor quality or quantity (Taberlet et al, 1996) which is often the case when analysing crime stain samples.

The error rate in forensic laboratories is largely unknown but recent data indicate that based on case analysis, data provided by the Innocence Project, Cardozo School of Law (New York), in 86 DNA exonerated cases, forensic testing errors accounted for 63 per cent of wrongful convictions, while false or misleading testimonies by forensic scientists accounted for 27 per cent of wrongful convictions (Saks and Koehler, 2005). A survey of published mtDNA sequence data from 1981 to 2002 indicated that 56 per cent of papers published in forensic and legal medical journals contained sequence errors (Forster, 2003). Tests conducted by the California Association of Crime Laboratory Directors (CACLD) on three DNA laboratories in 1987 and 1988 revealed several instances of false positive errors. In an initial study, 50 samples were sent to each of the three laboratories. Sixty-six matches were reported by the first two laboratories, one of which was a false positive. The third laboratory typed 47 samples and misclassified one of them. In a follow-up study based on 50 samples, approximately 91 matches were reported by the first two laboratories, one of which was a false positive (Koehler, 1993). The fact that errors do happen in forensic testing is openly admitted by the Custodian of the NDNAD who lists various types of errors associated with DNA profiles deposited in the Database (ACPO, 2006). The possibility of genotyping errors was also raised during the Court of Appeal case *R v Gordon* [1995] 1 Cr. App. R. 290 where it transpired that '... results from the control tracks at the sides of the gel, which had not previously been measured, were not consistent with the known values for the control DNA or indeed with each other'.

In the UK, forensic testing laboratories have to meet the requirements of the international quality standard for testing laboratories, ISO 17025. In addition, laboratories also conduct internal assessment of the error rate and investigate suspected DNA profiles for possible errors (although results of these studies are not widely publicised and are difficult to obtain) but even in these cases, there is a possibility that an erroneous DNA profile would be reported.

Laboratory accreditation significantly reduces the chances of error because of correct monitoring procedures and processes of forensic DNA analysis by the laboratory staff. However, even in a hypothetical scenario where human error can be completely excluded due to the introduction of the certification, genotypic error will still be present, simply because enzymes used for PCR reaction have a well documented error rate; genotypic instruments can malfunction; and stochastic processes at minimal DNA concentrations can introduce uncertainty into the results, as we have seen above. In this case the best way to deal with the problem of genotypic errors is not by putting forward arguments that forensic science is error free because of the rigorous system of checks and quality controls, but rather by identifying the frequency of genotypic errors and taking them into account when calculating random match probabilities and likelihood ratios. One way to accomplish this is by blind external proficiency testing using realistic samples, which have to be conducted by agencies unaffiliated to the forensic laboratory. Needless to say, this information should be readily available to defence teams.

But even when blind external proficiency testing is conducted, the probability of laboratory error will still be difficult to assess as the tests are specific not only to a particular laboratory or technicians who performed the procedures but also to a particular criminal case. No blind testing will ever be able to mimic the exact circumstances of a particular case, such as the amount and state of recovered DNA, contamination and many others factors discussed above; all of them, as we have seen, have a profound effect on the final outcome of the testing process. Ultimately, it is for the jury to assess the probability that some error has occurred on the basis of the evidence presented (Balding, 2005). The jury in such a case has to be given information about what types of errors are possible in each particular case, the genotyping error rate of a particular laboratory (if it is available, ideally the results of external blind proficiency tests) and the effect of errors on probative value of DNA evidence. The jury also needs to be informed that even when the probability of false inclusion is very small, it still has to consider it when the probability of a random match is even smaller. In such a case the random match is so unlikely that the alternative possibility of the defendant's profile arising through genotyping error (or fraud) may well be much more likely and this possibility has to be considered (Balding, 2005). This subject is treated in more detail in Chapter 7.

6.2 Reporting errors

When a genotype is reported incorrectly it can have the same effect on the trial as genotyping errors discussed in the previous section. This can happen when data are not copied correctly from laboratory journals, and when there have been errors entering data into computer programmes or errors during the writing up of forensic reports. Typing (i.e., keyboard) errors are more frequent than other laboratory errors and no matter how sophisticated the error catching system implemented in the laboratory, they often crop up in reports presented in court. It has to be accepted by forensic scientists that a DNA report may, and probably does, contain errors and that it has to be thoroughly checked for their presence by both the prosecution and the defence.

Usually, the most abundant type of error in DNA reports is a spelling or typing error although more serious errors, such as reporting the wrong value of random match probability, or likelihood ratio, or genotype of one of the samples, are also found in prosecution expert witness statements. In one of the court cases in which the author was involved the report of the prosecution scientist referred to a mixed sample which contained DNA from 'at least one male contributor'. However, the genotypes of all five different DNA profiles from this particular evidential item were given as female. When confronted by the leader of the defence, the reporting officer admitted that this was due to an error when typing the results of amelogenin genotyping. The scientist did not bother to type the genotype at the amelogenin locus every time but simply copied it to all the profiles.

To reduce the rate of reporting errors, any DNA report should be checked not only by the reporting scientist but also by a second person, and all calculations for random match probabilities or likelihood ratios used in the report should be verified. When the report contains information about genotypes of the samples, each allele should be checked against the outputs from the genotyping instrument.

Checking for potential report errors also needs to be done by the defence DNA expert witness as they are more likely than any other type of laboratory errors. The defence should ask the prosecution to provide raw genotyping data for each of the samples mentioned in the report and the reported genotypes should be thoroughly checked. The prosecution should also provide the defence with the reference to the method employed for calculating the random match probability or other relevant forensic statistic as well as the frequencies of the alleles and the values of the co-ancestry coefficients used for calculating these indices, so that the defence expert could verify that there was no error in reporting them.

Chapter 7

DNA evidence interpretation errors

The strength of DNA evidence is reflected by the value of the probability of a random match between DNA profiles from the crime sample and the accused. Any probabilistic approach introduces uncertainly into the interpretation of scientific evidence which, if not properly understood, can give rise to a misunderstanding of the evidence and inaccurate conclusions as to what the evidence really means. To be able to deal with errors of evidence misinterpretation, it is important to know their origin and how they can affect the proceedings.

Several types of DNA data interpretation errors are known. Some errors affect the way random match probability is calculated, some affect mixture evaluation and others affect how DNA data is interpreted in court. It is possible to divide DNA data interpretation errors loosely into two major categories – (1) statistical errors and errors associated with data analysis methodology and (2) errors of DNA evidence misinterpretation in the courtroom. It is difficult to separate statistical errors from errors of misinterpretation of evidence as each feeds the other. Here I treat statistical errors as errors that lead to erroneous calculation of a random match probability or likelihood ratio, resulting from either incorrect methodology of data analysis or the wrong choice of parameters used for the calculation of these indices. The errors of misinterpretation of DNA evidence refer to logical errors by forensic scientists or lawyers that happen in the courtroom, which have a propensity to affect interpretation of evidence by the judge and the jury. Most of these errors are related in one way or another to a tendency to interpret DNA evidence as means of giving a comment on the truthfulness or otherwise of the prosecution's proposition (Aitken and Taroni, 2004) as to the source of the crime stain or the guilt of the accused.

7.1 Statistical errors and errors in data analysis methodology

DNA evidence is always supported by a statistical index reflecting how strong the evidence against the accused is. When calculating this parameter, various assumptions are taken into account, most of which deal with the structure of human populations and are based on theoretical models rather than real-life situations. The differences between the two can dramatically affect the interpretation of DNA results.

Statistical errors can arise when an unsuitable population database is used as a source of allelic frequencies, when the co-ancestry coefficient is not used to calculate the random match probability, when the value of the coefficient taken for calculations is wrong, when the chosen statistical approach is inappropriate for the type of evidence and for other reasons. A particular interpretation error can happen when DNA is analysed using several different marker systems and the random match probability is computed taking into account all the results.

In *R v Doheny* (1990) unreported (Manchester Crown Court), a woman was brutally assaulted and raped. Semen stains were found on the under-clothes of the victim and used for DNA analysis. DNA evidence was obtained using both multi-locus and single locus VNTR genotyping and the semen was also analysed for the presence of blood group antigens to deter-mine the blood group of the assailant. The results of the multi-locus VNTR analysis produced a random match probability of 1 in 840 while for the single locus genotyping, a probability of 1 in 6,900 was obtained. The forensic scientist who performed the analysis multiplied the results of the two DNA tests to produce the probability of a random match of 1 in 5.7 million and then multiplied it by 7 to account for the occurrence ratio of the blood group, producing a probability of 1 in 40 million. This approach is intrinsically flawed and the results of the analysis were successfully challenged in *R v Doheny and Adams* [1997] 1 Cr. App. R. 369.

Multi-locus VNTR genotyping produces information on a large number of alleles located on various chromosomes. The exact location of these alleles is largely unknown and some of them may be on the same chromosome and close enough to be inherited together. They can also be located in close proximity to the alleles of the single locus probe as well as the blood group alleles. One of the main requirements of a reliable DNA marker system is independent inheritance of the loci. This is achieved by choosing DNA loci which are located on different chromosomes and thus inherited independ-ently. However, in multi-locus VNTR genotyping there is no way of deter-mining whether bands identified by a particular probe are clustered together on the same chromosome or are located on different chromosomes. They cannot be assumed to be independent and consequently it is wrong to multi-ply the results of multi-locus and single locus genotyping when calculating the random match probability. The practice was specifically criticised in the ruling of *R v Doheny and Adams* [1997] 1 Cr. App. R. 369.

In order to be able to estimate the random match probability the allelic frequencies used for the calculation should be drawn from the population database which correctly reflects the population relevant to the crime in question, i.e., the population the offender comes from. This, in most cases, is not known even when the racial origin of the offender is not in any doubt. As we have seen above, major ethnic groups are not homogenous and within them there are sub-groups which have allelic frequencies different from those estimated for the general population. When the offender was identified as, say, a 'white male', the database for UK Caucasians may not be an adequate source of allelic frequencies as he may have come from a Caucasian population which is genetically different from the one which was used to estimate the frequencies. Political change in the world in the past fifty years has increased migration of populations and there are many people who may be phenotypically classified as Caucasian but who will be very different, genetically, from the majority of Caucasian population in the country. For example, frequencies of some alleles in the UK's Caucasian population and in the Russian Caucasian population may differ 10-fold! The error will be exacerbated when the offender is of mixed race or was born in a different country. In order to correct for such errors, forensic scientists use the sub-population correction, θ, which ameliorates the effect of population sub-division on the resultant value of the random match probability. Failure to take it into account may cause the probability bias towards the prosecution hypothesis and be unfavourable to the defendant.

When there is no information on the ethnic origin of the offender, which is often the case, the forensic scientist who conducts DNA analysis and data interpretation does not know from which DNA database allelic frequencies should be taken. In such a case, a common practice in the UK is to favour the accused and to report the most conservative result from the three results obtained with reference to the databases of Afro-Caribbean, Caucasian and Indo–Pakistani British populations. This seems to be a sound approach although it still suffers from the same problems as described above – the UK source population used for a particular racial group may be completely different from that which the offender comes from. In such a case the reported value of the random match probability may be either overestimated or underestimated.

7.2 Errors in DNA evidence interpretation in the courtroom

When DNA evidence is examined in court there is one issue that is crucial for determining how much weight should be given to it in the proceedings. The issue, though simple, is not trivial: is it possible to relate the DNA match between the accused and the crime stain, with the probability of the accused being the perpetrator of the crime s/he is being tried for? It is only for the judge and jury to assess the link between the evidence and the probability of guilt and not in any way the job of the prosecution DNA expert or the prosecutor to comment on it.

When the jury evaluates the probative value of DNA evidence in the context of a particular case, they proceed by building the following logical chain in reaching the decision on the ultimate probandum:

1. Evidence matches the accused; *following from this:*
2. The accused is the source of evidence; *following from this:*
3. The accused is the perpetrator of the crime.

Every following statement is independent from the previous ones and it is exclusively the domain of the jury to decide whether it is possible to infer Statement 2 from Statement 1 or Statement 3 from Statement 2. DNA evidence provides information only about the first statement. Using information about the strength of DNA evidence in conjunction with other relevant evidence in the case, the jury makes a decision whether Statement 2 can be inferred from Statement 1. The confusion and misunderstanding of DNA evidence occurs when, by giving information about Statement 1, the scientist expresses an opinion on Statement 2 or even Statement 3. In other words, instead of commenting on the evidence, s/he comments on the probability of the prosecution (or the defence) hypothesis.

DNA is circumstantial evidence. Circumstantial evidence allows a fact at issue to be proven inferentially rather than directly by providing factual information from which an inference may be drawn on the probability of the fact at issue (Emson, 2004). It is for the forensic scientist to provide the facts but for the jury to make this inference from them.

The instances of misunderstanding of DNA evidence in the courtroom are numerous. For example, when using DNA evidence in arriving at the decision as to the guilt of the accused, the jury may easily confuse the probability that the accused's DNA profile would match that of the criminal, given that s/he is innocent, with the probability that the accused is innocent, given that his/her DNA profile matches that of the real criminal.

This leads to a common error of misinterpretation of evidence, called 'the prosecutor's fallacy'. The prosecutor's fallacy can be detrimental to the case of the accused and has been the subject of many appeal cases. Other interpretation errors include the defendant's fallacy, the uniqueness fallacy etc.

Evidence interpretation errors are far too common in the courtroom and are committed not only by lawyers who in most cases do not have special statistical training but also by forensic scientists who should know better. Each of these errors deserves to be discussed separately. Koehler (1993) and Aitken and Taroni (2004) present an excellent treatment of the subject of errors in evidence interpretation. I will largely follow them in discussing the errors of DNA evidence interpretation here.

7.2.1 The prosecutor's fallacy

The prosecutor's fallacy is a specific case of a logical error of the transposed conditional (Thompson and Schumann, 1987) which arises when the probability of DNA evidence under a particular hypothesis is confused with the probability of the hypothesis given DNA evidence. This fallacy tends to favour the prosecution and was a subject of numerous publications in legal literature as well as a cause of many successful appeals (see for example *R v Deen* TLR 1994 Jan 10, *R v Adams, R v Adams (Denis)* [1996] 2 Cr. App. R. 467, *R v Doheny and Adams* [1997] 1 Cr. App. R. 369). In spite of this it still often happens, especially in cases when DNA evidence is involved.

The error of the transposed conditional is an elementary logical error in which the evidence interpreter assumes that if A implies B, then B implies A. Balding (2005) gives a simple explanation of this error. Let A denote 'a cow' and B denote 'has four legs' then a statement 'a cow has four legs' is not the same as 'if an animal has four legs it is a cow'. A cow is one of the possibilities but the animal can also be a sheep, a goat or a dog.

The reasoning behind the prosecutor's fallacy is similar to this logical error, only in terms of probabilities. This can be illustrated by the following example. If there are 100 four-legged animals living on a farm, of which 10 are cows and 90 are sheep then the probability of randomly picking a four-legged animal which will be a cow is 0.1 (i.e., every tenth animal is a cow). Assume that the probability of having four legs if you are a cow on the farm is 1 (i.e., every cow on the farm has four legs; I disregard here rare genetic anomalies and accidents leading to amputation of limbs). In such a case the probability of the statement 'a cow has four legs' is 1 while the probability of the statement 'a four-legged animal on the farm is a cow' is only 0.1. The first statement is the probability of evidence ('four legs') under a particular hypothesis ('is a cow'), the second statement is a probability of a particular hypothesis ('is a cow') given evidence ('has four legs').

In relation to DNA evidence the prosecutor's fallacy is the confusion of the probability of a match between the accused and the crime stain (Statement 1 in the previous section) with the probability that the accused is the source of the crime stain (Statement 2) or with the probability of accused being guilty of the offence (Statement 3). The former fallacy is called the source probability error while the latter one is the ultimate issue error.

7.2.1.1 The source probability error

The source probability error is the most common type of the prosecutor's fallacy. This error happens when the probability of DNA evidence (e.g., the random match probability) is equated with the probability of the accused being the source of the crime stain sample. Equating these two probabilities tends to exaggerate the strength of the prosecution hypothesis and is detrimental to the defendant. The information on the source is inferred from the factual information provided by the expert and it is exclusively the prerogative of the jury to make such an inference from adduced evidence. Because of this, it is not for the expert to express his/her opinion on the source of evidence; this lies in the domain of the jury.

Examples of the source probability error are numerous. When the probability of a random match is, say, 1 in 80,000, statements like the one made by the prosecution expert witness in *R v Lonsdale* [1995] 2 Cr. App. R. 565 are fallacious:

> Mr Greenhalgh, for the prosecution . . . considered it 80,000 times more likely that the semen had come from the appellant than from another.

Forensic scientists, when adducing DNA evidence, sometimes make just such an error in front of the jury. Forensic evidence in the trials of Doheny and Adams, although presented by different scientists, both contained the source probability error, which was discussed at length during the Court of Appeal hearing in *R v Doheny and Adams* [1997] 1 Cr. App. R. 369.

Doheny:

> A. I calculated the chance of finding all of those bands and the conventional blood groups to be about 1 in 40 million.
> Q. The likelihood of it being anybody other than Alan Doheny?
> A. Is about 1 in 40 million.
> Q. You deal habitually with these things, the jury have to say, of (p. 378) course, on the evidence, whether they are satisfied beyond doubt that it is he. You have done the analysis, are you sure that it is he?
> A. Yes.

and Adams:

> Q. Is it possible that the semen could have come from a different person from the person who provided the blood sample?
> A. It is possible but it is so unlikely as to really not be credible. I can calculate; I can estimate the chances of this semen having come from a man other than the provider of the blood sample. I can work out the chances as being less than 1 in 27 million.

A correct version of these statements should involve a conditional statement of the form 'if the defendant were not the source, then the probability . . .' (Balding, 2005).

Forensic scientists are specially trained not to commit the errors of transposed conditional in their statements but the above examples indicate these types of errors are likely to be committed when the scientist is asked about the meaning of evidence in court. A legitimate question arises about the extent to which experts are responsible for the mischaracterisation of their scientific testimony by others. Under the activity and stress of direct and cross-examinations, it may not be reasonable to expect an expert to catch and correct all subtle distortions and misunderstandings expressed within the courtroom (Koehler, 1993).

7.2.1.2 The ultimate issue error

The source probability error is often extended to comment on the probability that the accused is guilty of the crime s/he is tried for. This is known as the ultimate issue error.

When scientists report the probability of a random match between the accused and the crime samples as, say, 1 in 100 million, they may erroneously be interpreted by the judge, jurors or prosecutor as meaning that the probability of the accused being innocent is also 1 in 100 million. An example of the reasoning leading to the ultimate issue error is given in *R v Doheny and Adams* [1997] 1 Cr. App. R. 369:

> If one person in a million has a DNA profile which matches that obtained from the crime stain, then the suspect will be 1 of perhaps 26 men in the United Kingdom who share that characteristic. If no fact is known about the Defendant, other than that he was in the United Kingdom at the time of the crime, the DNA evidence tells us no more than that there is a statistical probability that he was the criminal of 1 in 26.

The ultimate issue error often arises when the prosecutor or judge asks the scientist who presents the evidence a question in the form of a transposed conditional. Koehler (1993) gives an example of a dialogue between the prosecutor and the DNA expert witness after he reported a random match probability between the DNA profile of the accused and the crime stain samples as 1 in 5 billion:

> Q. So that in the event that the accused sitting in this chair would happen to be White, you're telling the members of this jury that there would [be] a one in 5 billion chance that anybody else could have committed the crime; is that correct?
> A. One in 5 billion, correct.

As illustrated by this dialogue, it is very easy for an expert witness to get caught by such a question and give an erroneous testimony. As well as experts, it is thought that ultimate source errors are committed by the judges and jurors, even when the experts don't commit them (Koehler, 1993). As this is often the case, the defence has to emphasise to the jury that DNA evidence does not give any information as to the guilt or otherwise of the accused, but only indicates the likelihood of him/her being the donor of DNA from the crime stain.

7.2.1.3 The false positive fallacy

In the previous chapter we saw that a match between the accused and the crime stain can either be true or be false, because of a false positive error. Many consider that for correct evaluation of DNA evidence, it is important only to have information about the value of the random match probability. However, it is also necessary to have valid data on the false positive error rate in the forensic laboratory, to be able to evaluate the evidence correctly.

The false positive fallacy happens when a scientist mistakenly assumes that if the false positive probability is low in the laboratory then the probability of a false match in the case in question must also be low (Aitken and Taroni, 2004). A scientist may think that if the probability of a false positive match in the laboratory is 0.001 then the probability of a true match reported in a particular case is 0.999. This fallacy, which is a version of the prosecutor's fallacy, arises from mistakenly equating the conditional probability of a match being reported when the samples do not match (the false positive probability) with the probability that the samples do not match when a match has been reported (Aitken and Taroni, 2004). These two probabilities are not the same.

The false positive probability depends only on the probability of genotyping (and/or human) error in the laboratory and is the probability that a match between the accused's sample and the crime sample will be reported, when there is no match. The probability that the samples do not match when a match has been reported depends on both the probability of genotyping (and/or human) error and the prior odds that such a match will occur. The assumption that the false positive probability is equal to the probability that the samples do not match when the match is reported, is fallacious because it ignores the prior probability that the accused's profile matches the crime profile (Aitken and Taroni, 2004). In a simple case, assuming there are no false negatives, the probability $Pr(M \mid R)$ of a true match M between the accused and the crime sample, given that a true match R has been reported, can be calculated using the following formula (Aitken and Taroni, 2004):

$$Pr(M \mid R) = \frac{1}{1 + kPr(R \mid \bar{M})}$$

where k are the prior odds that the accused's profile matches that from the crime scene and $Pr(R \mid \bar{M})$ is the false positive probability.

A more complex formula, which takes into account the probability of false negatives, can be found in the same work.

Aitken and Taroni (2004) provide a compelling example illustrating the false positive fallacy. Let assume that the prior odds of the accused matching the crime sample is 1 in 1,000, because the accused was identified by a DNA search and appeared initially to be an unlikely perpetrator. The match between the accused and the crime stain was obtained. Further, let the probability of the false positive match in the forensic laboratory which analysed the samples be 0.01. The false positive fallacy would suggest that because the false positive error in the laboratory is 0.01 the probability of a match reported correctly in this particular case would be 0.99. In reality, this probability is:

$$Pr\ (M\mid R) = \frac{1}{1 + 1000 \times 0.01} = 0.0909$$

which is almost 11 times smaller than that assumed under the false positive fallacy.

7.2.2 The defendant's fallacy

Besides the prosecutor's fallacy, the other logical error commonly heard in the courtroom is the defendant's fallacy (Thompson and Schumann, 1987) which, as the name states, usually favours the defendant.

To illustrate this fallacy let us examine the example from *R v Doheny and Adams* [1997] 1 Cr. App. R. 369, which illustrates the ultimate issue error. The crime was committed by a male. Suppose the total UK male population is 26 million. The random match probability reported for the case is 1 in 1 million. The defendant's fallacy would be to claim that as there are 26 people in the UK who have the DNA profile matching that from the crime scene, the probability that the defendant is the culprit is only 1 in 26 or less than 4 per cent. Some may go even further and argue that because the number of possible culprits is high the probative value of DNA evidence is low and it should be ignored.

Strictly speaking, the defendant's fallacy is not a fallacy in the sense of the prosecutor's fallacy. The logic behind the defendant's fallacy's reasoning would be correct if it were assumed that everyone was equally likely to be guilty (which of course contradicts the main principle of criminal law – innocent until proven guilty). In practice, though, this assumption is very unlikely. Even when there is no evidence directly incriminating the accused of the crime, there is usually enough background evidence related to the location and nature of the crime to exclude some individuals from the number of potential perpetrators and make others more plausible suspects. In addition, the DNA evidence in the above example has reduced the number of possible perpetrators from 26 million to 26 individuals, the accused being one of them, and increased the odds in favour of his guilt 1 million times. In other words, the evidence is 1 million times more likely if the accused is the perpetrator of the crime than if he is innocent.

7.2.3 The uniqueness fallacy

Another fallacy which often crops up in cases when DNA evidence is used is the uniqueness fallacy. This fallacy arises when the match probability for an unrelated perpetrator is small enough to imply that no other individual with the same profile could be found in the relevant population.

An example of the uniqueness fallacy could be found in *R v Doheny and Adams* [1997] 1 Cr. App. R. 369. In the case of Gary Adams, the prosecution expert reported a random match of 1 in 27 million. The following dialogue between the prosecutor and the expert witness ensued:

Q.   So, it is really a very high degree of probability indeed that the semen stain came from the same person who provided the blood sample?

A.   Yes. You really have to consider the size of the group of individuals (p. 384) who could possibly be the source of this semen. Now, there probably are only 27 million male people in the whole of the United Kingdom so a figure of 1 in 27 million does tend to imply that it is extremely likely there is only really one man in the whole of the United Kingdom who has this DNA profile.

In his summing up the case, the judge at the original trial concluded:

'. . . I do not know what the population of the United Kingdom is but I should not think there were more than 27 million males in the United Kingdom, which means that it is unique.'

The uniqueness fallacy misinterprets the role of forensic scientist in criminal proceedings and the role of statistics in forensic inference. It stems from taking the value of random match probability literally. Because of relatedness, the actual number of people who might have the same DNA profile as Gary Adams is higher. In the above case, it is wrong to assume that there are 27 million males in the UK who are unrelated to each other. This number is significantly lower than the one assumed by the prosecutor and the judge and is probably in the region of 3–5 million males if we consider the meaning of the word 'unrelated' as 'second cousin'.

Instead of having a literal meaning, the value of the random match probability indicates how strong the evidence against the defendant is and how much weight the jury should assign to it. The analogy here is the use of break horse power (bhp) to measure the power of a car engine and estimate the speed of the car. If the car has a top speed of 155 mph, 0–60 mph acceleration of 5.5 seconds and the engine power of 250 bhp it only indicates that the gross power of the engine will be equal to the power of 250 horses (obviously assuming that each horse has a power of 0.746 kW) and is not directly relevant to the top speed of the car or acceleration. Two hundred and fifty horses harnessed together will never achieve the speed of 155 mph or reach 0–60 mph in 5.5 seconds. At the same time, when we compare two cars, one with an engine of 100 bhp, the other with an engine of 250 bhp we can confidently say that the latter should be faster, even though the car speed cannot be expressed in break horse power units.

If all 7 billion people living on the planet were not related to each other, probably, a match probability which is several orders of magnitude smaller than the 1 in 7 billion would be sufficient to judge that a profile is unique and no identical one can be found. However, this is not the case. All people are related to each other to a certain degree, especially island populations like the one we have in the UK (the situation is even more complicated in Iceland whose 300,000 population originated from a few hundred original settlers in the ninth and tenth centuries). Because of this, the chances of finding another individual with an identical DNA profile are not negligible, making the claim of uniqueness statistically unsubstantiated, even when calculations of the random match accounted for co-ancestry. When the match probability is 1 in 27 million, it does not mean that we need to test 27 million people to find the matching profile. There is a high probability that the number of people needed to be tested to find the matching profile is significantly lower. This is discussed in more detail in the next section. But even in the hypothetical case when all people on the planet are not related to each other, because of the non-DNA evidence there seems to be no satisfactory way for an expert witness to address the question of uniqueness in court (Balding, 1993).

The other logical error in the uniqueness fallacy is related to misunderstanding of the law of evidence, the mechanics of proof in criminal proceedings and the role of the jury during a criminal trial. In expressing the fallacy the scientist usurps the right of the jury to draw conclusions as to the identity of the source. In making a statement on uniqueness of the DNA profile, the scientist has to account for the size of the relevant population of potential perpetrators. Because the size of this population depends on other evidence, besides demographic characteristics, the scientist will, in expressing his/her opinion on uniqueness, always be using the population of the wrong size as this other evidence is not available to him/her. It is also not in the domain of the scientist to regard some sections of the population as more capable of committing the crime than the other ones.

7.2.4 The probability of another match error

The logical flaw of the probability of another match error is similar to the uniqueness fallacy. This error stems from a mistaken belief that the probability of a random match is the same as the probability of finding another person in the population with the same DNA profile.

Again, let use the example from *R v Doheny and Adams* [1997] 1 Cr. App. R. 369 which deals with the appeal of Gary Adams. The judge in the original trial considered that, as the crime stain profile matched Gary Adams, the chances of finding this profile were 1 in 27 million because there were (in his estimate) no more than 27 million males in the UK; the probability that there was some other male with the DNA profile identical to Gary Adams' was also 1 in 27 million, and hence Gary Adams' profile could be considered unique. The trial judge in this case has mistaken the probability that a randomly selected UK male would have the profile identical to Gary Adams, which is 1 in 27 million, with the probability that some male in the population has the same profile as Gary Adams. The latter probability may be greater than the former.

Let N denote the size of the relevant population and F the frequency of a particular crime profile. Then the probability that a randomly selected person will not match the crime profile will be $1 - F$, while the probability that not a single member of the relevant population will match the crime profile will be $(1 - F)^N$. It follows from this that the complement probability θ, that at least one match will be found in the population is $\theta = 1 - (1 - F)^N$ (Aitken and Taroni, 2004).

In the case of Gary Adams, the random occurrence ratio of the crime profile F was 1 in 27 million and the size of the relevant population N was considered to be 27 million. Then the probability of finding at least one other person in the population with DNA profile matching Gary Adams will be:

$$\theta = 1 - (1 - F)^N = 1 - (1 - 1/27,000,000)^{27,000,000} = 0.632321 \text{ or } 63.2\%$$

It may be extremely unlikely to randomly pick a male whose DNA profile matches that of Gary Adams (1 in 27,000,000 chances) but the probability that at least one such man exists is 63.2 per cent.

If, for the sake of argument, I assume that the evidence in the case of Gary Adams was obtained using modern SGM Plus genotyping and the F reported was 1 in 1 billion, the probability of finding at least one match within UK's 27 million male population would still be 0.026639 or just short of 3 per cent. Can we consider that the 3 per cent probability of finding another match in the relevant population constitutes that the profile is unique? And what about 63.2 per cent?

7.2.5 The numerical conversion error

Sometimes, the random match probability may be incorrectly interpreted as the number of people who need to be tested until the second identical profile is found. A conclusion that when the probability of a random match is, say, 1 in 27 million, the number of people who need to be tested until the matching profile is found is 27 million is fallacious and is known as the numeric conversion error. This error exaggerates the number of people who would need to be tested before a match may be expected and thus exaggerates the probative value of DNA evidence (Koehler, 1993)

Koehler (1993) gives an example of a scientist committing a numerical conversion error in a Texas case. The expert was questioned about the match probability of 1 in 23 million he provided:

> Q.   Could you explain briefly to the jury what 1 in 23 million means in reference to this case? What does that mean?
> A.   It means that we calculated a match for four probes and that the pattern for the suspect in this case occurs in 1 in approximately every 23 million people. If we continued typing people until we reach 23 million, we would not expect to find someone else that matched for those four probes until after we had reached or exceeded 23 million people.

As in the previous example, let N denote the relevant population, F be the frequency of a particular crime profile and n be the minimum number of people who would have to be tested before another match was found. The numerical conversion error is to equate N with n.

As above, the probability that a randomly selected person will not match the crime profile will be $1 - F$, while the probability that, for n randomly selected individuals, none will match the crime profile will be $(1 - F)^n$. The probability that at least one match will be found is $1 - (1 - F)^n$. For a match to be more likely that not, the probability of a match has to be greater than 0.5, so, $(1 - F)^n < 0.5$ (Aitken and Taroni, 2004). Solving this inequality for n we obtain the formula for calculating the number of people needed to be tested before we might expect the match to be more likely than not:

$$n = \frac{\ln(0.5)}{\ln(1 - 1/F)}$$

Taking the same F that has been reported in the case of Gary Adams we would expect to find a match after testing 18.7 million males which is more than 8 million people smaller than the total number of UK males estimated by the expert. At the same time, the number of males that need to be tested to ensure that finding a match is guaranteed (say, with the probability of 0.99) is a staggering 124.3 million people, almost four times the estimated male population of the UK!

7.2.6 Other interpretation difficulties

Besides the abovementioned errors and fallacies forensic reports sometimes contain statements that have a potential for causing misinterpretation of DNA evidence. Some of these statements are discussed below.

7.2.6.1 Relative frequency of occurrence

Sometimes an expert statement contains, instead of the match probability, the reference to the frequency of occurrence of a particular DNA profile in the population. In such a case, the report includes a statement about the DNA evidence along the following lines: 'The DNA profile of a particular type occurs in about one person in 100,000 of the population'. There are several major objections to this approach (Aitken and Taroni, 2004).

1. When the relevant population is greater than the inversed frequency of occurrence, then it is possible by this approach to estimate the number of potential perpetrators and use DNA evidence as prior odds when evaluating the remaining evidence in this case. For example, when the size of the relevant population is 1 million and the frequency of the DNA profile is 1 in 100,000 then the number of potential perpetrators will be $1,000,000 \times (1/100,000) = 10$. However, if the inversed frequency of occurrence is bigger than the relevant population (the frequency is, say, 1 in 1 billion while the relevant population is 1 million) we would not expect to see another profile like this, which makes it impossible to combine DNA evidence with other evidence that might provide the support or an alibi for the defence case.

2. When a relative of the accused is considered as a potential perpetrator, a statement like 'The DNA profile in question occurs in about one brother in 400' does not make sense. The scientist has to find alternative ways of expressing the meaning of this statement, which may be even more confusing to the jury.

3. When assessing DNA evidence, there are at least two conflicting hypotheses – the prosecution hypothesis, which states that the accused is the donor of the crime stain, and the defence hypothesis, stating that the accused is not the donor of the crime stain but owing to chance his/her DNA profile matches that of the real perpetrator. This means that there is another person in the population with the profile matching that of the accused. In contrast to frequency, the concept of a match involves two profiles which permits evaluating both prosecution and defence theories. It is not the relative frequency of a particular DNA profile or the probability of finding a particular profile in the population that is essential for a criminal identification but rather the probability of finding a particular DNA profile in the population, given that the accused has this

profile. It is important to emphasise that in human populations, because of relatedness and population subdivisions, the match probability exceeds the probability of finding a particular profile in the population (Balding, 2005). Thus, the use of DNA profile frequency instead of the match probability favours prosecution and should be avoided in criminal trials.

4.   When a mixed profile is obtained from the crime stain or in cases of paternity testing or identification of victims of mass disasters, it is impossible to use the profile frequency to state the value of DNA evidence as these types of profiles cannot be expressed in the form of 'one in . . .'.

7.2.6.2 The 'Could be' approach

Often, forensic scientists use statements regarding the source of DNA evidence of the form 'it is 280,000 times more likely that the accused could be the donor of the DNA recovered from the left pocket of the trousers' or 'in my opinion the blood stains on the track suit bottoms could have come from the victim' and so on. This type of statement may be treated as the source probability error as they express a view on the probability of a hypothesis (the accused is the donor of the crime stain).

7.2.6.3 The 'Could not be excluded' approach

Another type of statement commonly found in forensic reports is that 'the accused cannot be excluded from being a donor of the crime stain'. We have discussed the exclusion probabilities approach in evaluating DNA evidence in Chapter 3. Under this approach the probability that a random man or a contributor to the mix will be excluded as the donor of the DNA from the crime scene is calculated. However, such a probability only states the proportion of the population which would be excluded; it is thus the measure of efficacy of a particular test (Robertson and Vignaux, 1992) as it answers the question 'how likely is an individual to be the donor of the crime stain'. However, the other question is much more important in criminal identification, namely 'how much more likely is the evidence if the accused is the donor of the crime stain than a randomly taken individual' (Aitken and Taroni, 2004). The 'could not be excluded' approach does not give an answer to this question and the probability of exclusion is not relevant for evaluating DNA evidence in such a case.

7.2.6.4 Statements about identical twins

The author has several times come across statements which are now rarely made in court but often in the press, that 'only identical twins have identical

DNA profiles' or 'no two people in the world have matching DNA profiles apart from identical twins'. These statements are not correct. Identical twins indeed have matching DNA profiles, however other people may have matching profiles owing to chance or because they are related. The chances of such a match happening are expressed by a random match probability and, however rare, a match between two unrelated individuals can happen.

7.3 Why interpretation errors happen

Most errors of DNA evidence interpretation tend to exaggerate the probative value of the evidence. Koehler (1993) in his review of interpretation errors addressed this issue. He investigated several potential factors, such as deliberate exaggeration of the probative value by scientists who wish to 'puff up' the utility of their science, or by prosecutors, determined to win their case. He concluded that the most plausible explanation for this sort of error is ignorance in the legal profession of statistics and rules for evidence interpretation.

In a review of court cases conducted by Koehler it transpired that DNA experts generally begin the interpretation part of their testimony with statements about population frequencies and comparison with a 'random man'. Although, as we have seen, there may be errors in these statements they are not deliberate and the very use of such statements indicate that the scientist tries to give an unbiased opinion. The errors in the testimony begin to appear in most cases only after the expert re-describes his/her findings in response to the questions from the prosecutor. It has to be kept in mind that while, for a prosecutor, a court hearing is part of the daily job, the expert witness is often under immense pressure both because of his/her role in the proceedings and also because of the adversarial nature of the criminal trial. In such circumstances, even highly experienced scientists can make errors in answering a logically erroneous question.

Because very few lawyers are trained in statistics and evidence interpretation they may misunderstand the subtleties of probabilistic inference and have trouble differentiating probabilistic information from probabilistic hypotheses that the information suggests (Koehler, 1993). All this indicates that the solution to the problem is specialised training of lawyers in matters dealing with evidence interpretation and probabilistic inference.

Chapter 8

DNA evidence during trial

8.1 Pre-trial disclosure of evidence against the accused

Given the right of the accused to a fair trial the prosecution should disclose to the accused in advance of the trial the nature of the allegation against him/her and all the evidence on which the prosecution is to rely to secure conviction. This includes DNA evidence. The procedure of the primary disclosure of evidence is set out in the Criminal Procedure and Investigations Act 1996 as amended by the Criminal Justice Act 2003 (CPIA). As directed by para 57 of the Attorney-General's Guidelines on Disclosure (updated April 2005) the prosecutor should, 'in addition to complying with the obligations under the Act, provide to the defence all evidence upon which the Crown proposes to rely in a summary trial. Such provision should allow the accused and their legal advisers sufficient time properly to consider the evidence before it is called.'

As provided by s 13(1) of the CPIA the prosecution is obliged to comply with primary disclosure under s 3 as soon as reasonably possible after the accused has been committed for trial. In addition to disclosure of the evidence which will be used by the prosecutor against the defendant, s 3(1) of the CPIA stipulates that the prosecutor must disclose to the accused any prosecution material that has not previously been disclosed to the accused and that might reasonably be considered capable of undermining the case for the prosecution against the accused or of assisting the case for the accused. Paragraph 10 of the Attorney-General's Guidelines on Disclosure states that, in making the decision as to whether to disclose the evidence that might undermine the prosecution case or assist the defence case, the prosecutor has to consider whether the evidence to be disclosed includes anything that tends to show a fact inconsistent with the elements of the case that must be proved by the prosecution and, at the trial, could lead to exclusion of evidence, a stay of proceedings, or finding that accused rights were breached under the European Convention on Human Rights. In making the decision as to the disclosure, the prosecutor has to consider whether this evidence could be used by the defence to undermine the prosecution case in cross-examination or suggest an explanation or partial explanation of the accused's actions.

Examples of material that might reasonably be considered capable of undermining the prosecution case or of assisting the case for the accused are:

- any material casting doubt upon the accuracy of any prosecution evidence;
- any material that may point to another person, whether charged or not (including a co-accused) having involvement in the commission of the offence;
- any material that may cast doubt upon the reliability of a confession;
- any material that might undermine the credibility of a prosecution witness;
- any material that might support a defence that is either raised by the defence or apparent from the prosecution papers; or
- any material that may have a bearing on the admissibility of any prosecution evidence.

These should include DNA profiles and reports that were not used by the prosecution, information about the proficiency of the forensic laboratory, genetic information about the relatives of the accused who may reasonably be believed to have committed the crime in question, and information on the competence and qualification of the DNA prosecution expert witness to name just a few. It should also be borne in mind that while an item taken in isolation may reasonably be considered not to be capable of undermining the prosecution case or assisting the accused, several items together can be.

When DNA samples are obtained from a defendant but the prosecution does not intend to adduce DNA evidence at the trial, it will be prudent of the defence to ask the prosecution to provide all necessary materials in relation to DNA examination of the crime samples and comparison with the DNA sample taken from the accused. In preparation for the case, the defence needs to know whether or not, as a result of examination, DNA profiles from the crime samples were obtained, what was the result of comparison between these profiles and the DNA profile of the defendant, and why the prosecution does not intend to adduce DNA evidence at the trial. It has to be remembered that the absence of evidence is not the evidence of absence.

If a DNA profile obtained from a crime scene does not match that of the defendant, it is powerful evidence supporting the defendant's case which the jury should consider in reaching its verdict. This point was commented on by the Court of Appeal in *R v Mitchell* [2004] *The Times*, 8 July. The accused was convicted of kidnapping, rape and three offences of indecent assault. The prosecution case depended almost entirely on the evidence of an eye witness, who knew the defendant and said she saw him with a girl when the offences took place. The accused claimed mistaken identity. During the trial it transpired that the accused's DNA profile did not match that from the crime scene. The judge at the original trial directed the jury that the expert DNA evidence was neutral and neither lent support to nor detracted from either case. Allowing the appeal it was held that:

> ... at trial, particularly where proof remained on the prosecution ... a non-match DNA profile was powerful evidence in the accused's favour which the jury should consider and weigh in the scale of the prosecution evidence.
>
> In respect of DNA evidence, judges should consider the way scientific evidence was used for the purposes of a jury's logical and common-sense decision making, with great care and not raise scientific speculative possibilities in a way which detracted from evidence an accused could genuinely rely on.

Additional weight to this argument was added by the fact that, during the accused's appeal against conviction, the crime stain profile was matched to another man.

Upon receiving all relevant evidence and information from the Crown, the accused is required by s 5(5) of the CPIA to serve on the Court and the prosecution a 'defence statement' within 14 days of primary disclosure having being made. In this statement the defence has to outline what the accused disputes about the prosecution case, including *inter alia* reliability and relevance of DNA evidence, and the reasons for it.

As provided by s 7 of the CPIA the prosecutor must keep under review the question whether, at any given time, following the defence statement, there is prosecution material that has not been disclosed to the accused or that might reasonably be considered capable of undermining the case for the prosecution against the accused or of assisting the case for the accused. Any such material is required to be disclosed to the accused as soon as is reasonably practicable. If the prosecutor considers that there is no such material, s/he must give a written statement to the defence. When the defence has reasonable cause to believe that there is such prosecution material they may apply to the court for an order requiring the prosecutor to disclose such material.

Statements dealing with DNA evidence which the prosecution intends to adduce at the trial typically conform to a format devised by the FSS, although statements provided by other laboratories may show minor variations. The statement dealing with DNA analysis typically consists of the following sections:

- Name, expertise, experience and qualifications of the expert
- Items received

- Information given to the scientist about the alleged circumstances of the case
- Purpose of examination
- Technical issues
- Examination and results
- Conclusions
- Appendix (usually DNA profiles of crime samples, the accused, etc.)

The scientist assigned to a case is referred to as a Reporting Officer. Where the analysis has been performed by a team of scientists, this should be clearly stated in the statement and the contribution of each member of the team indicated. Usually this is provided separately from the statement in a Forensic Examination Record, which is neither a statement nor an exhibit and is served separately.

The role and responsibilities of an expert witness have been addressed by the Court of Appeal in *R v Harris* [2006] 1 Cr. App R. 5 and *R v Bowman* [2006] EWCA Crim 417. The obligations of an expert witness in court are outlined in *R v Harris* [2006] 1 Cr. App R. 5:

> (p. 116) Expert evidence presented to the court should be and seen to be the independent product of the expert uninfluenced as to form or content by the exigencies of litigation.
>
> An expert witness should provide independent assistance to the court by way of objective unbiased opinion in relation to matters within his expertise. An expert witness in the High Court should never assume the role of advocate.
>
> An expert witness should state the facts or assumptions on which his opinion is based. He should not omit to consider material facts which detract from his concluded opinions.
>
> An expert should make it clear when a particular question or issue falls outside his expertise.
>
> If an expert's opinion is not properly researched because he considers that insufficient data is available then this must be stated with an indication that the opinion is no more than a provisional one.
>
> If after exchange of reports, an expert witness changes his view on material matters, such change of view should be communicated to the other side without delay and when appropriate to the court.

The decision in *R v Bowman* [2006] EWCA Crim 417 has re-iterated that the duties of an expert witness in a criminal trial are owed to the court and override any obligation to the person from whom the expert received instruction or by whom he was paid. This has implications for both prosecution and defence expert witnesses as, despite being instructed by a party to the trial, the expert statement is produced for the benefit of the court. The decision of the Court of Appeal expanded the above guidelines on how expert witness evidence is to be presented in court by outlining requirements of expert witness statements. According to the Court of Appeal, expert reports should include:

> (p. 60) Details of the expert's academic and professional qualifications, experience and accreditation relevant to the opinions expressed in the report and the range and extent of the expertise and any limitations upon the expertise.
>
> A statement setting out the substance of all the instructions received (with written or oral), questions upon which an opinion is sought, the materials provided and considered, and the documents, statements, evidence, information or assumptions which are material to the opinions expressed or upon which those opinions are based.
>
> Information relating to who has carried out measurements, examinations, tests etc and the methodology used, and whether or not such measurements etc were carried out under the expert's supervision.
>
> (p. 61) Where there is a range of opinion in the matters dealt with in the report a summary of the range of opinion and the reasons for the opinion given. In this connection any material facts or matters which detract from the expert's opinions and any points which should fairly be made against any opinions expressed should be set out.
>
> Relevant extracts of literature or any other material which might assist the court.
>
> A statement to the effect that the expert has complied with his/her duty to the court to provide independent assistance by way of objective unbiased opinion in relation to matters within his or her expertise and an acknowledgment that the expert will inform all parties and where appropriate the court in the event that his/her opinion changes on any material issues.
>
> Where on an exchange of experts' reports matters arise which require a further or supplemental report the above guidelines should, of course, be complied with.

It is paramount for successful defence that, during the preparation period for the trial, the defence team includes an expert on interpretation of DNA evidence. In some cases the defence may employ several experts who are specialists in various aspects of DNA evidence such as DNA technology or statistical interpretation of results of DNA testing. Even, when the probative value of DNA evidence seems to be very high, it is still necessary to have it examined by a DNA expert who may be able to identify week points or even faults in methodology or statistical approaches used by prosecution scientists for evaluation of DNA evidence.

8.2 Presentation of DNA evidence during trial

When the defence decides to challenge the admissibility of DNA evidence as a matter of law or make a case for the evidence to be excluded by the judge in the exercise of his/her common law discretion, it has to make appropriate submission to the judge on the *voir dire* in the absence of the jury. This is usually the case when, in the opinion of the defence, the probative value of DNA evidence is low and is exceeded by the prejudicial effect, or when there were serious errors committed when obtaining the evidence which could deny the accused the right of a fair trial. Should the DNA evidence impact on the fairness of the trial, an application pursuant of s 78 of PACE can be made. If the judge rules that the evidence ought to be admitted then the prosecution is free to adduce it.

Being an area of specialised knowledge, DNA evidence needs to be properly explained to the jury. This is done by a scientist, either personally involved in obtaining the evidence, or who personally supervised the team of scientists who produced the data. The purpose of the expert is to provide the jury with the information which is outside the scope of their knowledge to help them to form the opinion on issues linking the defendant and the scene of crime.

In England and Wales the guidelines for presenting DNA evidence in court were laid out in the ruling of *R v Doheny and Adams* [1997] 1 Cr. App. R. 369:

> The scientist should adduce the evidence of the DNA comparisons between the crime stain and the defendant's sample together with his/her calculations of the random occurrence ratio.
>
> Whenever DNA evidence is to be adduced the Crown should serve on the defence details as to how the calculations have been carried out which are sufficient to enable the defence to scrutinise the basis of the calculations.
>
> The Forensic Science Service should make available to a defence expert, if requested, the databases upon which the calculations have been based.
>
> Any issue of expert evidence should be identified and, if possible, resolved before trial. This area should be explored by the court in the pre-trial review.
>
> In giving evidence the expert will explain to the jury the nature of the matching DNA characteristics between the DNA in the crime stain and the DNA in the defendant's blood sample.
>
> The expert will, on the basis of empirical statistical data, give the jury the random occurrence ratio – the frequency with which the matching DNA characteristics are likely to be found in the population at large.
>
> Provided that the expert has the necessary data, it may then be

appropriate for him/her to indicate how many people with the matching characteristics are likely to be found in the United Kingdom or a more limited relevant sub-group, for instance, the Caucasian, sexually active males in the Manchester area.

It is then for members of the jury to decide, having regard to all the relevant evidence, whether they are sure that it was the defendant who left the crime stain, or whether it is possible that it was left by someone else with the same matching DNA characteristics.

The expert should not be asked his/her opinion on the likelihood that it was the defendant who left the crime stain, nor when giving (p. 370) evidence should s/he use terminology which may lead the jury to believe that s/he is expressing such an opinion.

It is inappropriate for an expert to expound a statistical approach to evaluating the likelihood that the defendant left the crime stain, since unnecessary theory and complexity deflect the jury from its proper task.

In the summing-up careful directions are required in respect of any issues of expert evidence and guidance should be given to avoid confusion caused by areas of expert evidence where no real issue exists.

The judge should explain to the jury the relevance of the random occurrence ratio in arriving at their verdict and draw attention to the extraneous evidence which provides the context which gives that ratio its significance, and to that which conflicts with the conclusion that the defendant was responsible for the crime stain.

In relation to the random occurrence ratio, a direction along the following lines may be appropriate, tailored to the facts of the particular case:

> Members of the jury, if you accept the scientific evidence called by the Crown this indicates that there are probably only four or five white males in the United Kingdom from whom that semen stain could have come. The defendant is one of them. If that is the position, the decision you have to reach, on all the evidence, is whether you are sure that it was the defendant who left that stain or whether it is possible that it was one of that other small group of men who share the same DNA characteristics.

These principles have been recently confirmed in *Pringle v R* [2003] WL 116971.

When assessing DNA evidence (as well as other types of evidence) in criminal proceedings the problem the law has to confront is the extent to which experts are allowed to influence the jury's decision on disputed issues (Emson, 2004). The issues which belong to the domain of the jury, the ultimate issues, upon which the final verdict will depend, have to be clearly separated in the mind of the expert from those on which s/he is entitled to give an opinion. It is unacceptable at common law for the ultimate issues to be commented on by an expert witness. These issues are for the jury to decide according to the standard of proof determined by law. The expert must not abuse his/her position, deliberately or inadvertently, by expressing opinion on the matters s/he is not entitled to, nor should s/he be asked to express such an opinion.

In relation to DNA evidence, specific issues on which the prosecution scientist must not comment are as follows (the list is by no means exhaustive and there may be other issues specific to the circumstances of a case):

whether or not the accused is the source of DNA found in the crime stain;

> It is in the domain of jury to decide whether the accused is the source of DNA basing their conclusion on the probability of random match and all other evidence and witness testimonies available to them.

give personal opinion as to the weight of DNA evidence expressed in a non-numerical way (as opposed to presenting a numerical value to the court and letting the jury assign a non-numerical value of strength to it);

> The expert witness should report a numerical value of the probability of a random match but must not express whether this probability represents, for example, weak support or support of any other strength for the hypothesis that the accused is the donor of examined DNA from the crime stain.

whether as a result of a specific act, the accused left his/her DNA at the scene of crime;

> When, for example, the source of examined DNA is semen obtained from a vaginal smear, it is not in the domain of the expert to comment how the semen got inside the vagina of the victim. This statement relates to the Activity Level of propositions (Chapter 3) and is the domain of the jury to form their opinion based on the evidence available to them. Some scientist in their reports on DNA evidence can go as far as state that 'In my opinion, if it is accepted that biological material from the victim is present on the penile swabs of the accused then the scientific findings provide very strong support for the views that the accused has had a vaginal intercourse with the victim'. The defence in this particular case had a completely different explanation as to the origin of victim's DNA on a accused's penile shaft (a common towel) of which the DNA expert was not aware.

the chances of the accused leaving his/her DNA at the crime scene prior
to the crime being committed ('prior odds');

> The opinion on the 'prior odds' is not expressed numerically and
> is formed in the minds of the jury based on the evidence adduced
> prior to DNA evidence. This evidence is not available to the foren-
> sic scientist putting him/her in no position to comment on the
> prior odds.

the number of people who could have contributed their DNA to the
crime sample (as opposed to giving the minimum number of contributors
to the DNA mixture, based on the results of DNA analysis);

> The scientist could estimate the number of contributors to a DNA
> mixture by analysing the number of peaks and their morphology.
> However, the jury is in a position to know how many people have
> been at the scene of crime and, consequently, can estimate the num-
> ber of people who could have contributed to the mixture. Usually,
> when reporting results of mixture evaluation, forensic scientists give
> the number of potential contributors in the form of 'no less than',
> thus indicating the minimum number of the individuals who could
> have contributed their DNA to the mixture.

the likelihood of error during examination of DNA evidence;

> It is for the jury to decide whether or not the results of DNA analysis
> have been affected by a laboratory or other error, taking into con-
> sideration the information about the types of laboratory and report-
> ing errors possible in each particular case, the genotyping error rate
> of a particular laboratory (if it is available, ideally the results of
> external blind proficiency tests) and the effect of errors on the proba-
> tive value of DNA evidence.

The limitations to what the expert is allowed to comment on stem from
the fact that in court proceedings the experts are allowed to give their
opinion only on matters which fall within their field of expertise and at the
same time are outside the general knowledge of the jury. Considering the
scientific expertise and authority of the expert, the jury may accept his/her
opinion without questioning and abrogate their responsibility to find the
true facts (Emson, 2004). Should the prosecution expert, during the testimony, express an opinion on the subject s/he is not entitled to, the defence
may find it appropriate to ask the judge to instruct the jury to disregard this
part of the expert's testimony or even apply for the evidence be ruled
inadmissible.

The main and in most cases the only purpose of DNA examination in the
contents of a criminal trial is identification. Interpretation of DNA evidence

is based on a big volume of scientific data and statistical reasoning. No other system of identification, past or present, has such a solid scientific basis as does identification using DNA analysis. While an expert presenting the results of identification by other means, like fingerprint or ear print examination, can express his/her personal opinion as to the identity of the source of the evidence, a DNA expert is prohibited to do so by the rules laid down by the Court of Appeal. This practice causes much criticism within UK's forensic community which seems not to be entirely unjustified.

From the legal standpoint, it is in the realm of the jury to decide whether or not the accused is the source of the DNA from the crime stain sample and, consequently, whether or not the accused was at the scene when the crime was committed. In arriving to this decision the jury bases its conclusion on a vast amount of evidential information provided to them by the prosecution and defence. Even more importantly, the jury possesses the means of verifying this information. The forensic scientist does not have access to any of this. S/he cannot be sure whether or not the background information about the case, provided to him/her by police, is true and does not have any means to check this. However, for more than a century, a fingerprint expert could express the strength of the evidence as 'in my opinion the finger mark on the glass was left by defendant's thumb' or in a similar fashion. In the view of many forensic scientists this is regrettable considering that fingerprint evidence has never been thoroughly checked and scientifically validated. In his brilliant review of the problem, Ian Evett (2000), an eminent UK forensic scientist, wrote that:

> ... no other area of forensic science has been explored statistically in anything remotely approaching the extent of the study of DNA profiling. Paradoxically, DNA profiling represents the only forensic science pursuit where the scientist, in the United Kingdom at least, is barred by precedent from expressing an opinion of identity of source. The DNA scientist is limited to presenting a match probability and, as yet, the jury have been given little assistance in comprehending its interaction with the other evidence.

When DNA evidence was presented in the original trials of *R v Doheny* (1990) unreported (Manchester Crown Court) and *R v Adams* (1991) unreported (Stafford Crown Court) the DNA analysis was performed using VNTR genotyping. This technique achieved relatively modest match probabilities. The introduction of the SGM Plus permitted generating match probabilities several orders of magnitude smaller. In most cases, for a complete match, they will be less than 1 in several billions. The 1997 guidance for presenting DNA evidence seems to be less adequate when very small probabilities of random match are presented in court, and to resolve this issue a dialogue between forensic scientists and the judiciary is needed (Evett, 2000).

Expert witnesses should provide their opinions comprehensively and in an unbiased manner. In formulating their opinions, experts may often need to rely on certain facts pertinent to the case and to refer to various extraneous sources of information (e.g., articles and data published in scientific journals) to justify their opinions. When experts have to rely on the facts resulting from the case these facts have to be proved by admissible evidence. Otherwise, the evidence is inadmissible under the hearsay rule. The implication of the hearsay rule with regards to admissibility of DNA evidence is discussed in the next chapter.

In contrast to the facts resulting from the case, published works of reference, documents prepared by public officials, scientific reports and publications in reputable journals all constitute exceptions to the hearsay rule under common law and can be relied upon by the expert when presenting the results of DNA examination. The reason for this is that information published in reputable sources has already been thoroughly examined by experts in the field and can be accepted to prove statements contained therein (Emson, 2004). Such documents may often need to be admitted to explain to the judge and jury how the expert reached his/her conclusions. Among information from published sources routinely used by DNA experts are allelic frequencies and the values of the co-ancestry coefficient as well as some specific technical information regarding a particular procedure or part of a DNA examination protocol.

The rules laid out in *R v Doheny and Adams* [1997] 1 Cr. App. R. 369 clearly indicate that the main information which the expert needs to provide to the judge and jury is the 'random occurrence ratio – the frequency with which the matching DNA characteristics are likely to be found in the population at large', and that the expert 'should not be asked his opinion on the likelihood that it was the defendant who left the crime stain nor when giving evidence [nor] use terminology which may lead the jury to believe that he is expressing such an opinion'. Unfortunately as we have discussed in Chapter 3, many expert witness statements contain expressions of personal opinion of the scientist. If the scientist decides to provide such an opinion in his/her report it should be only for the purpose of informing the prosecution and the defence on his/her personal opinion regarding the strength of evidence against the accused. It is typically put in brackets within the Conclusion section of the statement with a disclaiming note similar to this one:

> My opinion on the source of the DNA is provided here for the benefit of the prosecution and defence. In the event of a not guilty plea, all words within these square brackets should be deleted from my statement to avoid contravening the Court of Appeal ruling in *R v Doheny and Adams* (1997).

When the report contains personal opinion of the expert on the strength of

DNA evidence, this opinion should never be allowed to be aired in court as it will contravene the decision of the Court of Appeal. If the prosecution expert during his/her testimony expresses a personal opinion on the strength of evidence, the defence should make an application to the judge to instruct the jury to disregard this part of the expert's testimony.

Although the above arguments are the subject of some debate, there is, regrettably, a major error in the decision of the Court of Appeal over which DNA index should be reported by the prosecution scientist. It seems that, not being specialists in forensic DNA analysis, the Court of Appeal mistook the match probability for the random occurrence ratio, which are very different in nature, and the way they are calculated.

The random occurrence ratio, which is recommended by the Court of Appeal ruling to be reported by the expert, is the frequency of a particular DNA profile in the population. As we saw in Chapter 7, it is erroneous to report a profile frequency as the indicator of the probability that it was the accused who is the donor of the DNA from the crime stain because the concept of frequency does not allow the evaluation of both prosecution and defence hypotheses simultaneously. When a match between the crime stain profile and that of the accused is obtained, the defence does not usually dispute the fact of the match (although they may dispute the value of the statistic describing how strong the match is). Their theory is usually that the match is observed because the accused's DNA profile matches that of the real perpetrator of the crime in question. Reporting the profile frequency does not take this theory into account. In addition, because of the way it is calculated, the profile frequency favours the prosecution and could be detrimental to the defence case.

The correct measure of probability of a match between the accused and the crime stain is the random match probability which takes into account both alternative hypotheses and indicates how many times more likely is the view of events put forward by the prosecution (the accused is the donor of DNA in the crime sample) than that by the defence (another man with the profile identical to that of the accused is the donor). Forensic scientists in the UK recognise the difference between the frequency of a profile and the probability of a random match and give the latter in their statements. However, in cases where the frequency of the DNA profile is reported instead of match probability, the defence may raise an objection to the use of this parameter in relation to DNA evidence. Although the Court of Appeal recommends the use of random occurrence ratio, in almost every case heard by the Court of Appeal since Doheny and Adams the strength of DNA evidence has been reported as random match probability and this fact can be used by the defence to justify their position.

After DNA evidence has been adduced the defence may challenge it on one or several points. This may be done during the cross-examination of the prosecution expert or the evidence may be challenged by defence's own expert evidence. The ways DNA evidence can be challenged are discussed in the next chapter.

8.3 Is conviction based solely on DNA evidence possible?

In the process of establishing the guilt of the accused, the jury evaluates all evidence adduced at the trial and in doing so, assigns appropriate weights to each evidential fact. Some evidence may have much probative value and, in the minds of the jurors, give much reliable information regarding the probability of a fact at issue and, ultimately, the guilt or innocence of the accused, while other evidence could be less informative. DNA evidence is one of many types of evidence that is adduced at a trial and how much weight a jury assigns to it depends on how strong this evidence is as well as how convincing were the arguments of the defence in challenging the evidence. Whether or not the members of the jury decide to disregard other evidence in favour of DNA evidence or consider other types of evidence less informative is up to them. But, in any case, when DNA evidence is not the only type of evidence adduced at the trial (which is in the great majority of cases), the jury, in making its decision as to the guilt or innocence of the accused, analyses DNA evidence in conjunction with all other types of evidence and gives its verdict based on all evidence available to them.

Therefore, the question whether or not DNA evidence on its own is enough to convict an accused should be rephrased as 'in the absence of any other evidence, is DNA evidence enough to make a decision as to the guilt of the accused'. This is one of the most talked-about points regarding DNA evidence and there exist two contrasting opinions on the matter. The adherents of the 'yes' camp accept that conviction on DNA evidence alone is justified while the adherents of the 'no' camp believe that it is wrong to convict based solely on DNA evidence as the probability of miscarriage of justice in such a case is unacceptably high.

The judgment in the case of *R v Adams (Denis)* [1996] 2 Cr. App. R. 467 makes a special reference to the fact that '(p. 469) There is no principle of law that DNA evidence is in itself incapable of establishing guilt' and then on p. 470 '. . . There is . . . nothing inherent in the nature of DNA evidence which makes it inadmissible in itself or which justifies a special, unique rule, that evidence falling into such a category cannot found a conviction in the absence of other evidence'. This point of view was reiterated by the judgment in *R v Hanraty* [2002] 2 Cr. App. R. 30 where the Court of Appeal accepted that standing alone DNA was certain proof of the defendant's guilt.

The alternative opinion, which is also supported by many forensic scientists, was expressed by Kay LJ, who in the ruling of *R v Watters* [2000] WL 1791491 said:

Every case . . . has to be judged on its own facts. There is no rule that enables the court to say, well, when a figure [DNA match probability] reaches a certain level then it is safe to leave it to the jury, but below that it is not. But in every case one has to put the DNA evidence in the context of the rest of the evidence and decide whether taken as a whole it does amount to a prima facie case [and also, that it is] . . . necessary to look to see whether . . . the rest of the evidence in some way supported the DNA evidence so that, taken together, a proper inference of guilt could be drawn.

The issue whether or not DNA evidence alone is enough to convict the accused of the crime is an issue both of legal theory and practice. Instead of asking the question whether DNA evidence on its own can prove the guilt of the suspect, one has to ask whether DNA evidence on its own is enough to prove each element of *actus reus* and *mens rea* of the crime in question as well as their coincidence in time. DNA evidence can place the accused within an exceedingly small cohort of potential perpetrators. Whether on its own this proves both the *actus reus* and *mens rea* is questionable as a single type of circumstantial evidence cannot at the same time prove both. If either the *actus reus* or *mens rea* is absent it will not be possible to prove that the accused has committed the crime no matter how evil it is. For example, when semen is found on a vaginal swab from a rape victim and DNA evidence strongly supports that the source of DNA in the semen is the accused, this does not automatically indicate that the accused raped the victim, as absence of consent has to be proved by other evidence. Even in an offence of rape of a child (the offence where there is no opportunity for a plea of consent) the prosecution has to prove that penetration was intentional and this must be done by adducing other evidence or testimony. So, if DNA evidence is the only evidence in the trial and no circumstantial or other evidence is available, then from the theoretical perspective the DNA evidence seems incapable of proving both necessary components of a crime. When DNA evidence proves the act, something else must prove the intent.

Besides considerations with regard to the *actus reus* or *mens rea* of a particular crime, whether or not DNA evidence is enough to prove the guilt of the accused is intricately linked to who bears the legal burden of proof, to the standard of proof required to secure such a conviction, which in criminal proceedings is 'beyond reasonable doubt' and also, to the size of the population within which uniqueness of the DNA profile is claimed. It follows from this that it is also related to the problem of the uniqueness of a DNA profile itself, the probability of finding at least one DNA profile matching the accused in the relevant population, the probability of a false match, and the rules for choosing which relevant population the perpetrator of the crime comes from.

The purpose of adducing DNA evidence is to link a suspect with the crime scene. Because of its high cogency, DNA evidence is powerful enough to put a suspect within a small group of individuals who can be linked to the scene. When the probability of a random match is low, there may be only three or four people in the country besides the accused who could have committed the crime based on DNA evidence. In cases when a full match between DNA profiles from the crime stain and the suspect is obtained, the probability is usually reported as less than 1 in 1 billion meaning that the accused is put within an exceedingly small group of potential perpetrators. Whether this fact on its own is enough to prove the guilt beyond reasonable doubt is disputable.

The concept of random match probability is based on the assumption that the 'random man' is a person who is not related to the accused. When the probability of a random match is less then 1 in 1 billion, for anyone who is related to the accused, the value will be significantly higher. For example, the probability of a random full SGM Plus profile match for brothers will be only 1 in 10,000 (Foreman and Evett, 2001) and it is not the accused but his brother who could be the real perpetrator of the crime (in *R v Adams (Denis)* [1996] 2 Cr. App. R. 467 it was alleged by the defence that it was the brother of the accused who was the real perpetrator of the crime Denis Adams was convicted of). When the accused has an identical twin, DNA is powerless in discriminating between them. The prosecution may not have information about involvement of a relative of the accused in the crime, but, by the same token, it may not have any information about involvement of the accused with the single exception that his/her DNA profile was found to match that from the crime scene sample. If the match originated from speculative searching of the NDNAD, the fact that the accused was a suspect or a perpetrator in an unrelated crime committed sometime in the past makes him/her instantly the prime suspect in the crime s/he is tried for.

When members of the jury evaluate DNA evidence it is important to explain to them that a small match probability does not automatically establish guilt. Balding and Donnelly (1994) provide a good example of the dangers of establishing guilt solely on the basis of DNA evidence. Let assume that a crime was committed and no evidence, other than DNA evidence, is available to the prosecution. The match probability between the accused and the crime stain is 1 in 1,000,000. What is the probability that the accused is innocent? If the crime was committed in a big city, for example, like Birmingham, where the number of potential perpetrators could be as high as 500,000, the probability that the defendant is innocent after taking DNA into account will be at least one-third (for the calculation of the probability of innocence in this case see Balding and Donnelly, 1994). Does this fall within the 'beyond reasonable doubt' standard of proof? Apparently not! Simon and Mahan (1971) questioned judges, jurors and sociology students on the probability of guilt they would require to achieve to be satisfied that it was proven beyond reasonable doubt. Not surprisingly, the more serious the crime, the higher the probability of guilt needed to be achieved, but it ranged in jurors from 74 per cent for petty larceny to 86 per cent for murder. In Balding and Donnelly's example the probability of guilt is less than 70 per cent meaning that it probably would not be enough to convict the accused of the crime, obviously, assuming the above assumptions as to the match probability and the potential number of perpetrators. When, however, the probability of a random match is 1 in 1 billion and the number of potential perpetrators stays the same, the probability of innocence will decrease to the level when the probability of guilt may satisfy the jury that the issue has been proven beyond reasonable doubt.

This leads to the conclusion that when the match probability is extremely low, the possibility of a false positive match is excluded, the relevant population is reasonably small, there is no evidence whatsoever that a relative of the accused could be the real perpetrator of the crime, and that the real perpetrator of the crime was a UK resident at the time the crime was committed, then the DNA profile of the accused could be considered as unique by the jury who may be entitled to infer that the accused is guilty basing their decision on DNA evidence even in the absence of any other evidence (Emson, 2004).

It is difficult to argue that there is something inherent in the nature of DNA evidence that makes it in itself incapable of establishing guilt. However, this decision is conditional on the supposition that all the above-mentioned assumptions are valid. Yet they are usually among the most difficult ones to prove. The definition of the relevant population is often tentative and is related to the population resident within a certain area close to the scene of crime. However, the perpetrator may not necessarily be a local person but may live several hundred miles away. There may be relatives of the accused about whom neither s/he nor his/her family have any information (this is discussed in more detail in the next chapter) and one of them could be the real perpetrator of the crime. The fact that the offender was not a visitor to the UK from another country could also be hard to establish. This means that the debate continues as to whether or not it is possible to convict someone on DNA evidence alone.

Chapter 9

Challenging DNA evidence in the courtroom

When DNA evidence was first used in criminal practice it was considered impregnable and almost certain. Even now there is a belief among some criminal lawyers and barristers that DNA evidence is an unassailable proof of guilt. Throughout this book I have tried to show that this point of view is wrong. Despite being the most accurate method of human identification, DNA evidence is not infallible, although this does not mean that it is inherently flawed. As any other form of scientific evidence, the DNA testing procedure has a potential for error and DNA evidence also suffers from the same problems as other, more conventional, evidence, such as shoe print or fingerprint evidence.

I have already discussed many issues related to reliability of DNA evidence which could be explored by the defence in order to build a successful strategy for challenging this type of evidence in court. DNA evidence is subject to the same challenges as any other evidence and because of its scientific nature these can include contamination, inappropriate testing methodology, unreliability and statistical inaccuracy and many others (Chalmers, 2005b). It goes without saying that when the defence is successful in challenging the evidence it will have less or even no impact on the decision made by the tribunal of fact as to the ultimate issue and in some cases (e.g., *R v Mitchell* [2004] *The Times*, 8 July) it will even support the defence theory that the accused is not guilty.

In many instances DNA evidence has been successfully challenged in UK courts and courts in other countries, producing several landmark cases described below and elsewhere throughout this book. In most cases, challenges to DNA evidence are focused on admissibility, technical, laboratory and interpretation issues. These include challenges based on breaches of continuity, contamination of DNA samples in the laboratory and incorrect interpretation of DNA results.

In order to be able to develop a successful strategy for challenging DNA evidence it is paramount for the defence team to include specialists on DNA profiling and data interpretation. In some cases a defence team may enlist the help of several experts, such as an expert on statistical evaluation of DNA evidence and an expert on DNA technology issues, as illustrated by the example in *R v Doheny and Adams* [1997] 1 Cr. App. R. 369 when the defence in the case of Gary Adams used two distinguished experts in the fields of molecular biology and statistics to successfully attack the evidence presented by the prosecution.

Within the defence team, the role of the expert is not only to re-evaluate the evidence against the accused but also to explain the meaning of the evidence to other members of the team and 'coach' the leader of the defence on matters that will be used in cross-examining the prosecution expert. Even when the defence is not planning to submit their own statement on DNA evidence, the help of the expert will be vital in preparing an effective cross-examination strategy.

Assuming the DNA evidence was properly admitted it can be criticised by the defence in two ways – in cross-examination of the prosecution expert and in examination of the defence's own DNA expert. During the cross-examination, the defence can highlight to the jury the shortcomings of the prosecution DNA analysis, errors in statistical interpretation and some laboratory issues such as contamination and technical errors. When in the course of the cross-examination it transpires that, during the analysis, some of the above could have taken place, it will give a very powerful message to the jury as to reliability of the adduced DNA evidence and whether or not they should put much weight to it. During his/her testimony, the defence's expert can present his/her opinion on the evidence adduced by the prosecution and what in the defence's point of view are its shortcomings and flaws. The expert needs to explain to the jury in plain language why his/her theory is more accurate than that presented by his/her prosecution peer and what effect it will have on the weight the jury should be giving to the evidence. It will also be helpful for the defence's cause to explain to the jury the complexities and uncertainties of DNA testing, as jury members may have the misconception that DNA results are always accurate and infallible.

When the prosecution is intending to adduce DNA evidence against the accused, the defence team has to address as many issues, in relation to various aspects of DNA testing and results analysis (most of which are covered in this book), as practically possible. Freckleton and Selby (2005) provide a checklist of points that need to be explored when planning the efficient defence strategy. With several additions and modifications these are as follows:

- Examination of non-DNA forensic science that impacts on DNA analysis
- Existence of stated protocols of DNA analysis mentioned in the report and whether these protocols were adhered to
- Expertise and experience of the expert witness in generation and interpretation of the type of DNA evidence which is to be adduced at the trial

- Identity of laboratory staff who carried out DNA testing and analysis of the results and the contribution of each member of the team
- Existence of proficiency testing within the laboratory
- Results of internal and external quality control of the laboratory
- Information about the error rate within the laboratory
- Cross-checking all the stages of DNA analysis by a second scientist
- Cross-checking the results and their interpretation by at least one other scientist
- Continuity of exhibits
- Continuity of DNA samples in the laboratory
- Continuity of DNA samples between laboratories
- Potential for degradation and contamination of samples prior to DNA extraction
- Potential for degradation and contamination of samples and DNA extracted from the samples in the laboratory
- Use of controls (i.e., negative controls) to ensure absence of contamination
- Impact of degradation of samples on the results of DNA analysis
- Impact of contamination of samples on the results of DNA analysis
- Potential technical problems during DNA extraction, PCR and electrophoresis
- Use of genotyping software for allele identification
- Potential for the effect of DNA concentration on the outcome of analysis (stochastic effect)
- Heterozygote imbalance
- Pull-up peaks
- Stutter peaks
- Null alleles
- Which statistic was used to evaluate DNA evidence (profile frequency or match probability)
- Use (and value) of the sub-population correction in calculating the reported DNA statistic
- Size and relevance of the database used as source of allele frequencies
- Availability of all laboratory records for peer review
- Availability of samples to be used by the defence to confirm prosecution findings
- Utilisation of mathematical evidence
- Medical history of the suspect, victim and other potential suspects especially in relation to bone marrow transplantation, organ transplantation and recent blood transfusion.

Once relevant information has been obtained from the laboratory the strategy of attacking the evidence may be designed. Some of the possible points on which DNA evidence can be challenged are discussed below.

9.1 Continuity (chain-of-custody) issues

Successful challenges to the admissibility of DNA evidence often address the initial collection, preservation, and subsequent handling of the biological evidence recovered at the scene of crime. Continuity or chain-of-custody issues are of paramount importance for admitting DNA evidence, as only evidence that is related to the issue of fact should be admitted. At the crime scene biological material is collected by a forensic team, which then passes it on to another police force and so on until it reaches the destination laboratory which can be hundreds of miles away. Thus, when biological evidence was collected, for example, somewhere in a Cornish village, the samples will have to be delivered for analysis to the FSS laboratory in London or Birmingham. If it is then necessary to conduct LCN DNA testing on the samples, this may need to be done in the FSS laboratory in Wetherby. Because biological evidence collected at the scene will be passed through the hands of many people the possibility of a muddle is a very real one. It is important to be sure that the DNA samples from which the evidence was produced have been derived from the biological samples collected at the crime scene in question. This puts additional emphasis on the way crime scene samples are collected, recorded and stored.

The process of transporting the samples from the crime scene to the laboratory has to be meticulously documented. It is important that the defence scrutinise the way biological evidence was collected and transported – in cases of any major mistakes, the DNA evidence may be successfully challenged and prevented from being admitted. When the defence suspects that continuity may be an issue they have to ask the prosecution to provide evidence supporting the continuity.

The issue of continuity in relation to DNA evidence was addressed by the Court of Appeal in *R v P (Steven)* [2004] EWCA Crim. 2288. A woman was burgled and indecently assaulted in 1999. In 2001 a man was arrested for an unrelated matter and his DNA sample was found to match that obtained from the victim of the 1999 burglary and indecent assault. Following the match, the man was arrested and convicted for these crimes in 2002. Before the original trial, the prosecution did not put forward evidence supporting continuity and, at the beginning of the trial, the Crown admitted that continuity in relation to both evidential sample and that from the accused had not been proven. Only after the trial judge refused the request of the Crown to discharge the jury and order a retrial did the Crown serve a large number of notices of additional evidence in relation to continuity and integrity of the DNA evidence. The judge at his discretion allowed the admission of all these notices of additional evidence as evidence in the case, which was one of the main grounds for the appeal. Rejecting the appeal it was ruled that, although the prosecution had not produced evidence before the trial to make out continuity of DNA evidence, the state of the continuity evidence at the end of the trial was such that a jury would be properly satisfied that the issue of continuity had been made out. In reaching this conclusion the Court of Appeal prioritised 'the interests of justice in arriving at the truth' over the 'interests of the appellant in having a fair opportunity to meet the Crown's case and present his own case'. The approach the Court of Appeal has adopted in this situation seems to tolerate a certain degree of unfairness in the proceedings towards the defence case, most likely because of the high probative value and reliability of DNA evidence. However, there is little doubt that had the prosecution failed to satisfy the judge and the jury that the continuity of DNA evidence was intact the evidence would not have been admitted.

9.2 Hearsay issues

Analysis of DNA samples from a particular case usually involves a number of laboratory technical staff, sometimes as high as 30, and DNA samples from the same case are often analysed in more than one laboratory. In order to be able to present results of the analysis in court, the prosecution expert has to be personally involved in all the stages that are required to obtain the DNA evidence to be adduced, or has personally to supervise the staff involved in this process. Where the analysis is performed by a team of scientists or where assistants are used at some point during the analysis, this should be clearly indicated in the statement and the contribution of each member of the team specified. If the defence considers it necessary, a written report from a particular member of the team regarding his/her involvement in the process of analysis of a particular DNA sample could be obtained and this member of the team could be called as a witness.

If during his/her testimony the expert has to rely on the information or data obtained by other people who were not under his/her direct supervision, these have to be proved by admissible evidence. Failure to do this will result in the evidence being inadmissible under the hearsay rule. In *R v Loveridge* [2001] EWCA Crim. 734 the defendant was convicted of robbery on the basis of a complete match between his DNA profile and the profile from a balaclava recovered at the scene of crime. During the proceedings the prosecution expert witness admitted making her conclusion as to the probability of the match using DNA profiles produced by another laboratory and then made available to her. At the cross-examination, the prosecution expert acknowledged that she was not responsible for, nor supervised, the preparation of the DNA profiles. The Court of Appeal ruled that '. . . there simply was no admissible evidence before the court to make the DNA evidence admissible' and quashed the conviction. A similar issue was also raised in *R v Jackson* [1996] 2 Cr. App. R. 420.

9.3 Privilege

When a biological sample is provided by the accused for the purpose of criminal defence, the sample, the evidence derived from it and the expert opinion evidence of the scientist who analysed it are subject to legal privilege under s 10(1)(c) of PACE and thus cannot be used by the prosecution as evidence against the accused. In *R v R* [1995] 1 Cr. App. R. 183 the appellant appealed against his conviction of sexual offences. At the original trial the appellant, at the request of his solicitor, provided a blood sample to his general practitioner on the understanding that it would be used to obtain scientific advice to help with his defence. The trial judge granted leave to representatives of the prosecution to interview a scientist who had carried out DNA testing and at his discretion admitted the expert opinion evidence of the scientist. The Court of Appeal ruled that because the blood sample was provided as a result of legal advice in connection with legal proceedings and for the purposes of such proceedings, it was subject to legal privilege and the appellant was entitled to object to its production and to the production of opinion evidence based upon it. For this reason there is no discretion to admit privileged evidence without the consent of the accused.

9.4 Breach of PACE and the Code D

Taking DNA samples for criminal investigation is regulated by PACE which is also supplemented by the Code of Practice for the Identification of Persons by Police Officers (Code D). s 67(11) of PACE provides that in all criminal proceedings any Code of Practice shall be admissible in evidence and taken into account if any provision of a code appears to the court or tribunal conducting the proceedings to be relevant to any question arising in the proceedings. This means that any breaches of the Code D can result in the evidence being excluded at the discretion of the court (Laurie, 2005). In addition, s 78 of the Act provides that the court may refuse to allow evidence on which the prosecution proposes to rely if in the opinion of the court, having regard to all the circumstances, including the circumstances in which the evidence was obtained, the admission of the evidence would have such an adverse effect on the fairness of the proceedings that the court ought not to admit it.

However, even when DNA evidence is obtained in breach of the provisions laid out in PACE, the evidence may still be admitted as demonstrated by the decision in *R v Cooke* [1995] 1 Cr. App. R. 318. In this case, the samples on which DNA evidence was based were obtained outside the provisions of ss 63 and 65 of the Act but, in the view of the court, this breach did not affect the accuracy or the strength of the evidence. In reaching this decision the Court of Appeal discriminated between DNA evidence and a disputed confession, where the truth of the confession may well itself be at issue. In the view of the

Court, the strength and accuracy of DNA evidence will not have been affected by the way the evidence was obtained.

Because of the high cogency of DNA evidence it seems that, by admitting evidence obtained in breach of the relevant legislation, the benefit to the public good outweighs the fairness to the accused. As we have seen in Chapter 4 this point of view was also confirmed by the rulings in *Attorney-General's Reference (No. 3 of 1999)* [2000] 2 Cr. App. R. 416, *R v Chief Constable of the South Yorkshire Police ex parte S and Marper* [2004] 1 WLR 2196 and *R v Weir* [2000] 2 Cr. App. R. 416.

9.5 Relatives

When the random match probability is presented, it is explicitly stated that the value refers to an unrelated individual. However, the possibility that the crime in question has been committed by a relative of the accused is often alleged by the defence. In such a case, the random match probability will grossly overestimate the value of DNA evidence.

Where a full match between a crime stain and the accused is obtained using the SGM Plus marker system, the probability of a random match is reported by UK forensic laboratories as less than 1 in 1 billion. For relatives, though, it will be significantly higher (Table 9.1). The probability of a full match between brothers is some 100,000 times bigger than between two unrelated people. Even for uncle or nephew it will be 100 times bigger than the random match probability.

When the defence has information that the crime could have been committed by a close relative of the accused, it can argue that the value of the random match probability reported by a forensic scientist is not applicable to the particular case. DNA profiles of relatives are more likely to match than those of unrelated people and by using the probability of the former as opposed to the probability of the latter, the probative value of DNA evidence is significantly exaggerated. If it is assumed that all members of the relevant population are equally likely to have committed the crime in question and

Table 9.1 General match probability values recommended for use when reporting full SGM Plus profile matches (Foreman and Evett, 2001)

Relationship to the accused	Match probability
Sibling	1 in 10 thousand
Parent or child	1 in 1 million
Half-sibling	1 in 10 million
Uncle or aunt	1 in 10 million
Nephew or niece	1 in 10 million
First cousin	1 in 100 million
Unrelated	1 in 1 billion

relatives of the accused are within this population then, prior to the DNA test, they are as likely to be guilty as the accused (Aitken and Taroni, 2005). Where the only evidence against the accused is DNA (e.g., in *R v Adams (Denis)* [1996] 2 Cr. App. R. 467) the fact that a close relative could match the accused weakens the impact of DNA evidence against him/her. It has to be explained to the jury, as in the case of Denis Adams, that even when prosecution claims that it does not have any information regarding the involvement of a particular relative in the crime, it also does not have any information about the involvement of the accused apart from the fact that his/her DNA profile matches the crime scene sample which could have been deposited by a close relative of the accused.

The relevance of relatives in cases when DNA is the only evidence against the accused was highlighted in *R v Watters* [2000] WL 1791491. Robert Watters was arrested in 1998 in connection with two burglaries of which he was later acquitted. A DNA sample taken from him was found to match DNA profiles obtained from cigarette butts found at the scene of five sophisticated burglaries of commercial premises in Birmingham which had occurred in 1996 and which had similar features to the burglaries for which Watters was arrested. He was convicted and sentenced to six years' imprisonment. During the trial, the prosecution relied solely on the DNA evidence taken from the cigarette butts found at the scene of those burglaries. The prosecution claimed a random match probability of 1 in 86 million for DNA evidence obtained from the sites of the four burglaries and 1 in 79,000 for the evidence from the fifth burglary. When cross-examined the prosecution scientist conceded that if Watters had two brothers, the value of the match probability would be 1 in 267 and 1 in 32 for the first four and the fifth burglaries respectively. It turned out that Watters had two adult brothers, one of whom had been arrested in relation to these offences, and then released with no DNA sample taken from him. On appeal, the conviction was quashed. In giving the judgment Kay LJ said that, in reaching the verdict, the jury had:

> . . . to look to see whether, firstly, the rest of the evidence in some way supported the DNA evidence so that, taken together, a proper inference of guilt could be drawn. Secondly, it is necessary to see whether in relation to the brothers the jury could ever reach the conclusion. . . that they could exclude the brothers from involvement.

Although, in the view of the Court of Appeal, the odds in this case were substantial that the police charged the right brother, there was no evidence to exclude the other brothers from being perpetrators of the crimes in question and '. . . the principal piece of evidence . . . was not enough in itself for a jury to conclude with certainty that the appellant was responsible' for the burglaries. In conclusion, his Lordship remarked that:

> . . . every case has to be viewed on the totality of the evidence in that case. DNA evidence may have a greater significance where there is supporting evidence, dependent, of course, on the strength of that evidence.

It also has to be kept in mind that the real number of relatives the accused has may be higher than the number of relatives who are known to the defence or the prosecution. It should not be automatically assumed that people know all their own relatives (even close ones). This is not necessarily so. In real life people may have close relatives of whom they do not have any information. There are many factors contributing to this phenomenon. Some of them, like a full sibling or another child of one of the parents being put up for adoption, or born as a result of IVF treatment using donor sperm, are fairly rare; much more common are events of paternity discrepancy, when a child is biologically fathered by someone other than the man who believes he is the father. According to recent research (Bellis et al, 2005) the rate of paternity discrepancy estimated in various human populations ranges from 0 to 30 per cent. According to our own data (Semikhodskii, unpublished) based on the analysis of more than 1,500 DNA paternity testing cases in the UK, paternity discrepancy occurs in 28 per cent. Other scientists report figures of 15–18 per cent for the UK population, based on some 18,000 DNA paternity tests and 28–29 per cent for the USA population, based on some 300,000 DNA paternity tests (for more details see Bellis et al, 2005). Because the use of DNA testing in clinical and judicial procedures will lead to identification of more paternity discrepancy cases, it may be supposed that the estimated rate of paternity discrepancy will grow (Bellis et al, 2005).

Paternity discrepancy was found to be higher in those who live in deprivation, conceive younger and cohabit rather than marry. The first factor is associated with elevated crime rate in the UK and many other countries.

The high rate of paternity discrepancy means that an accused man may have a half brother of whom neither he nor the prosecution have any information, because the accused's father may be the biological father of a boy who is thought to be fathered by someone else, or the accused may not have been fathered by the man he considers to be his father but by another man, who may also have a son. This half brother could be of similar age to the accused and live within a distance from the crime scene that may well put him into the relevant population of potential perpetrators.

9.6 DNA technology issues

Although most DNA testing results presented in the court are obtained using STR genotyping, when a different technology has been used, the defence needs to be satisfied that the evidence obtained by using this new technology is reliable and the genotypic data are correct. Apart from genotyping technology there are other techniques used when obtaining DNA evidence. An old DNA isolation method can be modified or even replaced by completely new methods, or an additional purification step can be introduced, which allegedly provides better quality DNA for PCR. When such a method or technology is used to obtain DNA for the case, it is important to make sure that it produces reliable results, that this technology is not the research technology of a particular laboratory but was validated and adopted by several forensic laboratories for analysing casework samples, that results produced by using this technology have been published in reputable peer-reviewed forensic or related journals and, ultimately, that it has been used for obtaining DNA evidence in other cases. An expert opinion on technological issues may be requested to support or refute the data.

STR genotyping is currently the method of choice for forensic DNA analysis but the instrumentation used to obtain the profiles and genotyping software may vary. Genetic data can be obtained from a number of instruments with different resolutions, some of them using automated genotyping, some, manual identification of alleles. The defence has to be satisfied that the resolution of genotyping and allele scoring is acceptable for the types of data presented.

9.7 Laboratory issues

Laboratory examination of DNA is a complex and lengthy process involving many people and various techniques. Errors at any of these stages can invalidate the results or reduce the probative value of DNA evidence. Because various samples from the same case or from completely different cases are often processed together, there is a possibility of contamination of samples or of samples being switched. Reporting errors are also one of the most common types of laboratory error.

When a sample mistake is suspected, a request should be made for the laboratory to provide all information regarding sample tracking for the relevant case. Information about proficiency testing of the laboratory, the latest audit by a third party, internal quality control assessment and other documents, especially those related to the case in question, may also be required to assess whether or not it is likely for samples to have been mixed up. This information can also reveal some other problems with analysis of DNA evidence in the particular case. If the possibility of accidental switch of samples is suspected, the original DNA extracted from the evidential sample should be retested or a new extraction from the evidential sample done. It may also be necessary for the defence to obtain all relevant samples from the forensic laboratory as well as collect new DNA samples from the accused and perform its own analysis in another laboratory.

The possibility of a false match between the accused and the crime stain also needs to be investigated. The laboratory has to provide the internal genotyping error rate results and also the results of blind external proficiency testing using realistic samples. When the prosecution claims very small probabilities, the probability of random match of false inclusion can be several orders of magnitude higher and should not be discarded.

Sample contamination is commonly one of the key concerns for the defence and is probably the main source of laboratory-related errors. If there was an incidence of contamination of another DNA sample in the case in question, there is also a high possibility that DNA samples crucial for the defence case were also contaminated. When such an incident of contamination is admitted by the prosecution laboratory, the defence should cross-examine the reporting officer on why and when contamination of the other sample happened in this case, whether it happened before, during or after the crucial samples were analysed, what the cause was of this contamination, whether the person responsible for contamination worked with other samples, and whether there were any measures taken to make sure that such contamination would not happen in the future. It is important to emphasise that when the cause of contamination is unknown, it is impossible to set up measures directed to the prevention of the same error happening again.

Although sample contamination is a rare event, the incidents of contamination are typically commoner than reported by the laboratory, for the reason that the quality control system implemented in the laboratory can miss an isolated contamination event. If contamination happened because of human or technical error it is possible that such an error also caused contamination in other samples, analysed prior to the sample that was identified as being contaminated. If the same person or instrument responsible for contamination of other samples was used for examining crucial DNA samples, the possibility of their being contaminated should be investigated.

The most dangerous form of contamination occurs when the crime scene sample is contaminated by DNA from accused's sample. In addition, DNA from one crime scene can contaminate samples from the scene of an unrelated crime and thus falsely implicate the accused in the other crime. Unintentional contamination of evidential samples by laboratory staff is also fairly common.

Challenges regarding contamination have been used by the defence in many court cases. Thus, in the Californian case *People v Simpson* No. BA097211 Cal.Super.Ct. [1995] WL 479507 contamination of evidence was one of the two main assumptions in the defence's theory of origin of matches observed between OJ Simpson and evidence recovered at the crime scene.

OJ Simpson was arrested on suspicion of murdering his ex-wife Nicole and her male companion Ronald Goldman at Nicole's residence at South Bundy Drive. Several drops of blood were found at the crime scene near footprints made by a rare and expensive type of shoe – shoes that OJ wore and that proved to be his size. Next to the bodies was a bloodstained black leather glove that bore traces of fibre from Goldman's jeans. The glove's mate (which became known as the Rockingham glove), stained with blood consistent with

Simpson, was found on his property at Rockingham. One of the socks found at Simpson's home had a large blood stain which contained a DNA profile consistent with Nicole. Three additional samples from the same sock contained material consistent with Simpson. Blood consistent with Simpson was found on the pathway at his home. There were also traces of blood consistent with both victims lifted from inside Simpson's car and house, along with blood that contained his own DNA. In fact, his blood and Goldman's were found together on the car's console.

The defence argued that Simpson accidentally cut himself at home and left his samples inside the car and on the pathway at his home. At the cross-examination, one of the forensic scientists admitted that he accidentally spilled Simpson's blood from a reference vial at the evidence processing room and shortly afterwards handled the Rockingham glove as well as cotton swatches which contained droplets of blood collected at South Bundy Drive. The defence proposed that some of Simpson's blood was inadvertently transferred on the glove and swatches, which explains DNA profiles consistent with Simpson's (Thompson, 1996).

Apart from contamination, the defence put forward a theory that blood on many items was planted by police who wanted to frame Simpson for this crime. The planting theory was supported by the fact that the chemical ETDA, used for blood preservation, was found in blood stains which, according to the defence theory, were planted. These tactics severely undermined the cogency of DNA evidence, one of the key factors for the jury rejecting the prosecution account of the events and acquitting Simpson of both murders.

9.8 The choice of DNA test

The great majority of forensic samples in the UK are analysed by SGM Plus genotyping. However, in some cases, it may not be the best approach for obtaining DNA evidence. Each DNA test has advantages and limitations. To obtain reliable evidence, the test which produces the best results for specific samples has to be used. In rape cases, especially when a relative of the victim is accused of the crime, Y chromosome testing of DNA recovered from vaginal swab may give more reliable results than autosomal STR genotyping. In cases when a mixed profile is observed, Y chromosome testing can reduce the complexity of the profile. When a mixed profile results from DNA contributed by female and male donors, it may be the best approach to take.

Where, in the opinion of the defence DNA expert, a better approach could be used to test evidence, this should be conveyed to the jury and the prosecution expert cross-examined as to why the laboratory chose one type of test over the other. Sometimes, evidence, which may be vital for the defence case, is not tested by the forensic laboratory. In a recent case, a rootless hair found at the murder scene which, according to the defence, belonged to the murderer, was not tested by the prosecution forensic laboratory, which cited low probability of obtaining DNA evidence as the reason for not undertaking the analysis. The defence asked another forensic laboratory to perform analysis of the hair, and DNA evidence was successfully obtained.

9.9 Statements contravening the decision in *Doheny and Adams*

The decision of the Court of Appeal in *R v Doheny and Adams* [1997] 1 Cr. App. R. 369 provides guidance on presentation of DNA evidence in English courts, which should be followed by the prosecution DNA expert when preparing the witness statement or when giving the testimony. Otherwise the defence may find it necessary to challenge the evidence on the grounds of contravening the decision of the Court of Appeal.

As we have discussed in previous chapters the expert should not usurp the role of the jury by expressing his/her opinion on ultimate issues in relation to the source of DNA found in the crime stain, whether the accused left the crime stain as a result of a specific action, or comment on the number of people who could have contributed their DNA to the crime sample (as opposed to giving the minimum number of contributors to the DNA mixture based on the results of DNA analysis). The expert also should not express his/her personal opinion on the strength of support the DNA evidence provides to the prosecution hypothesis, or express an opinion of another scientist by reporting the strength of support in non-numerical way. Statements in the prosecution report dealing with the evidence which contravene this decision could be used by the defence as grounds for the evidence not to be admitted or, at the very least, for making an appropriate submission to the judge for these statements not to be adduced as part of the evidence.

9.10 DNA evidence interpretation issues

Challenges to the way DNA results are interpreted by the forensic scientist or by the prosecutor are probably among the most common challenges to DNA evidence. In almost every case, when the defence presents results of their own analysis, defence experts dispute the value of the random match probability or other statistical indices mentioned in the prosecution DNA report. In other cases, interpretation of the meaning of a reported DNA index by the prosecution can be attacked (e.g., in cases of the prosecution fallacy).

Logical errors in DNA evidence interpretation were discussed in Chapter 7. The defence should object if any of these are aired in court. Simple errors of the transposed conditional may be illustrated by examples given by Aitken and Taroni (2005): 'the probability of this DNA profile occurring at random is 1 in 18 billion; thus the likelihood that the DNA belongs to someone other that the suspect is 1 in 18 billion' or 'the probability of finding the evidence on an innocent person is 0.01 per cent (1 in 10,000) thus the likelihood that the suspect is guilty is 99.99 per cent' most likely will cause the jury to reach incorrect conclusions as to the guilt of the accused.

Because these errors are so powerful in influencing people's opinion, the defence needs to explain to the jury why such reasoning is logically flawed and how the evidence should be interpreted correctly.

The other group is comprised of challenges related to the statistical interpretation of DNA evidence. The choice of genetic database is important for correctly calculating random match probability. It is necessary to establish that the database chosen as the source of allelic frequencies is relevant to the ethnic origin of the accused. UK forensic laboratories use three databases for this purposes – Afro-Caribbean, Caucasian and Indo-Pakistani, however, these racial groups are not homogenous and include various sub-populations, where genetic frequencies can differ significantly from those of the general population. The issue is further complicated by interracial marriages and changes in migration patterns. Where the suspect comes from a community where close relative marriages are common, the chances of finding another individual with the profile matching the accused will be significantly higher and this will affect the interpretation of the data.

The defence should ask the prosecution laboratory to provide information about their choice of DNA database (this required by the guidance in *R v Doheny and Adams* [1997] 1 Cr. App. R. 369) and to provide relevant allelic frequencies and the values of the sub-population correction used for calculating the random match probability, so they can be used by the defence scientist to re-do the calculations. The methods used by the prosecution to compute the relevant statistics also need to be examined in relation to whether or not they are adequate for the type of evidence in question (e.g., whether or not the sub-population correction was used and if yes at what level etc).

In the case of mixed profiles it is important to establish whether or not the number of contributors has been determined correctly. Proving that the number of contributors is higher than that reported by the prosecution will greatly reduce the probative value of DNA evidence. When the number of contributors to the mixture is three or more, it is virtually impossible to estimate whether or not a particular individual had contributed his/her DNA to it.

Yet another challenge can be related to the type and size of the relevant population. Although it is in the domain of the jury to decide on what the relevant population in each particular case could be, the prosecution often uses a relevant population of the type and size it considers appropriate to the particular case when explaining the strength of DNA evidence. Obviously, should the defence disagree with the choice and size of the relevant population, it has to tell the jury why the prosecution theory regarding the relevant population is wrong and how the wrong choice of the relevant population could affect the case.

Chapter 10

Post-convictional DNA testing

The very first time DNA testing was used to solve a crime, it helped to exonerate an innocent man. Thus the power of DNA analysis can be used not only to convict the perpetrator but also to provide evidence that somebody is suspected, accused or even convicted of a crime s/he did not commit.

Post-convictional DNA testing is a powerful tool for rectifying miscarriages of justice. The best examples of DNA testing helping to exonerate people who were wrongfully convicted are provided by the work of the Innocence Project which was set up by Barry Scheck and Peter Neufeld in 1992 at Cardozo Law School in New York. The Innocence Project deals exclusively with cases in which post-convictional DNA testing can yield conclusive proof of innocence, and since its inception it has exonerated 173 innocent people (including 14 who had been sentenced to death). Regrettably, in the UK there is no organisation equivalent to the Innocence Project, however, suspected miscarriages of justice are investigated by the Criminal Case Review Commission (CCRC).

To be able to conduct post-convictional DNA testing, a convicted person has to seek leave to appeal against the conviction or sentence. Once it is granted, s/he is free to initiate all necessary steps, including post-convictional DNA testing, to prepare his/her appeal. However, in some cases, due to exceptional circumstances, it is possible to apply directly to CCRC which may consider the case and at their discretion refer it to the Court of Appeal under s 9(1) of the Criminal Appeal Act 1995.

This happened in the case of Joseph Otoo, whose conviction was quashed by the Court of Appeal in *R v Otoo* (2000) (unreported). The appellant was convicted in 1997 of armed robbery and the offence of possessing an imitation firearm, and sentenced to ten years' imprisonment. Throughout the original trial, the defence claimed mistaken identity and that the appellant was intimidated by the real perpetrator of the crime, whose identity was known. He was coerced into exchanging shoes with him, giving the real perpetrator the shoes worn when the crime was committed and which later became one of the main pieces of evidence against the appellant. Although DNA was extracted from items used in the robbery, no DNA evidence was adduced at the original trial. Also, no DNA sample was obtained from the person who the defence alleged was the real perpetrator of the crime. Upon representations made on behalf of the appellant, the police placed a marker on the alleged perpetrator's file to ensure that they would be notified if he were arrested at a later date. When he was arrested on an unconnected matter, intimate samples were taken from him and the DNA extracted from them was found to match DNA samples from the balaclava discarded at the scene of crime and the shoes used in the robbery. In the opinion of the Court of Appeal, DNA evidence was crucial in quashing the original conviction. It is worth noting that the profiling technique used to exonerate Joseph Otoo was not available at the time of the trial.

Advances in DNA testing methodology exonerated Michael Shirley, who spent 15 years in prison after been wrongfully convicted and sentenced to life imprisonment for raping and murdering a young girl in Portsmouth in 1988 (*Shirley v R* [2003] WL 21554724). At the original trial, no DNA evidence was adduced because the limitations of old technology did not allow DNA from intimate samples obtained from the victim to be compared with samples from the defendant. Only when such technology appeared (LCN DNA testing) was it possible to perform the comparison and exclude Michael Shirley from being the perpetrator of this horrendous crime.

Since its first use in the Enderby murder case, forensic DNA analysis has come a long way. Current DNA testing technology allows the obtaining of evidence from literally a single human cell. However, even 15 years ago large amounts of DNA were needed to obtain DNA evidence. In many cases, although biological samples were collected at the scene, it was impossible to obtain reliable DNA data using the contemporary technology. Even when the evidence was obtained, the probability of a random match was sufficiently high to leave doubts over whether the accused was the source of the analysed DNA from the crime stain.

The above examples highlight the two main situations in which post-convictional DNA can be helpful to establish the truth: cases in which biological evidence was not analysed due to insensitivity of old technology, and cases in which new facts are capable of providing irrefutable evidence in support of the innocence of the accused. In most of these cases, the original trial happened before SGM or LCN DNA testing was introduced into forensic casework. In addition to these, post-convictional DNA testing can be conducted in cases where modern DNA testing methodology could obtain better quality results than hitherto, which, because of its increased power of discrimination, may exclude the convicted individual from being the donor of DNA from the crime stain. Lastly, it is called in cases where the defence strongly believes that there were major errors of DNA analysis by the prosecution that led to the wrong conviction.

Chapter 11

Ethical aspects of DNA testing

DNA testing is an extremely powerful technique which allows various types of information about an individual to be obtained. DNA analysis can be used in crime investigations, for revealing disease predisposition, can provide information about the health of the individual, the skin colour and ethnic origin of the person can be deduced from analysing ancestry informative markers, while comparing two or more DNA samples can be used to determine the degree of relationship between people. The possibility of using DNA samples for obtaining information about a person which is irrelevant to crime investigation but, at the same time, is very sensitive from the privacy point of view poses many ethical questions. Even the way DNA samples and the data derived from them are used for criminal investigation pose legitimate concern to the general public and human rights groups.

Various ethical issues arising from the use of DNA for forensic purposes can be broadly grouped into two: issues associated with collection and retention of DNA samples and information, and issues related to DNA analysis and the use of genetic information obtained thus.

The question that concerns human rights groups the most is the question: what crimes merit collection of DNA samples? Current legislation allows obtaining DNA samples from all recordable offences no matter how serious they are. Do the same rules need to be applied to someone who is suspected or raping a woman as to someone who is suspecting of stealing a packet of cigarettes from a corner shop? The rationale beyond collecting DNA samples from all recordable crime is obvious – it is that someone who committed a crime (even a minor one) is assumed (rightfully or wrongfully) to be more likely to commit another, possibly serious, crime. This is debatable however. In many cases of murder or rape, convicted individuals were never suspected of committing a criminal offence before. Many people who committed a minor crime will never commit any other crime. On the other hand, in many instances, people who commit crimes go on to commit more serious ones. There have been many cases when an individual was arrested for a minor offence and his/her DNA profile matched the profile of the main suspect of a murder or a rape committed some time in the past.

Because of the high cogency of DNA evidence and several instances when the accused was convicted on DNA evidence alone (e.g., *R v Adams (Denis)* [1996] 2 Cr. App. R. 467), there is a danger that the current system may cause an innocent person be convicted for a crime s/he did not commit simply because his/her DNA (collected sometime during his/her life) matches that of the perpetrator of a crime. (This is especially true when only a partial DNA profile is available from the crime scene.) What will be someone's defence when a knife from a supermarket, which this individual touched but did not buy, was used as a murder weapon? Since 1995 more than 2.7 million unique DNA samples were collected in relation to crime investigation. This figure means that every seventh person in the UK has been a party to a criminal investigation either as a suspect or as the perpetrator within the past 11 years. The lifetime chance of a person giving a DNA sample in relation to invest-igation of a crime is thus very considerable. If the sample is collected five or ten years after an unsolved murder, in which the knife from a supermarket was used, will it be possible for the individual accused because of a DNA match to provide an alibi or recall exactly his/her movements on the day of the crime? Probably not.

This raises the issue about the fairness of the current system of collecting DNA samples for the purpose of criminal investigation. In this situation a proposal of a universal database finds growing support. The concept of a universal DNA database has been discussed by Williamson and Duncan (2002). In their view, the fairest but at the same time the most controversial would be collection of DNA samples from every member of society; collec-tion of DNA samples at birth; every member whose DNA sample has not yet been collected would have to provide one; as would every immigrant (and possibly even tourist). The last two points themselves pose considerable ethical as well as logistic problems.

There are advantages to collecting DNA samples at birth and then running samples recovered at crime scenes against the DNA database, as opposed to the current practice of profiling suspects. The rationale behind this pro-position is that, taking UK as an example, under the current system, DNA from Afro-Caribbean and other minority groups is more likely to go on the DNA database than that from Caucasians. Every third black man living in the UK has his DNA sample collected and the profile deposited on the NDNAND. In addition, DNA profiles from men are more likely to go to on the database than from women (more than 80 per cent of DNA profiles on the NDNAD are from men). The concern here is that these groups may be specifically targeted for mass screening.

When a mass collection of DNA is conducted by police for elimination purposes people who refuse, for whatever reason, to provide a DNA sample risk becoming suspects. It also goes against the principle of the presumption of innocence when an individual has to provide a DNA sample to exclude him/herself from the list of potential perpetrators. (At the same time there are ethical considerations, probably as important as the presumption of innocence, which induce a great proportion of the population to come forward and provide a DNA sample for elimination purposes.) Collecting DNA samples at birth will be able to overcome this problem.

The prison population does not reflect the ethnic and gender distribution of the whole country – there are significantly more imprisoned men than women and the proportion of ethnic minorities in prisons is significantly higher than in the general population. Are these strata of society intrinsically prone to be more criminally active or are there other factors which are contributing to such a situation, the rules for DNA collection being one of them? One argument in favour of universal DNA identification is that it might be fairer than collecting samples only from those coming into contact with the criminal justice system, who are disproportionately minorities and males.

DNA collection at birth would then not only act as a deterrent from crime for all members of the community but also could make catching criminals easier. Such a database, however, needs to be properly supervised and legislation safeguarding civil liberties and human rights needs to be put in place. The question of confidence in government is also vital to the idea of a universal DNA database.

The concern that a DNA database that includes all citizens of the UK will be a major intrusion into private life, is shared by many people and human rights organisations. Currently such a database is not planned but it seems to be possible in the future. Whether or not it will be implemented depends on whether the interests of an individual and his/her concern for privacy outweigh the interests of the general population to live in a crime-free society, or at least in a society where crime can be rapidly detected and the perpetrators punished.

Besides the issue of collecting DNA samples there is currently a debate over whether a DNA sample should be retained or destroyed after genotyping. I have discussed this issue in Chapter 4. Although retention of samples has the advantage of making the DNA available for future analysis using technologies which will eventually supersede SGM Plus, and the advantage of correcting potential miscarriages of justice, the practice is strongly opposed by some human rights organisations. Thus the UK's genetic watchdog GeneWatch UK in a recent report (GeneWatch UK, 2005) argues that storing DNA cannot be seen as a prerequisite for preventing miscarriage of justice because (1) the DNA profile of the subject is permanently logged into the database, (2) any new marker systems that will be adopted by the NDNAD will most likely include SGM and SGM Plus markers, i.e., the Database will be backward compatible once new technology is introduced and (3) should the subject become a suspect again, a new DNA sample will be obtained from him/her.

A major concern is that private information derived from DNA samples could be used against the individual now or sometime in the future. Because

DNA testing may predict illness, and because privacy protection may fail, it may be detrimental to the future employment or insurance of persons whose DNA was stored on the database, long after they have been acquitted, released, or paroled. On the other hand, storing the DNA identification profile alone cannot be said to be storing health-related information because the loci that samples are genotyped for do not represent functional genes.

There is another issue related to the future of the information stored on the database. Recent changes in legislation remove the obligation to destroy DNA samples and information derived from it from the database. However, what should happen to a sample (and the information derived therefrom) of an individual whose criminal record has been expunged? Should the sample be destroyed following the expunging or kept on the database? Since individuals can request that a criminal record be expunged in some circumstances or after a period of time, should they be allowed to request that their DNA identification profile together with the sample be destroyed as well?

Once a DNA sample has been collected and the information deposited on a DNA database, who should decide who is given access to the samples and the information and under what circumstances? How should the activities of any access-granting and accessing bodies be monitored and regulated? Will third parties, who are not involved in criminal justice, ever get access to the criminal DNA database? The concern here is that, because DNA data can provide information about whether a person has a genetic disorder or a predisposition to diseases and behavioural traits, this information becoming available to institutional third parties such as employers and insurers may stigmatise the individual concerned or produce unfavourably treatment (e.g., the refusal of insurance or employment). Even the knowledge of third parties that someone has a sample in a criminal DNA database (although access to the sample may be forbidden) could lead to discrimination.

Finally, the question of whether or not it is possible to use samples from the criminal DNA database for research purposes is also of major interest to human rights organisations. It has long being known that people's behaviour is genetically controlled. Because of the nature of the population on the database, there may be interest in doing research on behavioural predispositions, such as dispositions to addiction, antisocial behaviour, and violence. It is theoretically possible to compare samples of convicted individuals who murder their victims with samples of those who commit other violent crimes but never murder, to see whether these crimes have different genetic components, or samples from individuals who rape and murder their victims with samples of those who rape but never murder, to investigate whether there is a special gene or group of genes that make some criminals murder their victim after raping them.

Some human behavioural genetics research is controversial because of the possibility of stigmatisation, not only of individuals, but of entire racial groups. Should research be done with forensic DNA samples, and if so, what should be the limits? If the research on forensic samples is allowed, should informed consent from the individuals involved be required? If any commercially viable product is developed during such research, who will benefit from it? Will the individuals whose samples were used for the research get a share of the profits?

The Board of NDNAN does not consider it necessary to request consent for the DNA samples stored on the database to be used for research purposes (ACPO, 2006). They based this decision on the fact that as long as the purpose of research is related to the prevention and detection of crime, data protection considerations are complied with, and due account is taken of any independent ethical advice that has been provided, then there is no misuse of the samples or data, and no risk of the individual suffering adverse consequences.

As the NDNAD is currently a private database of the police, with no involvement of human rights organisations in its supervision, any proposed genetic research on DNA samples should, at the bare minimum, be approved by the Central Office for Research Ethics Committees, although even with such approval, the results of genetic research are considered by some groups to be misleading (GeneWatch UK, 2005). Proposed changes to the governance of the NDNAD (ACPO, 2006) are likely to ease the public concern about misuse of DNA samples and provide a safeguard for ethical treatment of stored genetic information.

References

Aitken, CGG and Taroni, F, *Statistics and the Evaluation of Evidence for Forensic Scientists*, 2004, Chichester: John Wiley & Sons

Anderson, S, Bankier, AT, Barrell, BG, de Bruijn, MH, Coulson, AR, Drouin, J, Eperon, IC, Nierlich, DP, Roe, BA, Sanger, F, Schreier, PH, Smith, AJ, Staden, R and Young, IG, 'Sequence and organization of the human mitochondrial genome', (1981) *Nature* 290:457–65

Andrews, RM, Kubacka, I, Chinnery, PF, Lightowlers, RN, Turnbull, DM and Howell, N, 'Reanalysis and revision of the Cambridge reference sequence for human mitochondrial DNA', (1999) *Nat Genet* 23:147

Association of Chief Police Officers, *The Forensic Science Service retention of case material. A memorandum of understanding between ACPO and FSS*, 2003. Available at http://www.acpo.police.uk/asp/policies/Data/baker_mou_retention_case_material_main.doc

Association of Chief Police Officers, *DNA Good Practice Manual*, 2nd edn. 2005. Available at: http://www.denverda.org/DNA_Documents/Final%20Document%20-%20DNA%20Good%20Practice.%20August%20%2705.pdf

Association of Chief Police Officers, *The National DNA Database Annual Report 2004–2005*, 2006. Available at http://www.acpo.police.uk/asp/policies/Data/NDNAD_AR_04_051.pdf

Bellis, MA, Hughes, K, Hughes, S and Ashton, JR, 'Measuring paternal discrepancy and its public health consequences', (2005) *J Epidemiol Community Health* 59:749–54

Balding, DJ, 'When can a DNA profile be regarded as unique?', (1993) *Sci Justice* 39:257–60

Balding, DJ, *Weight-of-evidence For Forensic DNA Profiles*, 2005, Chichester: John Wiley & Sons

Balding, DJ and Donnelly, P, 'How convincing is DNA evidence?', (1994) *Nature* 368:285–6

Brinkman, B, Sajantila, A, Goedde, HW, Matsumoto, H, Nishi, K and Wiegand, P, 'Population genetic comparisons among eight populations using allele frequency and sequence data from three microsatellite loci', (1996) *European Journal of Human Genetics* 4:175–82

Buckleton, J, Triggs, CM and Walsh, S (eds), *Forensic DNA Evidence Interpretation*, 2005, Boca Roca, London, New York, Washington DC: CRC Press

Buckleton, J, 'A framework for interpreting evidence', in Buckleton et al, 2005, 27–63

Buckleton, J, Clayton, T and Triggs, C, (2005a) 'Parentage testing', in Buckleton et al, 2005, 341–94

Buckleton, J and Gill, P, 'Low Copy Number', in Buckleton et al, 2005, 275–97

Buckleton, J, Triggs, C and Clayton, T, (2005b) 'Disaster victim identification, identification of missing persons and immigration cases', in Buckleton et al, 2005, 395–438, Boca Roca, London, New York, Washington DC: CRC Press.

Buckleton, J, Walsh, S and Harbison, S, (2005c) 'Nonautosomal Forensic Markers', in Buckleton et al, 2005, 299–340

Budowle, B, Allard, MW and Wilson, MR, 'Critique of interpretation of high levels of heteroplasmy in the human mitochondrial DNA hypervariable region I from hair', (2002) *Forensic Sci Int* 126:30–3

Budowle, B, Allard, MW, Wilson, MR and Chakraborty, R, 'Forensic and Mitochondrial DNA: Applications, Debates, and Foundations', (2003) *Annu Rev Genomics Hum Genet* 4:119–41

Butler, J, *Forensic DNA Typing*, 2nd edn, 2005, Amsterdam, London, New York: Elsevier

Chalmers, D (ed), *Genetic Testing and the Criminal Law*, 2005, London: UCL Press

Chalmers, D, (2005b) 'General Themes', in Chalmers, 2005, 177–186

Clayton, T and Buckleton, J, 'Mixtures', in Buckleton et al, 2005, 217–274

Clayton, TM, Whitaker, JR, Sparkes, R and Gill, P, 'Analysis and interpretation of mixed forensic stains using DNA STR profiling', (1998) *Forensic Sci Int* 91:55–70

Dauber, EM, Dorner, G, Mitterbauer, M, Wenda, S, Faeé, I, Glock, B and Mayr, WR, 'Discrepant results of samples taken from different tissues of a single individual', (2004) *Prog Forensic Genet* 10:48–9

Dijk, van, BA, Boomsma, DI and Man, de, AJ, 'Blood group chimerism in human multiple births is not rare', (1996) *Amer J Hum Genet* 61:264–8

Emson, R, *Evidence* (2nd edn), 2004, Basingstoke, Hampshire: PalgraveMacmillan

Evett, IW, 'Interpretation: a personal Odyssey', in Aitken, CGG and Stoney, DA (eds), *The Use of Statistics in Forensic Science*, 1991, 9–22, Chichester: Ellis Horwood

Evett, IW, 'DNA profiling: a discussion of issues relating to the reporting of very small match probabilities', (2000) *Crim L R* 341–55

Evett, IW and Gill, P, 'A discussion of the robustness of methods for assessing the evidential value of DNA single locus profiles in crime investigations', (1991) *Electrophoresis* 12:226–30

Evett, IW and Weir, BS, *Interpreting DNA Evidence*, 1998, Sunderland MA: Sinauer Associates

Ewen, KR, Bahlo, M, Treloar, SA, Levinson, DF, Mowry, B, Barlow, JW and Foote, SJ, 'Identification and analysis of error types in high-throughput genotyping', (2000) *Am J Hum Genet* 67:727–36

Foreman, LA and Evett, IW, 'Statistical analyses to support forensic interpretation for a new ten-locus STR profiling system', (2001) *Int J Legal Med* 114:147–55

Foreman, LA and Lambert, JA, 'Genetic differentiation within and between four UK ethnic groups', (2000) *Forensic Sci Int* 114:7–20

Forster, P, 'To err is human', (2003) *Annals Human Genetics* 67:2–4

Freckleton, I and Selby, H, *Expert Evidence: Law, Practice, Procedure and Advocacy* (3rd edn), 2005, Sydney: Lawbook Co

Fukshansky, N and Bär, W, 'DNA mixtures: biostatistics for mixed stains with haplotypic genetic markers', (2005) *Int J Legal Med* 119:285–90

GeneWatch UK, *The Police National DNA Database: Balancing Crime Detection, Human Rights and Privacy*, 2005. Available at: http://www.genewatch.org/HumanGen/Publications/Reports/NationalDNADatabase.pdf

Gill, P, 'Application of Low Copy Number DNA Profiling', (2001) *Croat Med J* 42:229–32

Gill, P and Buckleton, J, 'Biological Basis for DNA evidence', in Buckleton et al, 2005, 1–26

Gill, P, Werrett, DJ, Budowle, B and Guerrieri, R, 'An assessment of whether SNPs will replace STRs in national DNA databases – joint considerations of the DNA working group of the European Network of Forensic Science Institutes (ENFSI) and the Scientific Working Group on DNA Analysis Methods (SWGDAM)', (2004) *Sci Justice* 44:51–3

Gill, P, Whitaker, J, Flaxman, C, Brown, N and Buckleton, J, 'An investigation of the rigor of interpretation rules for STRs derived from less than 100 pg of DNA', (2000) *Forensic Sci Int* 112:17–40

HC Paper 26-I, *Home Affairs Committee. The Forensic Science Service. Session 1988–9*, 1989, London: HMSO

Herkenham, D, 'DNA database legislation and legal issues', 2002, *Profiles in DNA* 5(1). Available at http://www.promega.com/profiles/501/ProfilesInDNA_501_06.pdf

Home Office (1995) In: 'Criminal statistics England and Wales', supplementary tables 1994, Vol. 2: Proceedings in the Crown Court. Government Statistical Service, London, pp 6–25

Home Office (2000), HO Announcement 269/2000

Houck, MM and Budowle, B, 'Correlation of microscopic and mitochondrial DNA hair comparisons', (2002) *J Forensic Sci* 47(5):964–7

Howitt, T, 'Ensuring the integrity of results: a continuing challenge in forensic DNA analysis', in '*14th International Symposium on Human Identification, Phoenix (AZ), September 2003*', 2003, Madison: Promega Corporation. Available at: http://www.promega.com/geneticidproc/ussymp14proc/oralpresentations/howitt.pdf

Ivanov, PL, Wadhams, MJ, Roby, RK, Holland, MM, Weedn, VW and Parsons, TJ, 'Mitochondrial DNA sequence heteroplasmy in the Grand Duke of Russia Georgij Romanov establishes the authenticity of the remains of Tsar Nicholas II', (1996) *Nat Genet* 12:417–20

Jeffreys, AJ, Wilson, V and Thein, SL, 'Individual-specific "fingerprints" of human DNA', (1985) *Nature* 316:76–9

Jobling, MA, Pandya, A and Tyler-Smith, C, 'The Y chromosome in forensic analysis and paternity testing', (1997) *Int J Legal Med* 110:118–24

Kobilinsky, L, Liotti, TF and Oeser-Sweat, J, *DNA: Forensic and Legal Applications*, 2005, Hoboken: Wiley-Interscience

Koehler, JJ, 'Error and exaggeration in the presentation of DNA evidence', (1993) *Jurimetrics J* 34:21–39

Koehler, JJ, 'One in millions, billions and trillions: lessons from *People v Collins* (1968) for *People v Simpson* (1995)', (1997) *J Legal Education* 47:214–23

Laurie, G, 'United Kingdom', in Chalmers, 2005, 187–239

Locard, E, 'The analysis of dust traces', (1930) *American Journal of Police Science* 1:276–91

Meissner, C, von Wurmb, N, Schimansky, B and Oehmichen, M, 'Estimation of age at death based on quantitation of the 4977-bp deletion of human mitochondrial DNA in skeletal muscle', (1999) *Forensic Sci Int* 105:115–24

Melton, T, Dimick, G, Higgins, B, Lindstrom, L and Nelson, K, 'Forensic mitochondrial DNA analysis of 691 casework hairs' (2005) *J Forensic Sci* 50(1):73–80

Michikawa, Y, Mazzucchelli, F, Bresolin, N, Scarlato, G and Attardi, G, 'Aging-dependent large accumulation of point mutations in the human mtDNA control region for replication', (1999) *Science* 286:774–9

New Scientist (editorial), 'Your DNA in their hands', (2005) *New Scientist* 183(2494):3

Ohno, S, *Sex Chromosomes and the Sex Linked Genes*, 1967, Berlin: Springer Verlag

Oorschot, van, RAH and Jones, MK, 'DNA fingerprints from fingerprints', (1998) *Nature* 387:767

Parliamentary Office of Science and Technology, *The National DNA Database*, 2006, Number 258. Available at http://www.parliament.uk/documents/upload/postpn258.pdf

Pompanon, F, Bonin, A, Bellemain, E and Taberlet, P, 'Genotyping errors: causes, consequences and solutions', (2005) *Nat Rev Genet* 6:847–59

Primorac, D and Schanfield, MS, 'Application of forensic DNA testing in the legal system', (2000) *Croat Med J* 41:32–46

Robertson, B and Vignaux, GA, 'Unhelpful evidence in paternity cases', (1992) *New Zealand Law Journal* 9:315–17

Robertson, B and Vignaux, GA, *Interpreting Evidence*, 1995, Chichester: John Wiley & Sons

Roewer, L, Krawczak, M, Willuweit, S, Nagy, M, Alves, C, Amorim, A, Anslinger, K, Augustin, C, Betz, A, Bosch, E, Caglia, A, Carracedo, A, Corach, D, Dekairelle, AF, Dobosz, T, Dupuy, BM, Furedi, S, Gehrig, C, Gusmao, L, Henke, J, Henke, L, Hidding, M, Hohoff, C, Hoste, B, Jobling, MA, Kargel, HJ, de Knijff, P, Lessig, R, Liebeherr, E, Lorente, M, Martinez-Jarreta, B, Nievas, P, Nowak, M, Parson, W, Pascali, VL, Penacino, G, Ploski, R, Rolf, B, Sala, A, Schmidt, U, Schmitt, C, Schneider, PM, Szibor, R, Teifel-Greding, J and Kayser M, 'Online reference database of European Y-chromosomal short tandem repeat (STR) haplotypes', (2001) *Forensic Sci Int* 118:106–13

Romeo-Casabona, CM, Emaldi-Cirión, A, Uranga, AM and Nicolás-Jiménez, P, 'Spain', in Chalmers, 2005, 1–21

Saks, MJ and Koehler, JJ, 'The coming paradigm shift in forensic identification science', (2005) *Science* 309:893–5

Scientific Working Group on DNA Analysis Methods (SWGDAM), 'Guidelines for Mitochondrial DNA (mtDNA) Nucleotide Sequence Interpretation', (2003) *Forensic Sci Com* 5(2) [online]. Available at: http://www.fbi.gov/hq/lab/fsc/backissu/april2003/swgdammitodna.htm

Schulz, MM and Reichert, W, 'Archived or directly swabbed latent fingerprints as a DNA source for STR typing', (2002) *Forensic Sci Int* 127:128–30

Sekiguchi, K, Kasai, K and Levin, BC, 'Inter- and intragenerational transmission of a human mitochondrial DNA heteroplasmy among 13 maternally-related individuals and differences between and within tissues in two family members', (2003) *Mitochondrion* 2:401–14

Shriver, MD and Kittles, RA, 'Genetic ancestry and the search for personalized genetic histories', (2004) *Nature Rev Genet* 5:611–18

Simon, RJ and Mahan, L, 'Quantifying burdens of proof', (1971) *Law and Society Review* 5:319–30

Sobrino, B, Brion, M and Carracedo, A, 'SNPs in forensic genetics: a review on SNP typing methodologies', (2005) *Forensic Sci Int* 154:181–94

Sturm, RA and Frudakis, TN, 'Eye colour: portals into pigmentation genes and ancestry', (2004) *Trends Genet* 20:327–32

Sullivan, K, Johnson, P, Rowlands, D and Allen, H, 'New developments and challenges in the use of the UK DNA Database: addressing the issue of contaminated consumables', (2004) *Forensic Sci Int* 146S:S175–S176

Taberlet, P, Griffin, S, Goossens, B, Questiau, S, Manceau, V, Escaravage, N, Waits, LP and Bouvet, J, 'Reliable genotyping of samples with very low DNA quantities using PCR', (1996) *Nucleic Acids Res* 24:3189–94

Thangaraj, K, Reddy, AG and Singh, L, 'Is the amelogenin gene reliable for gender identification in forensic casework and prenatal diagnosis?', (2002) *Int J Legal Med* 116:121–3

Thompson, WC and Schumann, EL, 'Interpretation of statistical evidence in criminal trials: the prosecutor's fallacy and the defence attorney's fallacy', (1987) *Law Hum Behav* 11:167–87

Thompson, W, 'DNA evidence in the O.J. Simpson trial', (1996) *U Colo L Rev* 67:827–57

Tsuji, A, Ishiko, A, Takasaki, T and Ikeda, N, 'Estimating age of humans based on telomere shortening', (2002) *Forensic Sci Int* 126:197–9

Tully, G, Bar, W, Brinkmann, B, Carracedo, A, Gill, P, Morling, N, Parson, W and Schneider, P, 'Considerations by the European DNA profiling (EDNAP) group on the working practices, nomenclature and interpretation of mitochondrial DNA profiles', (2001) *Forensic Sci Int* 124:83–91

Whitaker, J, Cotton, EP and Gill, P, 'A comparison of the characteristics of profiles produced with the AMPFlSTR SGM Plus multiplex system for both standard and low copy number (LCN) STR DNA analysis', (2001) *Forensic Sci Int* 123:215–23

Williams, R and Johnson, P, *Forensic DNA Databasing: A European Prospective. Interim report, June 2005*, 2005. Available at http://www.dur.ac.uk/p.j.johnson/EU_Interim_Report_2005.pdf

Williamson, R and Duncan, R, 'DNA testing for all', (2002) *Nature* 418:585–6

Wright, S, 'The genetical structure of populations', (1951) *Ann Eugen* 15:323–54

Valverde, P, Healy, E, Jackson, I, Rees, JL and Thody, AJ, 'Variants of the melanocyte-stimulation hormone receptor gene are associated with red hair and fair skin in humans', (1995) *Nature Genet* 11:328–30

Yu, N, Kruskall, MS, Yunis, JJ, Knoll, JH, Uhl, L, Alosco, S, Ohashi, M, Clavijo, O, Husain, Z, Yunis, EJ, Yunis, JJ and Yunis, EJ, 'Disputed maternity leading to identification of tetragametic chimerism', (2002) *N Eng J Med* 346:1545–52

Glossary

Adventitious match a chance match between two individuals who are not identical twins.

Allele a genetic variant, one of a series of possible alternative forms of a gene or a DNA marker.

Allele dropout the condition in which a particular allele cannot be detected.

Allele masking the condition that occurs when contributors to a mixture share alleles at a particular locus.

Allelic frequency the proportion of a particular allele among all the alleles for this locus in the population.

Amplicon the product of PCR amplification. The area flanked by the forward and reverse primers and which is the target area for PCR amplification.

Amplification an increase in the number of copies of a particular DNA fragment by the process of PCR

Ancestry informative marker (AIM) a DNA marker whose polymorphic variants exhibit substantial difference among various ethnic groups

Autosome a chromosome not involved in sex determination

Azoospermia the condition when the ejaculate is completely devoid of sperm

Base see nucleotide

bp base pair

Buccal swab mouth swab

Cell the smallest unit of a living organism capable of independent reproduction: in multi-cellular organisms, cells of the same type and performing the same function form a tissue

Chromosome a nuclear thread-like structure consisting of DNA and protein and carrying genetic information

CODIS COmbined DNA Identification System; the national DNA database established in the USA in 1998

Copy number   number of copies of a particular DNA fragment, allele, or chromosome

Crime scene sample   a biological sample recovered from a crime scene

Criminal justice sample   A non-intimate DNA sample taken under PACE from a suspect arrested, charged, reported or convicted for a recordable offence, primarily for intelligence purposes only

Deoxyribonucleic acid   the molecular basis of heredity, a double stranded molecule containing the genetic information of an organism

Diploid cell   a cell with two sets of chromosomes

DNA   Deoxyribonucleic acid

DNA fingerprinting   a process of making visible restricted DNA fragments using a multi-locus DNA probe

DNA marker   a DNA sequence used in genetic analysis to obtain information about the genetic differences between two or more organisms

DNA probe   a DNA sequence used for making visible immobilised DNA sequences by hybridisation

DNA profile   an alpha-numeric representation of individual's genotype for a number of loci: in forensic practice, the term DNA profile has replaced DNA fingerprint as the product of forensic DNA analysis

DNA profiling   the process of obtaining a DNA profile

Drop-in   the phenomenon of an allele appearing as a contaminant in a DNA profile – the drop-in effect is usually found in LCN testing

Electrophoresis   the process of separation of DNA molecules in an electric field

Erythrocyte   red blood cell

Eukaryotic cell   a cell that contains a true nucleus and is capable of dividing by meiosis

Exon   a DNA sequence within a gene, which encodes genetic information

Evidential sample   a biological sample recovered from a crime scene, which is analysed to obtain genetic information on the offender

Familial search   the process of interrogating a DNA database with a DNA profile from a crime scene sample in order to identify possible close relatives of the offender

Full profile   a DNA profile containing information on all alleles within a particular maker system – for the 11-locus SGM Plus system, a full DNA profile contains information on 22 alleles

Gametes   germ cells represented in men by sperm cells and in women by egg cells

Gene   a hereditary unit occupying a specific position (locus) within the genome or chromosome

Genetic drift   fluctuation of gene frequencies due to random processes

Genetic chimera   an individual composed of a mixture of genetically different cells

Genome   the entire haploid complement of a cell

Genomic DNA   nuclear DNA

Genotype   the genetic constitution of an organism (as distinct from its physical appearance, its phenotype). With respect to a particular DNA marker or gene, genotype means that the organism has a particular genetic variant of this marker or gene

Haemoglobin   the oxygen-carrying protein of red blood cells

Hardy-Weinberg law   the concept that in an infinitely large and inter-breeding population in which mating is random and there is no selection, migration or mutation, gene frequencies and genotype frequencies will remain constant from generation to generation

Haploid cell   a cell with a single number of chromosomes – in the human body the only haploid cells are the germ cells

Haplotype   a specific combination of alleles of linked loci on one chromosome; in forensic DNA testing, 'haplotype' usually refers to a specific combination of alleles on Y chromosome

Heterozygote imbalance   the differences in peak morphology (area and height) between two allelic peaks of a heterozygote

Heterozygous locus   a locus both of whose alleles are different

Heteroplasmy   the situation in which an individual has two different types of mtDNA

Higher-order mixture   a DNA mixture with more than two contributors

Homoplasmy   situation in which an individual has a single type of mtDNA

Homozygous locus   a locus both of whose alleles are the same

Intron   a DNA sequence within a gene, which does not encode genetic information

ISSOL   International Standard Set of Loci: the set of loci used by Interpol to facilitate DNA data exchange between the member countries

Karyotype   a chromosomal complement of a cell

LCN DNA testing   Low copy number DNA testing: a procedure that allows analysis of DNA from very small biological samples – the increased sensitivity of LCN is achieved by employing 34 cycles during PCR amplification

Length heteroplasmy   a type of heteroplasmy in which an individual has two types of mtDNA showing differences in the length of genotyped sequences

Leukocyte   white blood cell – the only type of blood cells containing DNA

Linkage equilibrium   an assumption of independent inheritance between loci

Locus (plural, loci)   a position that a gene (or a DNA marker) occupies on a chromosome or within a segment of DNA: the terms 'gene and locus' and 'DNA marker and locus' are used interchangeably

Major components   the components of a mixed DNA profile belonging to the individual(s) whose contribution of DNA is discernibly larger than that of others

Marker   a DNA variant with a known location on a chromosome used for determining genetic differences between individuals

Match probability   random match probability

Matrilineal inheritance   inheritance of genetic traits via the maternal line – a trait may be transmitted by the mother to all her children but only daughters can pass it on further

Meiosis   the type of cell division leading to production of gametes

Microsatellite   a form of repeated DNA that includes STR with a typical repeat length of two to eight bp, repeated ten to a hundred times

Microvariant   a rare STR allele which has some form of sequence variation compared to more common alleles

Minisatellites   a form of repeated DNA that includes VNTR with a typical repeat length larger than ten bp which is repeated several hundred times

Minor components   the components of a mixed DNA profile belonging to the individual(s) whose contribution of DNA is discernibly smaller than that of others

Mitotype   a specific combination of alleles of linked loci on mtDNA

mtDNA   mitochondrial DNA: the type of DNA found in mitochondria, a small circular molecule, of which two to ten copies on average are present per mitochondrion

mtDNA testing   analysis of mitochondrial DNA

Mitochondrion (plural, mitochondria)   a semi-autonomous cell organelle which provides energy for cellular biochemical reactions

Mixed profile   a DNA profile of a mixture of DNA from two or more contributors

Mixture proportion   a value describing the relative contribution of various individuals to a DNA mixture

Monomorphic locus   a locus in which the most common allele is found with a frequency exceeding 0.95

Multiplex   a type of PCR amplification which allows analysing several loci at once

Mutation   a change in DNA

Negative control   a special PCR amplification which includes all components of the reaction with a single exception of the DNA template: negative control allows checking components of PCR reaction for DNA contamination

Nucleotide   a building block of DNA, a monomeric unit which consists of a purine (A or G) or pyrimidine base (T or C), a sugar and a residue of phosphoric acid

Nucleus   a small spheroid structure, present in all eukaryotic cells, which contains chromosomes

Nuclear DNA   the type of DNA found in the nucleus, chromosomal DNA

Null allele   an allele which, for whatever reason, cannot be made visible

Numerical chromosome abnormalities   a type of chromosomal abnormality which causes an organism to have a different chromosomal complement from the typical one for the species

Obligate allele   an allele that must be inherited from the alleged parent if s/he is the biological parent of the child

Oligospermia   a medical condition in men in which the ejaculate has a small number of spermatozoa, typically less than 20 million

Organelle   an autonomous part within a cell

Partial profile   a DNA profile for which it has not been possible to obtain genetic information for all possible alleles

Parentage testing   a genetic test that determines whether an alleged parent is a biological parent of a child; there are two types of parentage testing – paternity testing and maternity testing

Parentage duo testing   a type of parentage test which involves analysis of DNA from the child and one of the parents

Parentage trio testing   a type of parentage test which involves analysis of DNA from the child and both parents

Patrilineal inheritance   inheritance of genetic traits via the paternal line in which the trait is passed by the father only to his sons

PCR   Polymerase chain reaction

Phenotype   the observable properties or physical appearance of an organism – the phenotype of the organism results from the interaction between the genotype and the environment

Platelets   thrombocytes, blood particles involved in blood clotting

Point heteroplasmy   a type of heteroplasmy in which an individual has two types of mtDNA which differ by a single nucleotide at a particular position

Polymerase chain reaction   a type of enzymatic reaction which allows amplification of a DNA fragment of interest millions of times – the typical 28-cycle PCR procedure, used for conventional SGM Plus genotyping, allows a 268,435,456-fold increase in the starting amount of a DNA area of interest

Polymorphism   the occurrence in a population of two or more distinct genetic variants at a specific locus

Polymorphic locus   a genetic locus with more than one allele in the population with the frequency of the most common allele less than 0.95

Positive control   a type of PCR amplification which includes all the components of the reaction and good quality known DNA template to control for efficiency of amplification

Product rule   the rule for calculating random match probability which is based on multiplication of random match probabilities across all the loci analysed, providing the loci are inherited independently of each other

Pull-up peaks   a DNA analysis artefact in which a minor peak labelled with one colour appears among peaks labelled with another colour

Random match probability   the probability of a random match between two DNA profiles

Recombination   the process in which homologous chromosomes exchange parts during cell division

Replication   the process of doubling of cell DNA content

Restriction enzyme   a type of an enzyme that cuts DNA at a specific recognised location

Restriction fragment length polymorphism   a within-population variation in the length of DNA fragments obtained by restriction with a specific restriction enzyme

RFLP   restriction fragment length polymorphism

RMNE   random man not excluded: a statistical approach to DNA evidence evaluation that determines the proportion of the population which cannot be excluded from being the source of DNA in the crime stain

Serological methods   methods of forensic testing of body fluids based on analysis of specific antibodies (e.g., the blood group)

Sex cell   germ cell

Sex chromosome   a chromosome involved in sex determination of an individual – in humans there are two sex chromosomes: X and Y

SGM   second generation mastermix: a forensic DNA marker system introduced in 1995 and used in forensic casework until 1999; SGM allows simultaneous testing of six informative DNA loci and a sex determination marker

SGM Plus   an updated version of SGM introduced into forensic casework in 1999 and currently used by forensic laboratories in the UK and other countries: SGM Plus allows simultaneous analysis of 10 informative DNA loci and a sex determination marker

Simple mixture   a DNA mixture with two contributors

Single locus probe   a VNTR probe that shows variation of a specific locus

Single profile   a DNA profile of a sample that contains DNA from only one contributor

SLP   single locus probe

Somatic cell   a cell with double chromosomal complement: any cell in eukaryotic organism other than the sex cell

Speculative searching   the process of searching a DNA database with a DNA profile obtained from a subject or crime scene, to identify matches with the profiles already on the database

SSR   simple sequence repeats, a synonym of STR

Structural chromosome abnormalities   a type of chromosome abnormality that involves DNA rearrangement within a single chromosome or between two chromosomes

Stuttering   a type of DNA profile artefact that causes extra peaks, usually for smaller DNA fragments, to appear together with the peak for the main allele: stutter peaks are caused by DNA polymerase slippage during PCR amplification

Simple tandem repeats   a type of DNA repetitive sequence, the same as microsatellites

STR   simple tandem repeats

Telomeres   special DNA sequences located on the ends of chromosomes

Thrombocytes   platelets

Trisomy   a type of numeric chromosome abnormality when an affected individual has three copies of a particular chromosome

Variable number tandem repeats   a type of DNA repetitive sequence, same as minisatellites

VNTR   variable number tandem repeats

Y chromosome testing   analysis of DNA markers located on the Y chromosome

Zygote   a fertilised egg

Index